Breaking Patterns

A map to finding love, joy, and contentment

By John Harradine
Psychotherapist & Social Ecologist

Breaking Patterns
A map to finding love, joy, and contentment

Copyright © 2017 by John Harradine

All rights reserved. No part of this book may be reproduced in any form by any electronic or mechanical means including photocopying, recording, or information storage and retrieval without permission in writing from the author.

Cover design by: Bluering Design and Jack Evan Johnson
Edited, designed and published by: Bloomwood Media

ISBN-13: 978-0-646-80978-6
ISBN-10: 1547266007

First Edition June 2017
A Bloomwood Media Publication

I dedicate this book to my Mum, Jean Evelyn Harradine, who, at age 91, lived love, joy, and contentment – notwithstanding the extraordinary challenges she faced.

Jean Evelyn Harradine (Née Groves)
18th July 1922 to 9th November 2013

Navigating the map to finding love, joy, and contentment

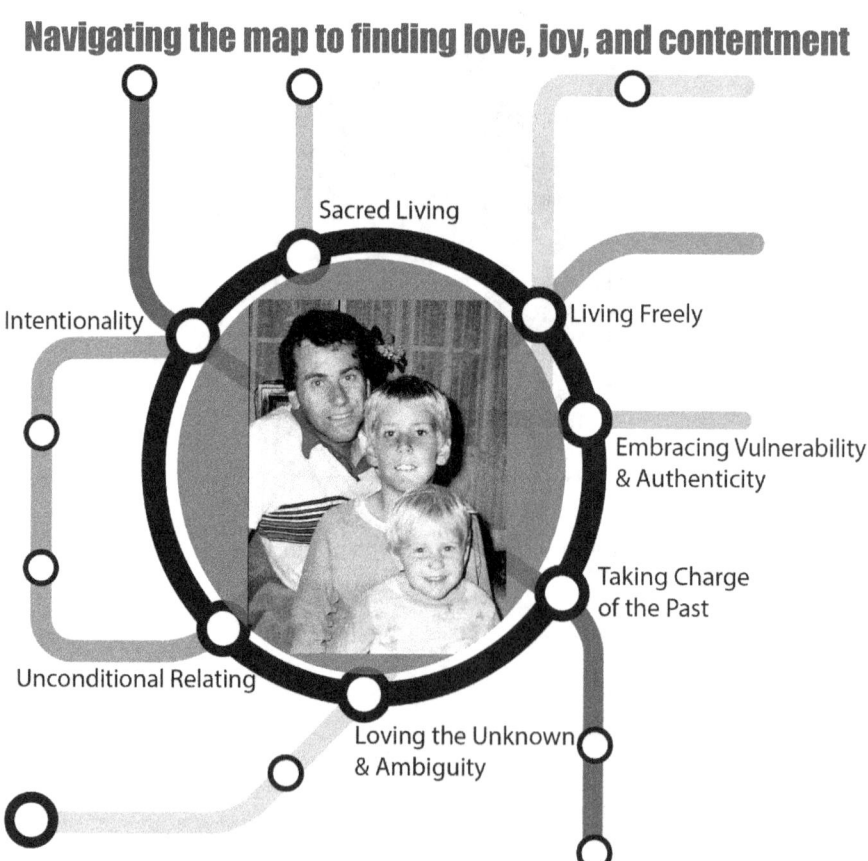

Sacred Living

Intentionality

Living Freely

Embracing Vulnerability & Authenticity

Taking Charge of the Past

Unconditional Relating

Loving the Unknown & Ambiguity

Table of Contents

Acknowledgements xi
Forward xiii
Introduction xv
Chapter 1: Living Freely 1
    Wanting Power and Control 1
    Seeking Possibility and Freedom 3
    Building a Bridge from Power and Control to Possibility and Freedom 5
    Integrating My Personal Story 9
    Questions I Ask Myself and Suggest for You 12
Chapter 2: Embracing Vulnerability and Authenticity 13
    Individual Deep Ecology 13
    Personal Transformation 17
    Developing Detachment 23
    Integrating My Personal Story 24
    Questions I Ask Myself and Suggest for You 28
Chapter 3: Taking Charge of the Past 29
    Transference from the Past to Today 29
    Transference from Our Parents 30
    Positive or Negative Transference – neither good nor bad 31
    Communication in Relationships and Transference 34
    The "Parent" in Us 35
    The "Adult" in Us 35
    The "Child" in Us 36
    Transactions 37
    Crossed Transactions 37
    Complementary Transactions 38
    Hidden Transactions 38
    Building Personal Effectiveness and More Robust Relationships ... 39
    Focusing on Greater Good Outcomes 39
    Integrating My Personal Story 40

Questions I Ask Myself and Suggest for You 46
Appendix - Listening for Potential 46
Chapter 4: Loving the Unknown and Ambiguity 49
Our Chaordic World 49
Learning Cycles 50
A Quantum Approach 51
The Individual 52
The Community 54
Personal Transformation in a Chaordic World 56
Growing and Effective Functioning in a Chaordic World 60
Integrating My Personal Story 62
Questions I Ask Myself and Suggest for You 68
Appendix: Glossary of Terms 68
Chapter 5: Unconditional Relating 71
Relationship Pathways 71
Relationship Characteristics 82
Integrating My Personal Story 87
Questions I Ask Myself and Suggest for You 90
Appendix - SBS Request for Comment 90
Chapter 6: Intentionality 95
Diving into Resistance 95
Defining Clear and Workable intentions 97
Uncovering Our Inner Intentions & Testing Alignment with Our Outer Goals 99
Knowing Our Unconscious Beliefs 102
Moving into Acceptance 105
Adopting and Attitude of Create, Promote and Allow 107
Being Present 108
Flowing with the Moment – Giving Way with Inner Ease 110
Integrating My Personal Story 112
Questions I Ask Myself and Suggest for You 116
Chapter 7: Sacred Living 117
Filling Our Pot of Gold 117
Sacred Living Defined 118

Thinking Holistically 119
Asking the Right Questions 120
How Beliefs and Intentions Define Our Levels of Sacred Living 123
Integrating My Personal Story 128
The Questions I ask Myself and Suggest for You 136

Figures

Chapter 1: Living Freely
- Figure 1.1: Unaware Consciousness 2
- Figure 1.2: Conscious Awareness 4
- Figure 1.3: Building a Bridge to Freedom 5

Chapter 2: Embracing Vulnerability and Authenticity
- Figure 2.1: Individual Conscious and Unconscious Ecology 14
- Figure 2.2: Individual Ecology and Beliefs 16
- Figure 2.3: Personal Transformation 17
- Figure 2.4: Life Scripts – Themes 18
- Figure 2.5: Core Drivers – The Six Buckets 20
- Figure 2.6: Emotional States of Task Actions 24

Chapter 3: Taking Charge of the Past
- Figure 3.1: The Three Brains 32
- Figure 3.2: Crossed Transactions 37
- Figure 3.3: Complementary Transactions 38
- Figure 3.4: Hidden Transactions 39

Chapter 4: Loving Ambiguity and the Unknown
- Figure 4.1: Our Chaordic World 50
- Figure 4.2: The Structure (Fractals) of Human Experience 52
- Figure 4.3: Individual Conscious and Unconscious Ecology (from Chapter 2) 53
- Figure 4.4: Personal Transformation in a Chaordic World 57
- Figure 4.5: Yesterday's Ordered World 57
- Figure 4.6: The Emerging Chaotic World 58
- Figure 4.7: Responding to a Chaotic World – AKA - Loving Ambiguity 58
- Figure 4.8: Attributes of a Chaordic World 59
- Figure 4.9: Tolerances for a Chaordic World 59

Figure 4.10: Transformative Learning 60
Figure 4.11: Ecology and Transformative Learning 61
Figure 4.12: Navigating the Path 64
Figure 4.13: Growing with Grace and Ease in our Refining Years 67

Chapter 5: Unconditional Relating
Figure 5.1: Relationship Pathway 72
Figure 5.2: Operating Ego – Primary & Disowned Selves 74
Figure 5.3: Archetypical Primary & Disowned Selves 75
Figure 5.4: Perfection & Discovery Approaches 77
Figure 5.5: Aware Ego – Primary & Disowned Selves 78
Figure 5.6: Building Relationships 83
Figure 5.7: Disconnected Relationship 83
Figure 5.8: Unbalanced Relationship 84
Figure 5.9: Conditional Relationship 84
Figure 5.10: Committed Relationship 86

Chapter 6: Intentionality
Figure 6.1: The Biology of Belief – New Science of Epigenetics 98
Figure 6.2: Intention Map 99
Figure 6.3: Engagement & Commitment Levels 101
Figure 6.4: Reframing beliefs 104
Figure 6.5: Building a Bridge to Freedom (from Chapter 1) 108
Figure 6.6: Our Chaordic World (from Chapter 4) 109
Figure 6.7: Levels of Conflict 111

Chapter 7: Sacred Living
Figure 7.1: The Social Ecology of Life 120
Figure 7.2: Life's Questions 121
Figure 7.3: Going Within to Avoid Going Without 123
Figure 7.4: Sacred Living 124
Figure 7.5: Surviving 124
Figure 7.6: Belonging 125
Figure 7.7: Winning 125
Figure 7.8: Joining 126
Figure 7.9: Succeeding 126
Figure 7.10: Caring 127

Figure 7.11: Integrating 127
Figure 7.12: Wisdom 128

Appendix: Companion Exercises to Support Your Understanding and Growth

Chapter 1: Living Freely
- Exercise 1: Letting go of the Power/Control Triangle.........................137
- Exercise 2: Moving to the Possibility/Freedom Triangle 138

Chapter 2: Embracing Our Vulnerability and Authenticity
- Exercise 3: Exploring Your Protective Selves 140
- Exercise 4: Reframing Beliefs..141
- Exercise 5: Early Steps to Developing an Authentic Self................... 145

Chapter 3: Taking Charge of the Past
- Exercise 6: Reviewing Our Early Story 147
- Exercise 7: Mapping Current Transactions in Your Relationship(s) 149

Chapter 4: Loving Ambiguity and the Unknown
- Exercise 8: Assess Your Focus on Order and Chaos 152

Chapter 5: Unconditional Relating
- Exercise 9: Knowing Your Primary/Disowned Selves 158
- Exercise 10: Relationship Assessment 161
- Exercise 11: Your Relationship Current State 164
- Exercise 12: Relationship Sharing Exercise 165

Chapter 6: Intentionality
- Exercise 13: Setting Personal Intentions and Goals 167
- Exercise 14: Aligning your personal intentions with those around you 167

Chapter 7: Sacred Living
- Exercise 15: Exploring Your Sacred Living Journey.......................... 169
- Exercise 16: Your Quest(s)..177

References, Recommended Readings and Movies 179
Author's Biography..189
Epilogue 203

Acknowledgements

I offer my heartfelt thanks and gratitude to some very special people who have guided me over the years and provided such valuable support in both good and challenging times.

I thank my Mum Jean (passed at 91 in 2013) to whom I have dedicated this book for her love and teaching me to grow old with joy regardless of what happens to me in life. My paternal grandmother Ada Lily Grace – I often called her by her full name – (passed at 94 in 1989), who provided unconditional loving in my early and middle years and taught me to stay strong in troubled times. This enabled me to find more of it in my first marriage and my current relationship. My father Dick (passed at 73 in 1994), who taught me to value education and learning. My children Mark and Christopher, now grown men living in the USA, have blessed my life with loving purpose and commitment to our family no matter its structure and circumstances. Their mother Diane brought stability and loving support into my early adult life when things were chaotic and unpredictable. Our son Glen (stillborn in April 1980) taught me the value of fully appreciating the whole of life in all its aspects.

Incredible long term friends (all over 20 years and some over 40 years), Jan, Ann (passed at 61 in 2005), Terri (including her generous editing contribution), Thyra, Susan, Steve (passed at 72 in 2012), Kevin, Marilyn, Andrew, Brian and Mr and Mrs G (now passed) have guided and chided me through life with nothing but my wellbeing in their hearts. My thanks also to those others who have supported me along the way. Finally, and oh so importantly, my partner Maxx has taught me unconditional acceptance, unswerving support and love in our 20-year relationship.

Forward

To reflect the concepts in this book, I've mapped summaries of my personal experiences. By world standards, mine is not a big story. By my standards, it's as big a story as I can tell. Along the way I have tried (and screwed up) and tried again – sometimes by trying to do the same things better, sometimes by changing what I do. Changing in a deliberate way led me to discover different tools to help me. Sometimes I had to create my own. What motivated me, always, was first a desire – which became a commitment – to not get stuck in my story.

We all tell ourselves stories about ourselves. We script others into our stories and make up stories about them, too. Sometimes our stories limit us. Sometimes we make up fairy tales. Sometimes we write a story about ourselves that inspires us. This handbook will help you write a better story for yourself – and help you make it real.

Whatever your own story is, make it is as big as it can be for you. That's what matters. How you make a difference to yourself is also how you make a difference for others and to your world – no matter how big or small your own story is, it matters. You matter.

Introduction

Much has been written in the fields of psychology and personal growth from the perspectives of psychodynamic and behavioural theory, or transpersonal psychology and spirituality. This book uses no labels. It is an eclectic mix of everything I find useful. It provides a practical approach to changing your life story, no matter what your existing beliefs and philosophies are. This book calls on you to move beyond the real and imagined limitations that, until now, have caused you to balk at claiming the fulfilment you truly want in life. Embrace the "gifts" – yes, gifts! – of your limitations. You have to pick them up so you can put them down.

As well as drawing from the knowledge and skills I acquired as part of my own pilgrim's progress, I have drawn on a myriad of experts in human development who have contributed to my learning and thinking over the years. A comprehensive recommended reading and viewing list is provided at the end of this handbook.

Like most of us, I have sometimes avoided life's challenges. I've also had to face them, sometimes voluntarily and at other times because I was forced to face them. I have learned to value the gifts that have come from all my experiences. I have also developed a sense of gratitude for all that has been good and even great in my life. At the end of each chapter I have included excerpts from my own life as an example of how the concepts presented have both challenged me, and also been put to practical use. This end section in each chapter was the most difficult to write. It certainly caused me to continue to reflect on my own story and how I was still writing it, even in the process of writing this handbook.

My hope is that you will find ways to link your own stories to the ideas presented. I hope the handbook will provide insights for your own personal learning, upliftment and growth. I have posed questions to help you practically integrate the ideas. An appendix of "Companion Exercises" for each chapter has also been included to assist you to anchor and live the concepts talked about. I have included frameworks (visual models) to help you picture and internalise the concepts. You will find a comprehensive list of the models in the table of contents. By themselves they tell a story.

Understanding the human condition has been a life's work for me. This book is written for professionals in the field of human development, for people who have been consciously pursuing personal growth and individuals who are new to examining their own lives and simply looking for a different way of living it. I offer this handbook to support your successful navigation through your changing life situations, daunting challenges and exciting opportunities. I hold that there is something here for each of you.

Each chapter represents a theme that we need to master to create the lives we want. Together the chapters provide a strategy for living a balanced, fulfilled and joyful life.

Chapter 1: *Living Freely* is about finding your way out of the dramas and power struggles that seem to affect us all. It provides the steps to empower yourself through a sense of possibility and freedom.

Chapter 2: *Embracing Vulnerability and Authenticity* explores how you can access who you truly are. You might not yet know. As you become more authentically yourself, your strengths will begin to emerge.

Chapter 3: *Taking Charge of the Past* asks you to let go of the past and find new ways to approach life, beyond what you have been "given", in order to strive for a new understanding of the communication patterns that are part of your history.

Chapter 4: *Loving Ambiguity and the Unknown* looks at how to control the patterns, conscious and unconscious, that keep you from adapting to an ever-changing chaotic world.

Chapter 5: *Unconditional Relating* examines the kinds of relationships we find ourselves in. You will now see how your ability to embrace the concepts in the earlier chapters will either hinder or support you to have the relationships you want – and create that sense of unconditional love we are all looking for.

Chapter 6: *Intentionality* sets the tone for the future and exposes how unconscious internal intentions trump any external goals we may set for ourselves – unless we have mastered past patterns. It provides a map to find a way out of your limitations every time you are pulled back into them.

Chapter 7: *Sacred Living* asks those questions you may not have dared to ask. Just how willing are you to challenge yourself and how big a life game do you want to play? This chapter helps you to get real about that and be happy with whatever level you choose.

I invite you to use the ideas in this book to assist you to map and then create your life story. As you move through each chapter these reflections will combine to show you how your way of being in the world either limits or expands you.

Integrating all parts of our lives is something we need to do, if we are to be fulfilled. We need to enjoy our lives moment by moment and that will lift us up to better enjoy – and write – our whole story. That's the first and last challenge of our life.

My wish for you is that you can (re)capture your own experiences by using this practical handbook. Believing that others will gain new ways of being in the world, by embracing these ideas, adds to the gifts I already have in life.

Thank you for making the time to read this heartfelt effort of mine and experience the exercises. Enjoy whatever you take from it. Leave whatever doesn't resonate with you. As one of my teachers once told me: "Don't believe anything I say; just check it out for yourself." I invite you to do the same.

Chapter 1: Living Freely

From Unaware Consciousness to Conscious Awareness!

I've heard it suggested that everything in life is about relationships. Relationships are formed by what appeals to us and what repels us, whether it's people, objects or experiences. Others have said that everything in life can be boiled down to three things: money, love and you. If we put these two ideas together, we have a relationship with money, love and ourselves – that is, what appeals to us about money, love and ourselves and what repels us from them. Our relationship with money enables our capacity to make choices; our relationship with love demonstrates what we value; our relationship with ourselves drives how we deal with every other relationship we have. Our attitudes and beliefs, not our circumstances, form the patterns that impact our relationship with life and our capability to live freely. They in turn influence our capacity for effective communication, which is the critical skill that nurtures or undermines our relationships.

Communication and relationships have a complexity that we don't often think about day-to-day. We fall into patterns of behaviour with people and usually stay there until something significant happens to push us out of them. Awareness of the patterns can help us to change our relationships into ones that are much more rewarding, effective and pleasurable. If your relationships work at the workplace, you get more done, more easily and feel more fulfilled. If your relationships work at home, you feel more peaceful, more supported and happier.

Wanting Power and Control

Have you ever wondered why some communication exchanges and relationships are easy and some are not? Or why you get on well with one person but with another it feels difficult? Or that your communication just isn't getting across the way you mean it to? Have you ever tried to control the situation to get your needs met or resist being controlled by another?

The Unaware Consciousness: Power/Control Triangle (Figure 1.1) depicts the dynamic that occurs when we want to control or want to resist being controlled. It forms what we might call the *"Operating Ego"* (Hal & Sidra Stone). We operate unconsciously, simply reacting to situations from either *"Persecutor"*, *"Rescuer"* or *"Victim"* consciousness (Eric Berne, 1967). It occurs whenever we have walked away from an exchange with another or others and at least one person has not been satisfied, is disappointed, angry, sad or hurting in some way. They are carrying some kind of negative energy.

This is a closed loop pattern. We can and do move from one role to another, playing different parts at different times with the same people or with different people. Nothing moves forward with this dynamic. The *Persecutor* criticises, the *Victim* is disempowered and the *Rescuer* tries to keep everyone from feeling bad by fixing it all. Judgement of what is right or wrong is present in all three roles. The word "should" around expectations of self and others will be felt even if unsaid.

Figure 1.1: Unaware Consciousness

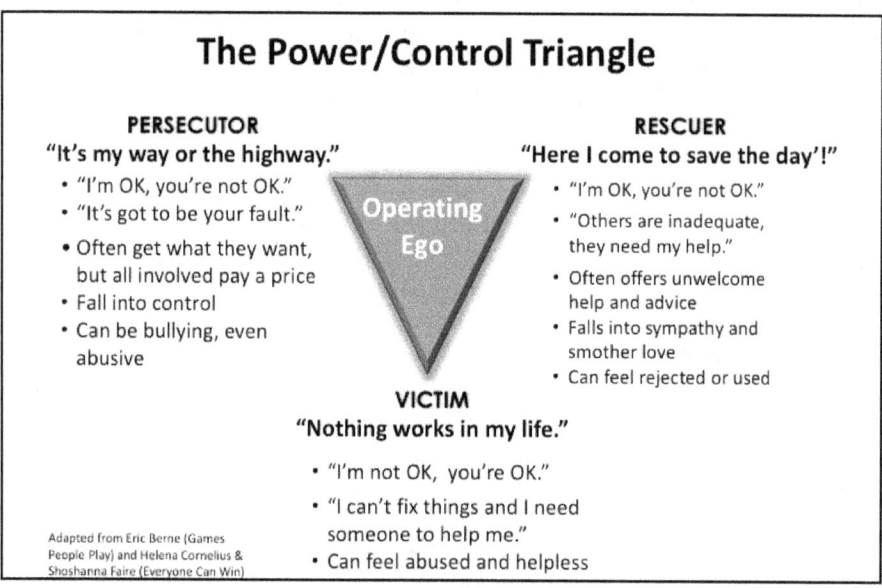

As we develop our approach to life, our strategy if you like, we tend to adopt one of these roles more often than the other two. There's a great book written called *"All I Really Needed to Know I Learned in Kindergarten"* by Robert Fulghum. Neuroscience now reinforces this notion suggesting our cellular memory of events in our unconscious will trump our conscious adult thinking every time. If we learnt as a youngster we got what we wanted by pushing others around (*Persecutor* energy) we will most likely continue with that strategy throughout our life. Of course, we may become more socially sophisticated about it. If we learnt to be recognised for helping others we are likely to adopt a "fix it" (*Rescuer*) approach. If we got a lot of attention and assistance from crying and/or acting helpless (*Victim*), we are likely to continue that strategy. These roles then become our primary ways to get what we want in our lives – our *Operating Ego*.

We may also reject one of the two roles more than the other two, forming negative attitudes about them. If we were bullied as a child and have adopted a *Victim* consciousness, we are very likely to judge *Persecutor* energy as definitely not okay. We will want to steer clear of it in others but even more so inside ourselves. We may not give ourselves permission to go into aggressive *Persecutor* behaviour. That doesn't mean to say we won't necessarily act in that way. It indicates we will have strong judgements on ourselves and others if we perceive ourselves or others acting in that way. Likewise, if we judge those who act in a helpless way, including ourselves, we will not give ourselves permission to engage with the *Victim* role. In this sense, we disown these roles. When we disown a limitation we also push down what it wants for us and the gift it offers. Although it ultimately doesn't work, in the short term it may appear to.

Our personal unconscious strategy becomes deeply embedded in our minds and out of our awareness. We formulate beliefs and reactive habits about these roles that keep us trapped in them. Bruce Lipton (2008) in his book "*The Biology of Beliefs*" shows from his neuroscience research that 5% of our personal life strategy is conscious and 95% unconscious. He adds that whenever there is a battle between the unconscious and the conscious mind, the unconscious will always win. We may think these approaches will get us what we want but eventually they run us into challenges and difficulties.

The Power/Control Triangle, far from being "wrong" however, is simply a limiting, reactive and unaware way of trying to get what we want. The only way out of the Power/Control Triangle's closed loop is to go through it. Trying to suppress or disengage from any of these roles only reinforces them, giving them more power over us. We need our *Persecutor* for backbone, to stand up for ourselves (to "*Create*"); we need our *Rescuer* for insight, compassion and giving support (to "*Promote*"); we need our *Victim* to be able to receive support and cooperate (to "*Allow*"). When we suppress the role we also suppress what it wants. It's like sitting on a beach ball in a swimming pool; it keeps coming up to the surface and bopping us on the head. A more effective approach is to allow ourselves to fall off the ball into the swimming pool and learn to play Olympic standard water polo with it. The water might seem a little, even a lot murky for a while, but the more we swim around in it the cleaner it gets.

Seeking Possibility and Freedom

We can take charge of ourselves and choose to adopt a different path. We need to get out of our own way to do it. That means owning our defences and suspending our judgements of ourselves and others. Simple but far from easy!

The Conscious Awareness: Possibility/Freedom Triangle (Figure 1.2) is a way we can take full responsibility for every interaction and outcome that we have, trusting that changing how we relate will ultimately create a different reaction in others. It takes just one person to change their approach in a communication to change the relationship dynamic. It also takes perseverance and small experiments with new ways to create a shift to more effective ways of relating. If we think that the person we are communicating with needs to change, think again; that will take us right back into the Power/Control Triangle. The change needs to start with ourselves if we really want to see a change in how our relationships work. Neale Walsch in his book *"Conversations with God"* suggests that "if you can't go within, you go without".

Building conscious awareness and ultimately, what eminent psychologists Hal and Sidra Stone (1989) call the *"Aware Ego"*, is a journey into understanding our deeper patterns. These live below our thoughts and behaviours. It requires us to become aware of, embrace and take charge of those parts of us that have seemingly protected us for years. These parts have a positive intention. Understanding what that is, is crucial. We may want to move on from limiting behaviours, attitudes and beliefs but we need to take their positive intentions along with us, reframing our beliefs and subsequent behaviours into something expansive that holds for the same positive intentions. Later chapters address the breadth and depth of this topic.

Figure 1.2: Conscious Awareness

The Possibility/Freedom Triangle

CREATOR
"I take action to achieve my intentions."
- Clarify clear and workable intentions
- Actions create greater good outcomes
- Be hard on the issue and soft on the person

Aware Ego

PROMOTER
"I stand for greater good outcomes."
- Explore how much help is appropriate
- Look after yourself first so you have strength to support others
- Encourage people to stand for themselves in constructive ways

ALLOWER
"I can hold the space and let things unfold."
- Be present with what is in the moment
- Use everything for your upliftment learning and growth
- Look for the positive intention in all behaviour

Adapted from John Roger (Do It – Get Off Your Buts) and Hal & Sidra Stone (Embracing Our Selves)

When we stand for ourselves (engage our backbone) without againstness, the *Persecutor* transforms positively into a *Creator* of what is possible. The *Creator* in us holds for assertiveness as distinct from aggression. Similarly, the *Rescuer* can promote compassion and support without reinforcing helplessness. It holds for encouragement as distinct from over-helping. The *Allower* can embrace their vulnerability without collapsing into it, thereby engendering deeper connection to self and others. The *Allower* holds for cooperation as distinct from compliance.

John-Roger, New York Times bestselling author, and Peter McWilliams (1997) authors of *"You Can't Afford the Luxury of a Negative Thought"*, proposed the idea that we *"create, promote and allow"* everything in our lives. There are, of course, natural and manmade disasters that may befall us and there may be genuine victims in these circumstances. However, when things happen to us, rather than retreat into the Power/Control Triangle roles, we can start by asking ourselves: "How did I *create, promote or allow* this to happen to me?" This way we take responsibility and accountability for our part rather than retreating into blaming ourselves or others for our circumstances, i.e. back into the limitations of the Power/Control Triangle. Another way of looking at this is to adopt an attitude of: it doesn't matter what happens to us in life; what matters is what we do with what happens to us.

When we have the resolve and then the skill to go for possibility and freedom without attachment to the past events and future outcomes we are much more likely to operate with authentic courage; relationships are more rewarding, effective and sustainable; outcomes are not only more easily achieved but also take on higher aspirations. Joy takes centre stage.

Building a Bridge from Power and Control to Possibility and Freedom

Figure 1.3 depicts the pathway to taking personal responsibility for our outcomes. The Bungee Zone warning is Neale Walsch's quote: "If you can't go within you go without". An unwillingness to do this flips us back to the *Operating Ego*.

Figure 1.3: BUILDING A BRIDGE TO FREEDOM

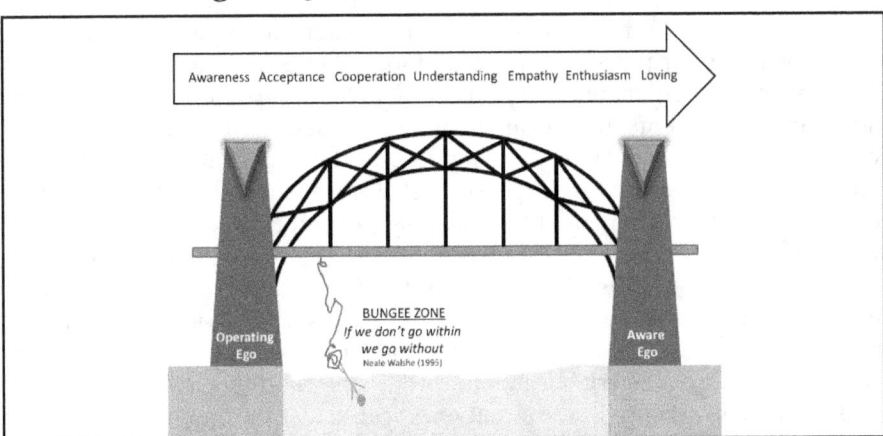

Awareness is the first stepping stone to move across the bridge. We can begin by asking: What am I *aware* of right now in this minute? Which triangle am I experiencing myself in? Which part of that triangle appears to be strongest? How does that feel? Is it expansive or contractive? Am I carrying any judgements on myself or others? Is there a sense of righteousness or justification about my position? Do I have an emotional charge or attachment to a particular outcome? How *neutral* am I about this present moment? Whatever our experience, do we want to change our state or stay in it? What might be the payoff we get from our choice? If we find ourselves in the Power/Control Triangle and want to stay there the payoff might be that we want to be right or we might think it will keep us safe somehow.

We can ask ourselves: "Would I rather be right or happy?" Still want to stay in the Power/Control Triangle? Most likely you are making being right more important than being happy. If so our next step across the bridge will be interesting! *We get more of what we focus on!* Whatever our initial assessment, how might our responses so far tell us something about the habits, patterns or beliefs we hold? How do they serve us? How do they hold us back? Ready to move to the next step?

Acceptance of "it is what it is" is a necessary state to embrace to move through past hurts, sadness, pain, fear, anger or disturbance of any kind. This is not to say acceptance equals begrudging compliance. Any compliance that contains a skerrick of upset, judgement or limiting emotion is not acceptance as it is meant here. It is where a state of emotional neutrality needs to be found. Not always easy of course.

Residual negativity of any kind is a cue to return to *awareness* and repeat any questions that might assist us to uncover what is disturbing us. It's like peeling an onion – layer within layer within layer – to find the source and core of what is preventing the neutrality needed to set ourselves free. If we experience ourselves challenged to let go then we might ponder how our resistance may be keeping us stuck: "what we resist we are stuck with"!

With *acceptance*, we can bend but not break; we can be truthful in all situations and beyond that seek the truth in them; we accept others as they are suspending our judgements and find forgiveness of ourselves and others. Forgiveness can be challenging, but without it we are held hostage to our upset and judgements and negative emotions. Challenging maybe; but often very necessary. We may not be able to forgive the behaviour and if we can so much the better, but we can forgive ourselves for the judgements we might be holding on ourselves and/or others. John-Roger and Paul Kaye (2009) suggest we start with "I forgive myself for judging myself for (insert your judgement, e.g. being angry)" and/or "I forgive myself for judging another (insert name) for (insert judgement, e.g. ignoring me)." We can keep repeating this over and over with either the same or additional judgements until we feel a sense of completion and our energy begins to settle. This is an indication that we are finding some *neutrality* in the situation. It can take time and practice. Fake it until you make it – even *faith* it until you make it! Forgiveness doesn't make a wrong right, but frees us to be generous with ourselves and others to move through and on from disturbances in our lives.

Cooperation: *Neutrality* paves the way to *cooperate* with the situation. We may be aware of some residual disturbance but we find we are simply noticing that. There is no desire to fight with it or flee from it. Sometimes we want to fight and flee at the same time. We may experience this in a situation which has triggered our anger or perhaps sadness, but we feel unable to say anything. Perhaps we want to avoid the fallout of such a confrontation with our boss or partner. And yet we feel obliged to stay in the situation. This can create a sense of freezing.

First notice what's happening for you and then see if you can identify something to "give way" on. Notice this is not a suggestion to "give in" as that will take you into either guilty or resentful compliance. You might simply say to yourself: "I choose to stay here and temporarily suspend my upset or judgements" or "I'll pick this up later".

The feelings and sensations in your body will give you clues about your *neutrality*. If it is tight, tense or rigid notice what it might be emotionally connected to. You can check if you can let it go, even temporarily, perhaps by focusing on your breath. If your thoughts are about what or who is right or wrong it is likely you are in righteous judgement. There is no neutrality in that. You can move your thoughts to something like: "This isn't working (for me, others or the situation). What can I *create, promote or allow* right here, right now?"

We can take charge of ourselves by looking for a greater good outcome. Hold an (I) win, (you) win, (we) win intention as best we can. There may not be a win, win, win outcome but an intention to stay with that as long as we can may assist us to get closer to that. It's called "go with the flow".

The alternative when things get tough in these circumstances is we are tempted to retreat into the Power/Control Triangle. If we keep doing that we are likely to feel frustrated and drained. We need to stay aware of our direction and just get up one more time than we fall. Above all: breathe!

Understanding: Do you know how electricity works? Even the experts are divided on it. If a light goes out what do we do? We change the globe. If that doesn't work we check the fuse. Still not working? Call an electrician. Moral: we don't need to know how electricity works to change a light bulb.

Many people want to know the detail of why. It's called analysis paralysis. It's not this level of understanding that we are going for here. Rather, understand how to change a light bulb or perhaps even a fuse and let the rest go. We only need to understand how to move not necessarily *why*. If we haven't fully moved through the *acceptance* and *cooperation* cycles, we may find ourselves poring over the detail still trying to explore or explain why this is happening. Again ask: "What can I create, promote and/or allow here?" to keep moving across the bridge. Otherwise our attempts to continually understand may have us standing under it all, unable to move in either direction.

Ultimately, we need *understanding* with compassion which reinforces *acceptance* and *cooperation*, freeing us from our judgements and needing to be right. Then we'll find ourselves moving to a state of *empathy* for ourselves and others. Rumi the great Sufi philosopher said, "On the other side of right and wrong is a field; I'll meet you there."

Empathy might be described as the expression of compassion. This includes compassion for ourselves as well as others. *Empathy* requires us to suspend judgement. Judgement often arrives when we use the word *should* – "I should", "You should", "They should", etc. The suggestion is no "shoulding" on ourselves or anybody else. "Shoulds" keep us in the Power/Control Triangle.

See if you can imagine yourself looking at what you and others are doing in the situation from a different physical position than you are in right at the moment, as if you were in the stalls of a theatre watching a movie about the situation. This metaphoric separation from ourselves and the situation can create new perspectives on what is happening. This distance can assist us to look for the positive intention of all parties, including ourselves. The scene in the movie Dead Poets Society where Robin Williams has Ethan Hawke stand on a table to see things from a different view is a beautiful example of this. Every behaviour has a positive intention at least for the individual acting out, e.g. to get something, keep ourselves safe or protect ourselves in some way.

Once we have identified a new perspective, new tactics and ideas can be employed to bring about the best possible "win, win, win" outcome. The big warning light again is judgement, fear or other limiting or negative thoughts and emotions. If these aren't embraced and worked through we will be catapulted back into the Power/Control Triangle. Crossing this bridge may feel like bungee jumping – our stomach and heart are in our throat at first and it may even feel like we are going to die, in the metaphoric sense at least; but on the other side is a sense of elation that can be indescribable until you've experienced it. Judgement and fear are the antithesis of enthusiasm and loving. If by this time, we are still in judgement or fear we can check out any payoff, especially unconscious payoff, we may be deriving from staying with it. Sometimes we may just unconsciously want the drama of the bungee jump.

Renewed **enthusiasm** is the natural outcome of holding ourselves through all the previous steps across the bridge. If we have cleared what seemed like roadblocks getting across the bridge and used them as stepping stones, our next challenge may just be to hang on to this renewal.

Old habits can die hard so limiting beliefs may re-surface, particularly our beliefs about our entitlement or otherwise to joy and happiness, not to mention success in life. These can be an opportunity to clear even deeper out of awareness limitations that have been blocked from view. Life is a moving process. It is not static and we are a work in progress; practice makes progress not perfection. Simply getting up one more time than we fall can be the key to faking it and faithing it until we make it. Sustained enthusiasm, including enthusiasm about our limitations requires us to think with an "abundance" consciousness. This means embracing the Possibility/Freedom Triangle and not retreating to the "lack" consciousness of the Power/Control Triangle.

Abundance consciousness sees limitations as gifts to grow and learn from. In this way we can find the upside of nearly all situations. We no longer need to "re-act" in old ways; we are able to respond – "response-able" with whatever crosses our path. Chapter 7 *"Sacred Living"*, pursues the transformation from lack to abundance consciousness by posing an extended array of questions that support us to find greater good outcomes.

It has been said that "Having it all is **loving** it all" (source unknown). Carl Rogers, renowned psychologist, proposed the concept of "unconditional positive regard", a concept not too far removed from *unconditional loving*. This does not mean that we condone all behaviours. It does mean we look for the frailty in humankind. It has been said: "We all do the best with what we have and what we know. If we knew better, we would do better" (source unknown). That can be a hard pill to swallow with behaviour that brings harm to oneself or others. Nonetheless if we want to live an *enthusiastic, abundant* and *loving* life it is essential to find a place inside that can at least consider such a possibility. There are no unconditional loving possibilities in the Power/Control Triangle. *Loving it all* is the key to freedom. Find the gifts; find the positive intentions in yourself and others. I think no one says it better than author John-Roger (1991):

- Don't hurt yourself and don't hurt others
- Take care of yourself so you have the strength to take care of others
- Use everything for your upliftment, learning and growth

Starting with some new behaviours, which aim to surrender ineffective habits, can support us to begin the journey. We may notice how our old habits fight back if any discomfort, such as awkwardness, not being in control or emotional upset, is felt. This is a clue to examine the underlying beliefs, values, needs and fears in our unconscious that can keep us trapped in the Power/Control Triangle. See Chapter 2, *"Embracing Vulnerability and Authenticity"* for more on this.

In the Power/Control Triangle life is lived from "have to". In the Possibility/Freedom Triangle life is lived from "choose to". The irony is that if you are living from "have to", you have chosen that. There are only two "have to's" in life: you have to die and you have to choose. People often say you have to pay taxes; no, you can choose to go to jail!

Integrating My Personal Story

At around 12 years of age I found myself developing a strong sense of needing to protect my mother and sister as my father experienced undiagnosed post-traumatic stress disorder (PTSD) problems. My **Rescuer** was born and has been with me for all my life. A close friend later gave it a name, "**St Francis of Assist You**". If he didn't work "**Mighty Mouse**" would arrive to save the day; and if he didn't work "**People Panel Beating Pete**" would arrive.

Later in my adult life I recall another friend suggesting: "You know John there is a little bit of you that thinks if everybody lived the way you thought they should they would be okay". My retort was: "That's rubbish; there's a whole lot of me that thinks that!" It took me quite a while to arrest the attachment I had to making the world a better place and when I did let go I became more effective at improving things around me. These days I find myself spending much more time in **Promoter** – thank heavens, for myself and those around me. However, **St Francis of Assist You** still rears his head with my partner, children and very close friends. Fortunately, they are robust enough and fun loving enough to let me know in loving ways.

It is not to say my **Persecutor** and **Victim** aren't in play. My **Persecutor** and **Victim** stood at the ready to play their part behind my **Rescuer** if it didn't solve what was going on. Standing my ground **aggressively** was a fall-back strategy. In my teenage life, I disowned my **Victim** and rarely gave into anything. When I went to high school I was allowed into a selective public school because my father went there albeit for only one year. My Dad wanted me to do languages because they were the "A" classes. His **Rescuer** was compensating for his lack of opportunity to continue high school; a state he was aggrieved about probably for all his life (**Victim**). I wanted to attend the "B" or "C" classes as they were commerce classes and interested me, but what did I know (**Persecutor/Victim**)? My dad was an upholsterer so they put me in "D", "E" and "F" classes for technical drawing, woodwork and metalwork. I was hopeless at all three and failed my final exams after three years, never achieving more than 35% in all three subjects and scraping through on the other five (**Victim**). I needed six to get through to senior years in high school. The school suggested I leave as I they said would never pass my matriculation. My **Persecutor** showed up to do battle with theirs. I turned up at school to the commerce classes to repeat the year. I was a year behind other students and the school resisted me doing this but I just kept showing up to defy them. I took to it easily and went through to matriculation.

With my father's PTSD and the school's lack of concern for my needs and not listening I developed a defiant **Persecutor** when pushed into a corner, refusing to be a **Victim** to anyone or anything in my mind – "I won't do it and you can't make me!" That part of me is still present today but happily tends to operate with much more cooperation to **create possibilities** others may resist or not see. **I stand for myself but not against others** as I did back then; well, most of the time!

At 23 my bike accident definitely resulted in me experiencing a **Victim** situation and my stubbornness turned into determination when doctors suggested my left leg might need amputating. I told them **they did not have permission to do that.** They saved it and then suggested I would never play tennis again. I had read *"Reach for the Sky"* in my first year at high school; a true story about Douglas Bader an ACE World War II pilot who crashes, loses both his legs from the knees down and with tin legs flies again and plays tennis and golf. I had also seen the film. I was inspired by this. I was a pretty good tennis player and within three weeks of getting both legs out of plaster I was hitting on a ball machine. I created, promoted and allowed a different outcome to what the doctors had predicted. I still play A Grade tennis today.

At 32, facing the loss of a full-term stillborn child, the most devastating thing that has ever happened to me, I found myself at odds with a system that had little idea about how to support such events. Diane (my ex-wife) and I decided to view it as something that might have been but never was and so we didn't see our son at all. She was unconscious during the birth and she too was in danger. That decision haunted me and later I set out to find his grave and name him. It took me nine years to convince authorities to let me find him. They started with: "We have no records of where he is." I persevered and eventually uncovered a system that kept records. Then I asked to name his grave. They said no as it was a nameless grave area. Then I said I wanted him exhumed and placed in a named area. Eventually a new curator compassionately challenged the system himself and was influential not only in letting me place a plaque on my son's grave but also invited other cemeteries in the country to do the same. As serendipity would have it they found the grave on the day of my Grandmother's (first mentor and guide) funeral.

The system changed as **I sought to influence what I could. I created, promoted and allowed** something I didn't expect and was **not attached to**. Today there are many plaques in the area where people have been given the opportunity to change their minds. My son's plaque reads: "Glen Harradine. Stillborn 13.4.80. Remembered and loved by his parents John & Diane, & older brother Mark. His gift to life was Christopher" (our next child). His gift was more than that, though, as if there could be more. His gift was my appreciation for life and my children, grown men now. Would I want to get that gift that way again? Hell no! But I have it.

My son Christopher once asked me the hardest question I have ever been asked. He said: "Dad, if you hadn't lost Glen would you have had me?" I can feel the goose bumps as I write this. I said: "All I know, Christopher, is that we were meant to have you and I wouldn't change that for anything." He has, since the day he was born, the most unconditionally loving heart I have experienced in anyone I know. I am blessed by his and Mark's presence in the world. When I think of this story in this way **I can't possibly find myself in Persecutor, Rescuer or Victim.** I was though – angry like never before with the specialist, the hospital, the funeral parlour and God as best I knew him/her back then. However, as time passed and life went on my deepest sadness morphed through forgiveness into joy for what I did and do have. I focused on what I could **create, promote and allow** from it. Beyond that I decided I would never subordinate myself to fear of anything ever again. When fear showed up I would embrace and live with it and know that it too shall pass.

Questions I Ask Myself and Suggest for You

From these experiences, regardless of any patterns I have developed in the Power/Control Triangle, the two fundamental questions I have learnt to ask myself in any challenging or opportunistic situations are:

1. How did I create, promote and/or allow myself to get here?
2. What can I create, promote and allow from here?

These two questions can stop me from retreating into power and control behaviours and open the door for new insights that may support better outcomes for all involved and at the very least, preserve and build better relationships as I hold myself accountable for my part in circumstances.

See the *Appendix – Companion Exercises to Support Your Understanding and Growth* for more ideas and questions to explore:

- Exercise 1: Letting go of the Power/Control Triangle, page 137
- Exercise 2: Moving into the Possibility/Freedom Triangle, page 138

Chapter 2
Embracing Our Vulnerability and Authenticity

What other people think of us is none of our business; it's their business!

Fishing for the human spirit – for who we truly and authentically are, is more than fishing from the rocks; it requires us to go scuba diving for the fish we seek. Not a task for the fainthearted but a necessary one if we truly want to know our "*selves*" – all of them – and what they want for us. It can be a chilling experience at first and we may shiver at the thought of such a deep exploration into what we may not want to know about our *selves*. Knowing who we truly are requires us to have a sense of our deeper *selves*, which can a bit if not very scary. When we can stand alongside of and hold our vulnerability without collapsing into it, we are truly strong. It just might turn out to be a fantastic adventure with the right wet suit. (We'll get really good at scuba diving, no matter what we encounter.)

Individual Deep Ecology

If you imagine you are an iceberg in the sea (Figure 2.1), you can get an image of how we are made up – what is visible and what is not. What is visible above "see" level are our **behaviours**; what we get a glimpse of are our **thoughts**, although many remain hidden. Our **emotions and feelings** are well hidden unless we consciously think about them. We can then either choose to express or suppress them. This choice depends on the **beliefs and values** we hold below our emotions, again either consciously or unconsciously.

Our beliefs and values will determine how appropriate we think the expression of the emotion or feeling is in a given situation. These beliefs and values over time can become *unconscious habits*, out of our conscious awareness. It's as if we are on automatic pilot as we develop what we might call a *"personal life strategy"* from them, holding on to what we think is right, good or serves us and rejecting what we think is wrong, bad or may harm us in some way.

Even deeper than our beliefs and values are our **needs and fears**. In working with people over many years I have found that two needs and two fears seem to underpin all others; *the need for control and the need for inclusion; the fear of failure and the fear of rejection.*

This model enables us to dive deeply into how we function. It is a "whole person" concept – **our individual ecology** if you like.

Figure 2.1: INDIVIDUAL CONSCIOUSNESS AND UNCONSCIOUS ECOLOGY

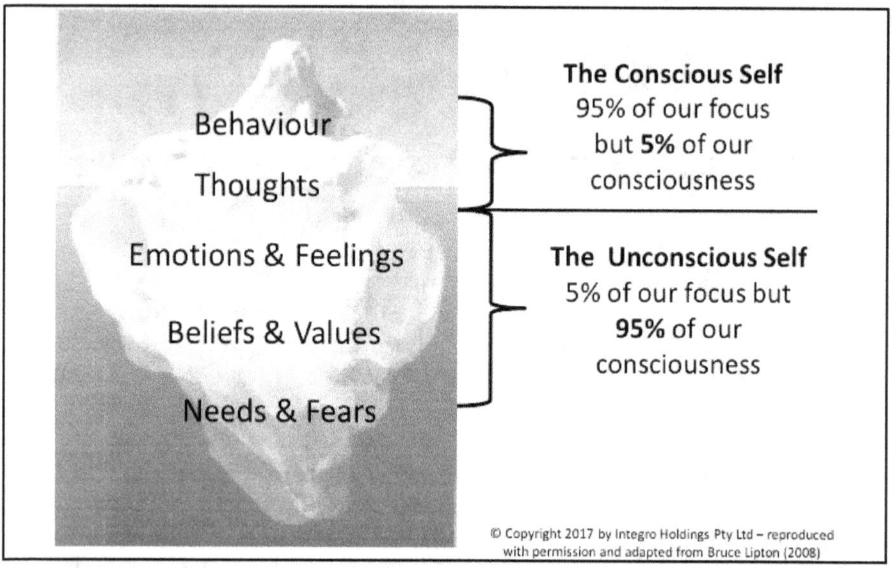

- Behaviour
- Thoughts

The Conscious Self
95% of our focus but **5%** of our consciousness

- Emotions & Feelings
- Beliefs & Values
- Needs & Fears

The Unconscious Self
5% of our focus but **95%** of our consciousness

© Copyright 2017 by Integro Holdings Pty Ltd – reproduced with permission and adapted from Bruce Lipton (2008)

Intentions and goals are nothing but thoughts until acted upon. Often when we set goals we can be out of step with our underlying beliefs and values. A simple example is to focus on our career and be passionate about it, but feel conflicted about how little time we are spending with our children or family. In today's world, this appears to be all too common.

Intentions are the results we get and not the goals we set. When our results do not match our stated goals, more powerful unconscious intentions are out of our awareness or have been consciously pushed down. In either case, inner conflict has arisen and if ignored, our iceberg will begin to crack. For example, if someone close to us, say a boss, asks or tells us to do something and we don't agree with the request or instruction, yet we feel their approval is important or want to avoid their disapproval, we may say yes to it but not fully commit. We then may go about looking like we are complying with what has been asked of us but somehow become distracted, perhaps even sabotaging our efforts. At the same time, we behave in ways that preserve our relationship with the person – which is the real intention. Vulnerability is the by-product of such a dilemma, producing various strategies to protect ourselves from embracing it. Chapter 6 explores the idea of *"Intentionality"* more deeply.

Neuroscience has now shed much light on how we function. Old neural pathways become embedded in our cellular memory (Bruce Lipton, 2008 – *"The Biology of Beliefs"*) and it's now known it is possible to develop new ones; some to replace old ones, some to circumvent them and some that simply enable new ways of being. In addition, what Lipton has shown (Figure 2.2) is that only 5% of our personal strategies are conscious (our behaviours, thoughts and some emotions) and 95% are unconscious (our buried feelings, beliefs, values, needs and fears). In the modern world 95% of our focus can be on our conscious thoughts and behaviours and only 5% on our unconscious, feelings, emotions, beliefs, values, needs and fears – below "see" level. Bruce Lipton has also demonstrated that when there is not alignment between the conscious and the unconscious, the unconscious will always win.

The proposition this evokes is that the more conscious we become, i.e. know all of our *selves* housed in our iceberg, the more likely we will achieve what we want and the greater the chance we have of relieving stress and living freely from a place of joy, spontaneity, enthusiasm, grace, ease and loving. To do this we need to be willing to fall off that beach ball we have been continually trying to sit on, fall into the water and learn to play Olympic standard water polo with it. Embracing our vulnerability is an essential stepping stone in this process. The popular belief that positive thinking alone can sustainably shift us is insufficient to effect long term genuine change and growth. Bruce Lipton adds credence to the idea that we need awareness of our unconscious programming to make the changes we want in our lives.

Most of us are taught to hide our vulnerability, especially in work and other public settings. Phrases like "They wear their heart on their sleeve" are said to indicate that a person is over-emotional, run by their emotions or not in control of themselves. We have been taught very early in life that behaving 'appropriately' gets us positive attention aka love and 'inappropriately' gets us negative attention (AKA less love). Either way we usually prefer any attention rather than none at all. Isolation, being left out or ignored is untenable for us as a way of being in the world, i.e. our need for inclusion and a fear of rejection is primary in developing our personal strategies.

We are socialised to toughen and be strong as we grow up. In the end, we come to associate vulnerability with weakness, too much emotion and lacking independence. So, we cover it up, bury it in our unconscious, aiming to present in a way that suggests we can handle whatever life hands us. God forbid we should express our anger, frustration, disappointment, sadness, hurt, fear or pain in anything other than socially acceptable ways. Sitting on that proverbial beach ball can get very tiring.

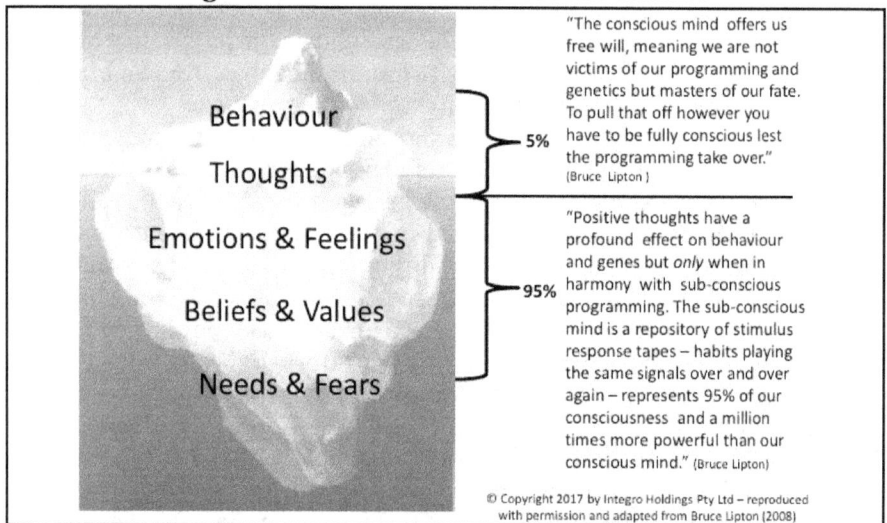

Figure 2.2: INDIVIDUAL ECOLOGY AND BELIEFS

"The conscious mind offers us free will, meaning we are not victims of our programming and genetics but masters of our fate. To pull that off however you have to be fully conscious lest the programming take over." (Bruce Lipton)

"Positive thoughts have a profound effect on behaviour and genes but *only* when in harmony with sub-conscious programming. The sub-conscious mind is a repository of stimulus response tapes – habits playing the same signals over and over again – represents 95% of our consciousness and a million times more powerful than our conscious mind." (Bruce Lipton)

© Copyright 2017 by Integro Holdings Pty Ltd – reproduced with permission and adapted from Bruce Lipton (2008)

The only way out is through. Our strategies of pushing our way through, tap dancing around issues, over analysing what is happening or has happened simply don't cut it in the long term. It has been suggested that two things create change; the pain is so great we can't stand it anymore or the opportunity is so big we can't leave it alone; unfortunately, most people are motivated by the former. Living in our comfort zone is living between these two extremes and does not sustain deep change.

When we look at all that comes our way as containing gifts, it is then we are empowered to better meet the challenges and opportunities in our lives. In some circumstances, it is harder to find the gifts than others and this is not to minimise tragedy that may befall us. Our vulnerability is front and centre in these situations so finding gifts may be the furthest thing from our minds, especially early on in events that have set us back.

The alternative to finding gifts in everything is to stay stuck in unconscious and often limiting patterns which are ruled by old beliefs and values. Even positive or expanding patterns can become limiting at some point. Many would say they are content to do this, often retreating to what is right and wrong in the world and how things "should" be. Try not "shoulding" on yourself or anybody else and see where it takes you.

Unconscious right/wrong patterns can run our lives – but would you rather be right or happy? Many if not most respond that they would rather be happy but spend 90% of their time trying to be right or at least not being wrong. Be right by all means but be prepared to take what goes with that. Guilt and resentment drive right/wrong thinking. Guilt is a great course corrector and can assist us to change but staying stuck in it is not useful. Deepak Chopra (1996) suggests that "resentment is like taking poison and expecting your enemy to die". These feelings aim to protect the vulnerability that lives underneath them. So, what is the way through?

Personal Transformation

One way of viewing our development and raising our consciousness is displayed in Figure 2.3.

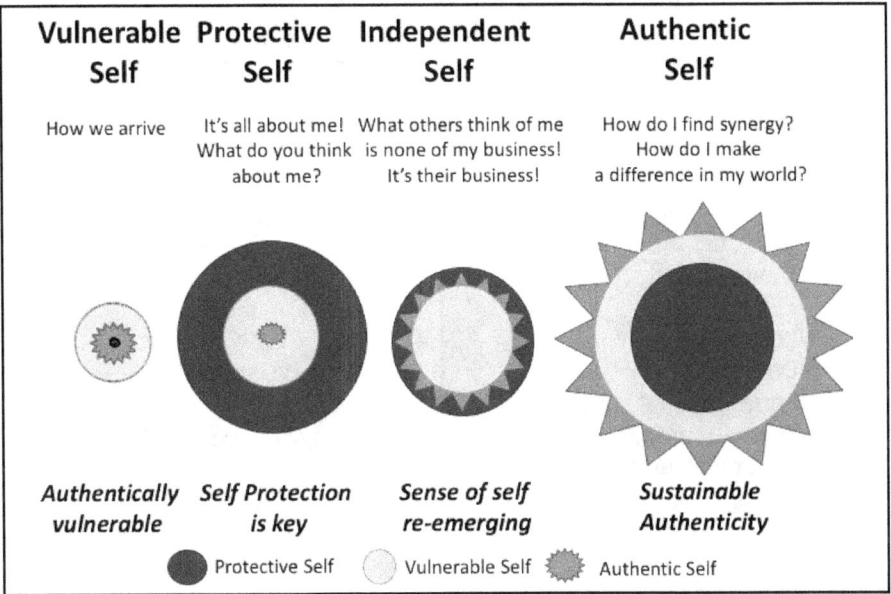

Figure 2.3: PERSONAL TRANSFORMATION

We are born vulnerable, needing to be taken care of on every level. In our vulnerability lies our authenticity. When we are hungry or soil ourselves we cry. We just go for it. Later as we are socialised to deny our vulnerability we also deny our authenticity. Both these parts (*selves*) of us are vital in finding a sense of purpose. Yet they become overshadowed as the world unfolds before us and we develop an unending array of "*Protective Selves*" aiming to strengthen us against what the world serves up and in the long run these *Protective Selves* weaken us. Once we have selected our range of protective selves we stop fishing and our unconscious habits inflexibly run our lives. When we can re-embrace our vulnerability, we can re-discover who we are in our authenticity.

Notice in Figure 2.3 how the *Protective Self* initially dominates both the vulnerable and "*Authentic Self*". Its aim is to prevent negative feelings emerging and to support us getting what we think we want. Building and maintaining *Protective Selves* takes energy and the longer we do it the more it weakens us, although we don't think so.

We think we find strength in the walls we have built around us. They can speed up illness and *"dis – ease"*. It's not that *Protective Selves* aren't legitimate and indeed necessary, but they come to run us rather than us having dominion over them. It is then that they become problematic and even dysfunctional.

In their classic work *"Born to Win"*, Muriel James and Dorothy Jongeward (1971) propose that we develop life scripts to defend ourselves. They form the basis of our *Protective Selves*. Figure 2.4 contains a list of life scripts put forward in their book and some I have added. It's of course not complete. Take a look and see if there are any you identify with. Make up your own if they come to you as you read them.

Figure 2.4: Life Scripts & Themes

• Be strong	• Driving people crazy
• Losing my mind	• Committing suicide
• Being the best	• Carrying my cross
• Saving sinners	• Building empires
• Being helpful	• Being miserable
• Having a ball	• Walking on eggshells
• Trying hard	• Missing the boat
• Bossing others	• Sorry for being alive
• Do it my way	• Getting stepped on
• Stumbling but recovering	• Looking for a pot of gold
• Succeeding then failing	• I have to be perfect
• Never getting anywhere	• It has to be perfect
• Saving for a rainy day	• Be perfect
• I have to get it right	• Give it to me
• I can't be wrong	• Being responsible
• I've got it wrong	• Pleasing others
• It's not enough	• I need to win
• I'm not enough	• I can't lose
• Being positive	• Do the right thing
• Poor me	• I'll do it my way
• Follow the rules	• It's hard to trust

Adapted and expanded from James and Jongeward – Born to Win (1971)

What might be the needs and fears, beliefs and values that have caused you to adopt the two or three scripts you have listed for yourself? How have these served you?

There is a payoff or positive intention for holding onto any aspect of our *selves*, even when we can identify we would be better off to let it go. The inner intention of what it wants for us is positive and can trump any thought or behaviour to the contrary if it forms part of your *Protective Self system*.

Every one of the above life scripts has a positive intention or payoff. See if you can work out what they are. That positive intention will keep us running the life script until we are aware of what is happening – the pain or the opportunity is big enough for us to want to find an alternative way to meet that intention and payoff. We might wonder what could be the positive intention of some of the above life scripts, for example: "sorry for being alive" – that could be something like gaining acceptance or depending on how it is said, to stand up for ourselves; what about "losing my mind" – why would we think that is positive? Well it could be that falling into that means we avoid being overwhelmed by too much responsibility. The positive intention of constantly being miserable (victim consciousness) is attention; the positive intention about pleasing others is to be liked. Both can be exhausting in different ways.

Every limitation we buy into wants something for us and we need to find out what that thing is if we want to move beyond our *Protective Self*; otherwise the need for that unconscious payoff will eventually drag us back to the limitation. Our job is to separate the positive intention from the limitation and build an expansive pathway that holds the positive intention and serves as an antidote to the limitation.

These life scripts along with their often-unconscious payoffs or positive intentions build to form part of our strategy to push, please, perfect, rationalise, avoid and judge our way through life.

As mentioned previously, two things create change: pain and opportunity, with pain the prime motivator. Everything between these two extremes is our comfort or familiar zone (also called our familiar zone). We don't learn anything in our comfort zone. We just reinforce what we think we already know or believe.

Start noticing what you are noticing about your defences. Build awareness about what triggers your defences, i.e. your *Protective Selves*. Don't try to fix them. At first just notice situations where you feel out of sorts; what people say, including compliments that you may push away; who that person is to you and how much you think they matter. Use the iceberg model to unpack what is going on at the deeper layers of your ecology: what are the behaviours you are noticing in yourself and others; what thoughts occur from those behaviours, especially judgements; what emotions and feelings are you experiencing and be prepared to own these no matter what they are – pushing them down has us back up on the beach ball; what beliefs and values might feel transgressed or violated in some way; lastly what needs and fears are present for you. This is where our vulnerability is likely to really show itself if not earlier on your fishing trip. When the fish are biting it's not normal to go into shore or a so called safe harbour – even when the weather gets a little stormy. Of course, if it stirs up too much and it feels like a tsunami is heading your way keep yourself safe, but be prepared to get back out to "see" when the storm passes.

When we first get in touch with some of our deeper vulnerability it can shake us up. As we learn to stand with it and not collapse into it then our strength grows and the opportunity for positive change arrives. To know where we are going and truly believe we can get there, we need to know where we are coming from, what we want to take with us and what we want or even need to leave behind. It is here that we can find our heart's desire and what we want at a soul level. This is not meant to be an exhaustive psychoanalysis, although in some cases it might be. We do need insight into our patterns, however, and know what triggers them. The "stuff" doesn't go away; we just get better at managing it.

Knowing our selves at the deepest levels, not something we are taught to do well, is the road to an *"Independent Self"* and an *"Authentic Self"* – the road to self-mastery.

The Vedic tradition suggests there are six core drivers in the deepest parts of us (Vladimir Dimitrov, 2003). See Figure 2.5.

Figure 2.5: CORE DRIVERS - THE SIX BUCKETS

Each bucket will have an *"equilibrium point"* for each individual, i.e. each person will need to fill each of the buckets to a point where there is a sense of personal satisfaction, especially from the emotions and feelings down to needs and fears, i.e. in our unconscious. If they are emptied below that point we will move heaven and earth to re-establish the homeostasis we have set for ourselves. In other words, if at the top of the iceberg our conscious mind (behaviour and thoughts) are at odds with a bucket being filled to equilibrium and ostensibly emptying it below its equilibrium point, our vulnerability will be triggered. We will feel conflicted internally and if our conscious mind pushes us to continue there will be a rebellion in the unconscious mind with a desire to refill whatever bucket(s) is below its equilibrium point. Equally if someone else triggers a defence in us it's because one of our buckets feels emptied by their remarks.

So, what happens if there is a battle between the unconscious and the conscious mind? The unconscious mind always wins out (Bruce Lipton, 2008). Our primary life strategy will determine how each of us will do that. However we do that it will involve a combination of *"fight"*, *"flight"*, *"freeze"* (concurrent fight and flight) or *"fragment"* (particularly if the internal disturbance continues for a while and we have been freezing) tactics. The alternative is to *"flow"* and that requires opening up to our deeper ecology, developing greater awareness of what is going on in our unconscious. That includes embracing our vulnerability which can be understood through the filters of the buckets.

We can generally identify two of the six buckets that tend to dominate the others, i.e. they need filling more than the others and/or if emptied below equilibrium are given greater attention to refill them. Often there is a presenting bucket that appears more important than the others. For example, we might think our *"Knowledge"* bucket is critical and study hard, build skills and competencies to fill it up. However underneath we might be looking for the recognition that comes from it. The real bucket we want to fill here is the *"Love"* bucket.

> Knowing our patterns and their related vulnerability is a fundamental first key to living an independent and authentic life.

The *Independent Self* cannot evolve without first understanding its protective strategies at the deepest levels. Once we are aware of them and of course all the associated vulnerabilities, we are in a position to run them rather than have them run us. You'll notice from Figure 2.3 that the *"Whole Self"* (the *Vulnerable*, *Protective*, *Independent* and *Authentic* selves) gets a little smaller in this stage. For a time as we learn and try new ways of being we might feel a little smaller. When we have practiced our protective strategies for many years they don't disappear overnight. Whilst we aim to pull back on our protective ways we can be unsure what to replace them with. It does however leave room for the vulnerability to seem bigger; the very thing we have being trying to avoid. But instead of using our *Protective Self* to quell the vulnerability, our awareness almost forces us to embrace it. Once we are aware of something we can never not be aware of it. Oh, we still might try and push it down but our unconscious, that has now become conscious, knows that.

So, what to do? Get in touch with the unconscious beliefs both that limit you and expand you. These are apparent from our self-talk at the conscious level and recognised through feelings and sensations. We can then begin to imagine and play with possible unconscious beliefs (the unspoken sub-text if you will) that might have been taken on in the past but buried in the unconscious. In this way, we begin our authentic journey. It is tenuous at first so we need to be patient with ourselves; we will want to retreat to old protective ways. We just need to notice that is what we are doing and bring ourselves back to moving towards breaking through to a place where the *Authentic Self* becomes primary.

The process itself yields even more vulnerability that has been out of our awareness. It may mean facing losses we have not previously allowed ourselves to experience. Friendships can change; life choices shift; we may find greater levels of conflict present themselves. These things are brought to us to determine how true to our core beliefs we are willing to be. The willingness to break through old protective patterns that can undermine our integrity is essential and it takes courage; sometimes even more courage than it did to face and embrace our vulnerability. Standing in "what other people think of me is none of my business; it's their business" is challenging. This is not an egocentric againstness I am proposing here. It is simply standing for us without judgement of ourselves or others; one may say standing for ourselves in loving. One technique to support yourself is to imagine yourself as far into the earth as you are tall, as if to form a statue that is secured into the ground as far as it is above it. This will make it much harder for the world to bounce you out of your authenticity than from your previous protective strategies. The walls of Jericho did eventually come tumbling down.

Developing an *Independent Self* assists us to grow into who we truly want to be. However, it doesn't necessarily connect us with others. We don't go up alone! To evolve into having our authenticity navigate our lives we need to let go of old patterns. This is perhaps one of the hardest things to do, especially if it disturbs how we have thought life "should" be. It is one thing to develop an *Independent Self* separated from others, but unless we want to live completely alone on a mountain or desert island for the rest of our lives we will inevitably meet and relate to others. Our *Independent Self* is most tested in these situations and none more than in our family of origin (FOO) and primary relationships with partners and children. Our vulnerability has an even larger presence when we choose to operate from an authentic position. If anything will have us regress back to old ways it is how we operate in our FOO and with our partner and children.

Imagine standing among your FOO, partners and children and being absolutely neutral about the negative or limiting dynamics that are playing out. Standing for yourself (as far into the earth as you are tall), no againstness and detached from any outcomes no matter what is served up to you. You could be in touch with your protective ways, the vulnerabilities they are managing and yet still be completely authentic in a way that supports yourself and all around you.

It is possible. Is it possible 100% of the time? Perhaps; but we are human. Authenticity is not about being the perfectly aligned human being; it is recognising when we are not aligned and declaring it – notice how the lines between the *selves* are less defined in the glyph. Gaining skill to live authentically is as essential as understanding our inner world. Much has been written about the skills we need and the references and recommended reading at the end of this book is a good start. I have also suggested skill building through the exercises provided in the *"Appendix – Companion Exercises to Deepen Your Understanding and Growth"*. The willingness to persevere with new ways is what it takes and simply to get up one more time than we fall.

Developing Detachment

A starting point for living authentically is to develop detachment. Some interpret this as indifference, disconnection, disengagement or uncaring. If you want to know more, take a look at works by Deepak Chopra, Wayne Dyer, Scott Peck, John-Roger and many others (see "*Recommend Readings*"). For now, let's settle on Deepak Chopra's (1996) definition from his book "*The Seven Spiritual Laws of Success*": "In order to acquire anything in the physical universe, you have to relinquish your attachment to it. This doesn't mean you give up your intention to create your desire. You give up your attachment to the result... Detachment is based on the unquestioned belief in the power of the true self."

When we are engaged with others we do so at different levels of importance to us. This can often determine how attached we get and when we are attached it is a sure-fire way to trigger our *Protective Selves*.

The idea of detachment is so counter to so many of us it is almost impossible for some to even contemplate. The business world has been built on behaviourist theory of carrot and stick motivation. I have had extensive experience in large worldwide corporations of what I now consider a fallacious philosophy that does more harm than good, all built around attachment to stated goals – for the most part unachievable goals thrust upon organisation leaders and employees to satisfy an insatiable share market.

The starting point for detachment is to buy into the concept. This means challenging some of our deeper unconscious beliefs. These beliefs have been installed by societal norms and have strong neural pathways. Figure 2.6 "*Emotional States of Task Actions*", describes what happens to us with varying levels of engagement and involvement in an activity and the corresponding levels of attachment/detachment.

What this diagram is depicting is that if we are not involved in something and we are highly attached to being so then we are likely to experience "*Frustration*". If we are not involved in something and we are also highly attached to being so we will experience being "*Perfectionistic*" and/or "*Painfully Resistant*" to what is happening. If we are not involved and not attached then "*Boredom*" is likely to occur. The irony is that *boredom* often shows up when we are about to learn something new that we don't really want to engage with.

These defensive strategies of *Frustration*, *Perfectionism*, *Resistance* and *Boredom* predispose us to invoke our *Protective Selves* and hide our vulnerability.

The alternative is maintaining high levels of participation and engagement and remaining *detached* from the result. This requires us to hold respect for ourselves and others. To sustain that we need to function from our *Authentic Self*; and to do that we must take a deep dive into the abyss of the unconscious, fishing at the bottom of the iceberg and catching the *vulnerability* that resides there, or swimming around in the pool with the beach ball, whichever metaphor suits you. Then we can resurface stronger in our *selves*, knowing our *selves* and living integrously from our *Authentic Self*. This leaves more room for holding a vision of what we want, letting go in a way that allows new things to show up that we may not yet have dreamed of. It also means listening to others, showing respect, to see what they have to offer.

Figure 2.6: EMOTIONAL STATES OF TASK ACTIONS

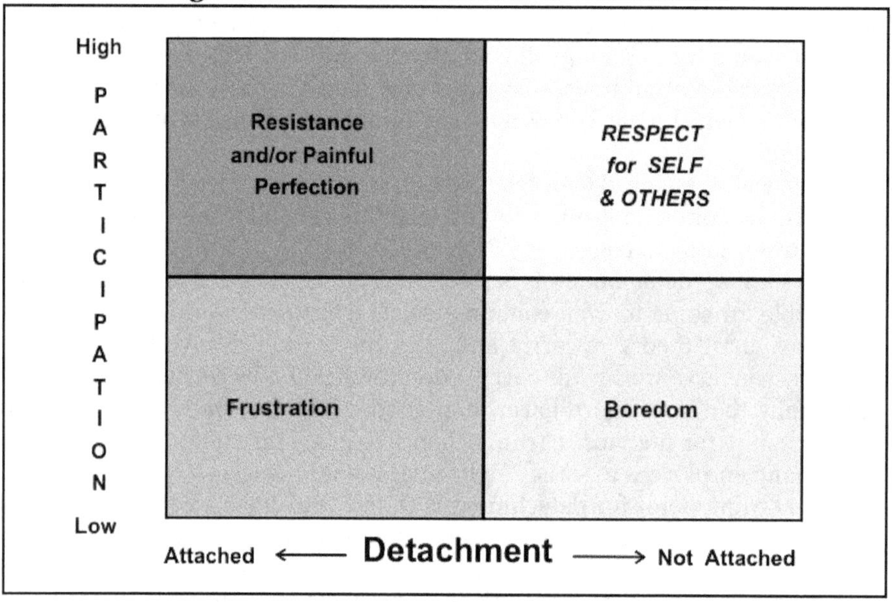

	Attached ←	Detachment → Not Attached
High PARTICIPATION	Resistance and/or Painful Perfection	RESPECT for SELF & OTHERS
Low	Frustration	Boredom

With detachment, we can suspend judgements and be objective; we can embrace emotions without collapsing into them; we can accept what we cannot change; we can observe ourselves without a pull in one direction or another; we can hold for a situation without becoming enmeshed in it; we can own our mistakes and course correct; we can let go and love it all.

Wayne Dyer (2004) in his book *"You'll See It When You Believe It"* suggests that *"we lose our mind and gain our senses."* This is a good starting point to build awareness and *awareness* is the first key to it all.

Integrating My Personal Story

Whilst I have written about the loss of Glen in Chapter 1, it bears a second mention. I can never remember **feeling more vulnerable before or since**; not during my father's outbursts and suicide attempts in my teenage years, not being retrenched in my middle 40s and not even leaving my wife and children when my marriage broke up, although that came close.

The sense of not knowing what was coming next in these circumstances exposed **Vulnerability** in ways no other circumstances have for me. It triggered an **authentic journey**, had me rebuild my relationship with my father and come to terms with who I really was. Many of my ***Protective Selves*** had served me well but they falter, as they do, during a crisis.

I started to question conventional ways of living. I saw a psychologist as some depression began to set in; something I had not experienced before, at least that I was aware of. The birth of Christopher re-enforced these conventional ways of living and I was glad he was here, but something in me was stirring that over time I was unable to quell. I was beginning in my mid to late 30s to question my sexuality. This, Glen's death and Christopher's birth threw everything into internal chaos. Of course, **St Francis of Assist You** made sure my external world was functioning; my lawns were mowed, the garden pristine, the house renovated, the pool sparkling, and the career on track (**all to perfection – one of my Protective Selves** – or so I thought).

My personal life was still working at a level. Diane and I had a good marriage and we loved and love our children. My career took off and it became a focal point as it does for so many with young families and the primary drive to provide subjugated any thought of separation or addressing my sexuality.

My career was so enjoyable and successful it was a halcyon time for me then. However, it reinforced shutting down any attempts at coming out and I wasn't even sure how to describe yet alone label what was happening. I just kept **pushing through** (*yet another Protective Self at play*). The pain was to get so great however I couldn't stand it anymore. It was my career that ultimately gave me the confidence to come to terms with my **Authentic** or **True Self**. I can't recall a time when I was so validated by the outside world. The **need for recognition and validation** *(another Protective Self)* stemmed from the criticism I had had as a child and I overcompensated for it by filling up my *Knowledge Bucket* to gain that recognition and defeat the messages I had received as a teenager.

My career at Digital Equipment Corporation (DEC) appeared to expunge so much from the past. However, as the top of my iceberg, i.e. behaviour and thoughts began to feel safe it unearthed **deeper needs** I was forced to recognise and come to terms with. Ironically it was the motivational system I was working with that triggered awareness of my own inner motivations. DEC was one of the most successful IT organisations in the world (in 1991 125,000 people around the world, debt free, $2bn USD in the bank). I managed the most sophisticated goaling, performance management and compensations systems in existence at the time and probably since that time. The founder of the company insisted that sales people not be paid commission; rather they were paid a substantially higher base rate and there was an attractive share option plan for high achievement. The shares at the time were worth about $135USD per share. The CEO had been on the front page of New York's Time Magazine as CEO of the decade and the company is cited in the best seller "*In Search of Excellence*" (Tom Peters and Robert Waterman).

As time passed and some new senior executives were recruited from competitors, pressure mounted to introduce incentives for sales people. The UK group had tried to introduce a 5% variable income component for sales people for a number of years and failed. I was sent to Geneva to their conference to figure out what were the blockages to getting it through. On the plane ride home I set an intention to achieve a 2% variable component within six months. I was told I was wasting my time. I wasn't attached to achieving it, interestingly enough, but I did believe in the idea at the time. I did it in five months and was hailed a hero. I received a handsome share option reward and was named employee of the year. It was one of the worst professional things that I could have done. It opened Pandora's Box to greater levels of variable income and the attachment to personal gain. It undermined cooperation across divisions, which was vital to the company's success in an incredibly fast changing market.

As I watched a culture move from group wide pride to desperation and decisions at the top based on personal agendas, I became very disillusioned with what I had thought was a reasonable way of operating. Then a peer of a competitive company referred me to a book called *"Punished by Rewards"* (Alphie Kohn, 1999). It opened my eyes to a new way of thinking. Alphie Kohn interviewed B.F. Skinner (psychologist famous for behaviourist theories) at the end of his life and was amazed to discover as many experiments in Skinner's archives that disproved his theories as supported them. Inside I became the behaviourist anti-Christ. I developed a penchant for different ways of understanding the human condition and motivation that are predicated on both individual and group well-being.

DEC was bought by Compaq in 1998 and then later by Hewlett Packard. Many have not even heard of DEC today and much contributed to its downfall. I firmly believe the impact of variable income on its culture of cooperation was one of those contributing factors. Self-interest replaced cooperation engendered by its founder Ken Olsen. When Compaq bought Digital I was later to discover that DEC was within three weeks of bankruptcy and this had not been declared publically. A book has been written by Ed Schein called *"DEC is Dead; Long Live DEC"*. It's about DEC employees who were retrenched in the 1990s (65,000 of them) and how they tried to create what they had at Digital everywhere else they were employed.

When I saw the negative impact of incentives introduced into DEC I left my role and established myself in organisational change work. I worked around the world and it kept my traditional life going until I was 47. The gift in the change was to embark on researching alternatives to attachment and behaviourist methodologies and lead me into a **deep personal and professional development journey**.

Today I am less attached to being the behaviourist anti-Christ. I now think it does have a place. However, when motivational thinking is only focused on behaviour at the conscious level and ignores the bottom layers of the iceberg I have come to deeply understand Bruce Lipton's view that unconscious programming must align with behavioural effort to sustainably effect desired change. This is the case not only at the individual level but also at the organisational, community and societal level. Western culture's love affair with behaviourism and its accompanying attachment underpinnings may explain why research has revealed 85% to 90% of change and large project efforts fail. What's that definition of insanity? "Doing the same thing over and over again and expecting a different result!"

Questions I ask myself and suggest for you:

The following questions are central to me now in any given situation. As you reflect on your own vulnerabilities and levels of authenticity, see if these questions can assist in supporting you to make greater good decisions.

1. What *Protective Selves* are present in this situation?
2. How are my *Protective Selves* playing out in this situation?
3. Are they lifting and/or supporting me to find a greater good outcome or holding me back?
4. If they are holding me back what judgements or fears am I running on myself and/others?
5. In the case of judgements on others, how are these judgements and fears a mirror of my own limitations?
6. What judgements and fears I have about myself and others am I prepared to forgive and let go of?
7. What judgements and fears I have about myself and others am I not prepared to forgive and I hold onto?
   a. What price do I pay for this?
   b. What is the payoff for me in holding on to the judgements?
   c. Which is bigger – the payoff or the price?
8. What *Protective Selves* might be responding if I am not willing to forgive the judgements on myself and others?
9. What buckets are being filled or emptied by my choices?
10. What attachments am I running? E.g. being right, not being wrong, winning, not losing?
11. What limiting beliefs are being inferred and triggering me emotionally in this situation?
    a. What is the positive intention of this belief?
12. How can I reframe any beliefs that are holding me back and retain the positive intention of the limiting belief?
    a. What are the positive qualities I can draw on to assist a more expansive perspective and to lift in this situation?

My experience is to simply get up one more time than I fall.

See the *Appendix – Companion Exercises to Support Your Understanding and Growth* for more ideas and questions to explore:

- Exercise 3: Exploring Your Protective Selves, page 140
- Exercise 4: Reframing Beliefs, page 141
- Exercise 5: Early Steps to Developing an *Authentic Self*, page 145

Chapter 3
Taking Charge of the Past

**Embracing our story in order to let it go –
what we resist we are stuck with!**

Transference from the Past to Today

Chapters 1 and 2 focused on the patterns we have developed to cope with life today. These patterns emerge very early in life. Researchers suggest they are formed by the time we are seven years old. For example, if we learnt that we got our own way pushing others around in the sand pit at kindergarten we'll develop a pattern to do that in other and later situations; if we learnt that we received a pat on the head for being a good boy or girl we'll please others as we get older; and if we were criticised a lot we'll learn to avoid criticism and the rejection that goes with it.

We link past experiences (positive and negative) to current situations and especially to intimate relationships. The psychological term for this is "transference". We are often unaware we are doing this, that is, it is unconscious. Mastering transference is not only a critical skill to sustain and uplift relationships, but also essential for us to take charge of our defences rather than have these run us, i.e. to be more in charge of our life and ultimately be happier, we need to let go of our past.

Many definitions of transference have been proposed: "Transference is the transference of past feelings, conflicts and attitudes into present relationships, situations and circumstances. It evolves from unresolved or unsatisfactory childhood experiences in relationships with parents or important figures." (Wilson & Kneisel, 1996) i.e. perceptions of how roles, especially authoritative roles, that have been formulated in one's mind and are applied to current situations.

Transference was first explored by Sigmund Freud as he witnessed how his patients brought past experiences of close relationships into his therapy sessions and applied these experiences to their relationships with him. Whether they were positive or negative experiences, the key was how patients unconsciously linked Freud with past significant others, especially authority figures and particularly parental figures. For example, if a patient experienced their father as distant and unfeeling they would likely experience Freud as distant and unfeeling; if they experienced their father as loving and protective they would attribute these qualities to Freud.

Transference knows no contextual constraints, i.e. without awareness it will filter into all aspects of our relationships, and especially those with significant adults. It doesn't stop there though. The Harvard Business Review's article *"The Power of Transference"* by Michael Maccoby (2004) addresses how transference plays out with authority figures and leadership in the business world. His research showed that invariably what one thought of as a good father also applied to how they viewed a good manager. Moreover, he found cultural differences between East and West. Where Westerners saw good fathers and managers as helpful and encouraging independence, Asians sought a more protective and teaching style in their fathers and leaders.

Transference is not presented here as a good or bad thing, but without awareness it can control us as we unconsciously react to any given situation. It shows up especially when we are feeling stressed and negative transference can dominate our approach in dealing with our stress. Transference doesn't stop with parents and authority figures, it also occurs amongst siblings. For example, if one child feels unfairly treated by one or both parents and they perceive other siblings are treated better, the sense of rejection that may emerge from that can be projected onto their later life partner where they encounter similar circumstances, e.g. a partner paying a lot of attention to a close relative.

Let's say a couple have two children and one parent who has felt unfairly treated by their family of origin compared to a sibling, witnesses their partner treat the two children differently. Their upset from their childhood is infused into the present situation and without awareness they may simply react critically toward their partner, perhaps out of proportion to the event. The partner, again without awareness, may react negatively to any feedback, especially if they have come from a family that is critical of wrong doing. We now have a negative bonding pattern built into their relationship that can eventually undermine and dominate the relationship if it persists. More can be discovered about bonding patterns in Chapter 5, *"Unconditional Relating"*.

Transference from Our Parents

According to Maccoby, maternal transference begins a little earlier than paternal transference. He suggests that a father figure is often perceived as distant and detached and looks for high performance. He also describes the mother archetype as an authority figure but also viewed as the deliverer of unconditional love as well as the first person to say "no" to us. He proposes this creates two mother archetypes in the child's mind that are presented in children's stories – fairy godmother and witch.

Societal norms about what constitutes good and bad parenting are enmeshed with our direct experience of our parents and formulate how we respond to life. A good demonstration of this has been the shift in society's views about physical discipline of children. Moving from the razor strap in the early 20th century, to caning at school extending into the middle and late 20th century, to a tan across the back of the legs with the bare hand being permissible and then to striking at all being outlawed. What is viewed today as child abuse was once seen as normal. Parents who hit are vilified today and yet the same behaviour 20 or more years ago would be acceptable. I have many clients who speak of being hit in one breath and then defend their parents by minimising the impact on them explaining "it was normal back then". A young child can harbour much resentment from being struck even mildly but if the bulk of the relationship is more loving can also feel guilty for upsetting the parent. This dynamic forms the foundation of conditional love that most of us experience. See Chapter 5, "*Unconditional Relating*" for more about this.

These feelings are carried forward into adulthood as we develop protective patterns to deal with the conflicts that arise in our lives. See Chapter 2, "*Embracing Vulnerability and Authenticity*" which explores our protective approaches more deeply and how we can redevelop our 'authentic selves'. What is important now is to understand how transference, if not brought into awareness and understood, can fuel conflict to a point where it is gridlocked and feels unresolvable. This can ultimately cause breakdown in our relationships with partners, children, family members, friends and work colleagues, including leaders.

Positive or Negative Transference – Neither Good nor Bad

Positive transference can be as limiting as negative transference. When we consistently bring forward idealised images of people we blind ourselves to their limitations – and we all carry limitations. As well as projecting our judgements on to others we can become over-critical of ourselves. Negative transference, if understood, can be a breakthrough to healing relationships not only in the present but from the past. When we are judgemental about another whether an idealised view or a critical one, the first step is to recognise our initial experience of the judgement. Then we can ask how much of this judgement is really what is happening right now and how much is a carryover from the past.

Identifying and owning our patterns of behaviour and thought are essential to healing the past, building more effective and open communication strategies, and creating better and more loving relationships. But it is not just thoughts and behaviours we need to address. We need to understand the emotions, feelings, beliefs, values, needs and fears that live inside of us, especially the unconscious habits we have formed in our life – how they serve us and how they limit us. Chapter 2, *"Living Freely"* explored how our judgemental ways trap us into either aiming to control others or not be controlled by others. Transference is at the source of the conflict.

Sorting the past from the present and not projecting either of these into the future, is fundamental to assigning appropriate meaning to current situations. To do that we must take responsibility for our own behaviours, thoughts, feelings, beliefs, values, needs and fears. To do that we need to pay attention to how neuroscience has shown that our unconscious mind is far more powerful than our conscious mind. See Chapter 2 for more about this.

As discussed previously, Bruce Lipton (2008), in his work *"The Biology of Beliefs"*, has demonstrated that 95% of our approach to life is unconscious and when there is a battle between the unconscious and the conscious minds, the unconscious will always win. Recognising what is going on in our unconscious mind can minimise the limiting effects of both positive and negative transference. Remember that any sort of transference at its core is neither good nor bad, right nor wrong. What is important is to know when it is triggering patterns that are limiting us.

Mastering transference requires understanding of what is going on in our three brains and how they interact. Table 3.1 below lists elements of our three brains.

Figure 3.1: THE THREE BRAINS (FROM DR SCOTT WALKER)

95%		5%
UNCONSCIOUS	SUB-CONSCIOUS	CONSCIOUS
REFLEXES (Reptilian)	EMOTIONAL REACTIONS (Mammalian)	COGNITIVE RESPONSES (Neocortex)
• Survival • Fight • Flight • Instinctual • Territoriality • Procreation • Physiological functions	• Emotions and feelings • Memory • Sexuality • Perception • Hormonal • Ideals • Beliefs	• Directed behaviour • Language • Structure • Reasoning • Interpretation • Ideas • Meaning

The reptilian and mammalian brains store composite images of our early caregivers including, but not limited to, their gaze (e.g. smiles and frowns), their voices, their emotions, how love was expressed between caregivers and to us (or not), and how conflict was handled (or not). The interactions between our caregivers, others and us were also lodged in these parts of your brain and as we grew our neo-cortex aimed to make sense of them all.

The reptilian brain is most interested in survival and the general neuropsychological view is that the brain is wired to detect threat i.e. negative stimuli over other experiences. Fear therefore can dominate the expression of love; for example, when in our early years a sense of distrust, shame or guilt is embedded through negative experiences with our caregivers. These negative experiences are like heat seeking missiles looking for somewhere to land. The meaning we make of our early experiences finds its way into adult relationships unless we learn to transform it.

Neuropsychology has explored how attachment patterns influence adult patterns from when we are very young, i.e. are transferred to later relationships. Connection with our loved ones, especially with partners and children has the potential to reveal all we need to know about our transference and its impact on those relationships. Chapter 2 explores the idea of "detachment". A precursor to developing detachment is to better understand what we are attached to. What we are attached to is created very early in life.

A number of researchers including neuroscientists have uncovered some powerful data about how our early years unconsciously influence our later ones if these early patterns are not interrupted by the effort to grow and learn about ourselves.

Louis Cozolino (2014) *The Neuroscience of Human Relationships – Attachment and the Developing Social Brain,* four attachment styles identifies: "Secure, Resistant (Ainsworth et al., 1978), Avoidant, Disorgansied." The research showed how various parenting (mothering) style impact very young children and how they emerge as adults.

According to Cozolino *Secure attachment* in children develops from mothers who are "emotionally available, perceptive and effective." Infants experiencing separation from and reunion with their parent moved toward their caregiver for comfort and support and were easily soothed. As adults, they demonstrated trust in the reliability of their partners. They had good memories and "narrative coherency".

Resistant attachment resulted from inconsistent availability from caregivers who he describes as "enmeshed and ambivalent". Whilst infants approached their caregiver after separation looking for comfort they displayed anger and resistance to comfort offered. They were too easily calmed and slow to return to play. As adults they were fearful of abandonment and could distrust their romantic partners' availability and commitment. They could also show jealousy and focussed on emotional connection. They also would be output focussed, concerned with intrusions, pressure, and ideals or rageful.

Avoidant attachment emerged when caregivers were "dismissive, distant and rejecting". Separation and reunion resulted in infants avoiding comfort offerings but neither did they seem upset. As adults they "avoid emotional dependence and deny their own attachment needs" as well as others' needs. They found it difficult to develop intimacy in romantic relationships. They showed low recall, would minimise, be dismissing, stay in denial and idealise.

Disorganised attachment revealed a "disorganised, disoriented frightening or frightened sexualised behaviours. The infant acts chaotically and can demonstrate "self-injurious' behaviour. As adults they are conflicted, disoriented and have "unresolved loss and traumatic history".

Of course, each attachment style does not represent a neat dividing line between each attachment pattern. We each may have aspects of more than one pattern. When looking at your own transference, the above figure may give you clues about how you impact your relationships, how others might impact you and the tensions that come from that.

Carl Jung (1975) in *"The Practice of Psychotherapy: Essays on the Psychology of the Transference and Other Subjects"* suggests that we need to sustain the tension of opposites. It supports us to transform. Other chapters provide several techniques to both understand our deeper unconscious layers that contain our "tension of opposites" as well as how they impact our relationships. The first step is to explore the patterns in our lives that consistently disturb or excite us and connect how these patterns are embedded in our closest relationships. A construct that helps us do that comes from a psychology modality of "Transactional Analysis" (TA). It can assist us to *manage our transference rather than have it manage us; we can learn to take care of our relationships, instead of asking the relationship to take care of us.*

Communication in Relationships and Transference

This extract draws on the work of Eric Berne (1967), author of *"Games People Play"*, Thomas Harris (1973), *"I'm OK You're OK"* and the work of Muriel James and Dorothy Jongward (1978), *"Born to Win"*; all authors of bestselling books in the field of human development and founders of TA.
Simply put, when two people communicate they enter into a "transaction". Understanding what happens during that exchange is the "analysis" part and where transference will occur.

Much has been researched and written now about how we store memories of events and how these memories are triggered in later life situations. Responses to those situations can be defensive or constructive depending on the level of awareness of each party. It is particularly tricky when individuals function from different awareness levels or consciousness. For more on levels of awareness see Chapter 2, *"Embracing Vulnerability and Authenticity"*. Our history informs our present in different ways depending on how aware we have become of old unconscious patterns.

The core assumption underpinning TA is that unless we make a conscious choice to depart from our history in a given situation, responses that we experienced in our childhood and developed as an unconscious life strategy will cause us to automatically react and defend.

TA aims to unpack our unconscious reactions, categorise them and have us make more conscious choices.
There are three "Ego States" that TA refers to:

- Parent – either "critical" or "nurturing"
- Adult – the part of us that rationalises and analyses
- Child – the part of us that feels and adapts or reacts

Acknowledging our own patterns among these three ego states and the unconscious sub-texts within them is key to managing transference, building personal effectiveness and developing successful caring relationships.

There is no "right" or "wrong" about what these patterns indicate; rather the intent is to notice how much the patterns drive us in relationship and provide more or less of what each of us want. Responsible (able to respond) and conscious, rather than reactive (re-act) and unconscious, access to all ego states is what is called for to support personal outcomes and uplifting relationships. This requires that the needs and fears of our unconscious minds be brought into focused awareness.

The "Parent" in Us

The events that happened in our first few years determine how we come to understand authority, control and power. The rules that we learn about and how we experience them being applied govern what we think is right and wrong. The "should" and "should nots" are incubated ready to be drawn upon as later life situations arise.

If our authority figures adopt a *critical* stance we too are likely to act in similar ways later in life. If the approach was *nurturing* or helpful that will also influence how we act.

The *"Critical Parent"* (*CP*) is directly controlling, demanding, prejudiced, moralises and/or punitive in nature. It can carry many of the attributes of the Persecutor described in Chapter 1.

The *"Nurturing Parent"* (*NP*) is empathetic, sympathetic, protective, supportive, encouraging and can be smothering; similar to the Rescuer described in Chapter 1.

The "Adult" in Us

This part of us wants to figure things out rationally and analytically. It's interested in the facts.

A precursor to the adult ego state is the *"Little Professor"*. It is a transition state that creates a pathway from the child ego state to developing a full *"Adult Ego State"*. It peaks at around 9 to 12 years of age. The *Little Professor* is very clever at figuring things out and aims to manipulate our environment to have our needs met. For example, it may play mum off against dad by sneakily and separately gaining their independent views about something and telling each of the parents that the other parent had told them that what they wanted was okay. If you ever did that as a child your *Little Professor* was running the show. It also has a sense of humour and will often use it to escape or avoid difficult situations. The word "cute" is a hallmark of this part of us. Overall this part of us carries our creativity, intuition, curiosity and even logical part of us. It is clever at manipulating its world.

Unless a fully developed *Adult Ego State* emerges the residue of the *Little Professor* can manifest negative relationship and family dynamics. It can also be a source of conflict in organisational and community life.

As one develops more consciousness in the *Adult Ego State* objectivity overtakes the manipulative nature of the *Little Professor*.

The *Adult Ego State* is not concerned with emotions and feelings. It is analytical and utilitarian. It can also be expedient. The *Adult* in us is necessary for objective assessment. It can be useful for moving us from the Power/Control Triangle to the Possibility/Freedom Triangle described in Chapter 1. In conflict and gridlock it is very useful for calming things down and opening new perspectives on an issue. Its downside is indeed its access to feelings, preferring to bypass them with facts and information. So, empathy available from the *Nurturing Parent* can be lost if it is overdone.

The "Child" in Us

This feeling part of us recorded experiences in our memory banks about the rules and controls that were put around us as children. These experiences are powerful and live in our cellular unconscious (reptilian and mammalian brains – see Figure 1) memory forever. If you think about a sour lemon for long enough your throat will begin to parch and your salivary glands will become active and yet you are not eating a lemon. Emotions and feelings operate the same way. Our emotional reactions to family dynamics and societal norms will formulate conclusions about ourselves and the world. We hold them in our physiology (reptilian) and emotional (mammalian) brains.

Life situations will trigger old experiences. Depending on other factors in our development we will feel things like frustration, anger, hurt, pain and fear; as well as joy, spontaneity, curiosity, creativity and imagination.

The *"Natural Child"* or *"Free Child"* (*FC*) wants what it wants when it wants it. It's insatiable. It is also fun loving, indeed in love with life. It is not interested in censorship and can be impulsive and rebellious. Alternatively, when we are fearful or emotionally aggressive our *Natural Child* is also at the forefront. It simply reacts to whatever is presented.

Very soon in life we learn it is important to get along with others and our *"Adaptive Child"* (*AC*) develops ways of accommodating and pleasing others. Politeness is central to the *Adaptive Child* and is often coupled with submission. It can withdraw if it gets "too hot in the kitchen". It does not like conflict. It's the one that knows how to say "sorry" and cooperate but can also become overly compliant and apologetic

The *"Wounded Child"* hurts at our core. On the upside, it's through this part of us that we can access our vulnerability. On the downside, other *Ego States* within us aim to ensure it is not exposed to harm and can overprotect it. For example, the *Nurturing Parent* can be keen to rescue the wounded child from hurt and upset but, if overplayed, the person doesn't feel safe or learn to stand for themselves. The ideas in Chapter 2, *"Embracing Vulnerability and Authenticity"* as well the companion exercises for this chapter provide approaches to embrace the *Wounded Child* in healthy ways.

Transactions

As we develop, our approach to life will predispose us to operate more from one or two *Ego States*. As two or more people connect, transference occurs, often unconsciously as the transactions unfold. As our preferences meet others' preferences, the exchanges form *"Bonding Patterns"* which can be either positive or negative experiences. For more on *Bonding Patterns*, see Chapter 5, *"Unconditional Relating"*.

There are different types of transactions between people that form *Bonding Patterns*. Here are some examples:

Crossed Transactions

Crossed transactions occur when one party aims to access a similar Ego State in the other but receives a response from an Ego State it didn't intend to trigger.

For example:

- Person 1: Did you do the shopping? – An objective factual request from the Adult Ego State.
- Person 2: Of course, I did. What? Don't you think I'm doing my part? – A reactive and subjective interpretation of Person 1's motivation, i.e. thinking Person 1 is coming from a Critical Parent perspective and reacting from their Rebellious Free Child.

It looks like this:

Figure 3.2: Crossed Transaction

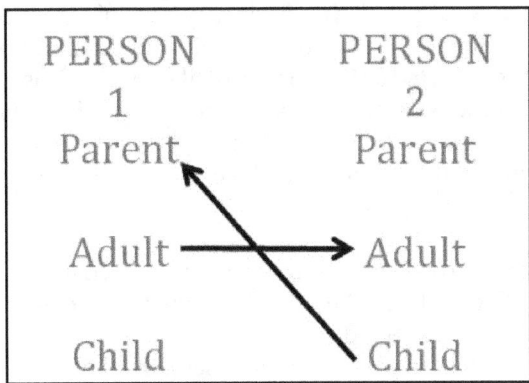

Complementary Transactions

This occurs when the Ego State aimed for is accessed in the other.

- Person 1: Did you do the shopping? – An objective factual request from the Adult Ego State.
- Person 2: Yes, I did. Was there anything else that you needed doing? Or: Were you concerned I might not get to it?

Figure 3.3: COMPLEMENTARY TRANSACTION

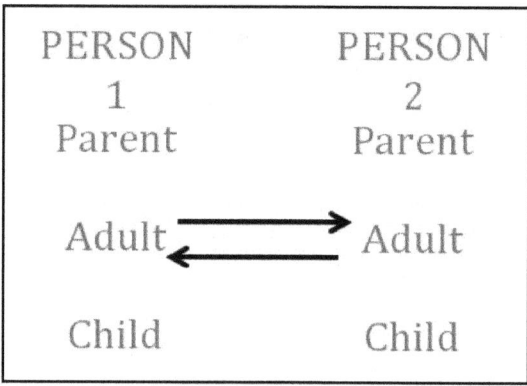

Complementary transactions are the most desirable because they create functional exchanges.

Hidden Transactions

The most problematic and diffcult to navigate, these transactions have the greatest chance of sabotaging relationships. They are often caught up in tone and body language even though the words may be adult or supportive. Humour and sarcasm are more obvious components of these transactions.

The result of the unstated criticism is most likely more *Crossed Transactions*, particularly if the other's awareness is unconscious of these dynamics.

Imagine in our example that the opening question was loaded with a disbelief or an untrusting energy. The words are the same but the tone is assumptive and critical.

- Person 1: Did you do the shopping? – An objective factual request from the Adult Ego State. Add in a critical tone with a demand on it from the Critical Parent Ego State.
- Person 2: Yes, I did. Don't ask me questions that you already know the answer to. Or: Who wants to know? Or: I'll do it in my own good time.

Figure 3.4: HIDDEN TRANSACTION

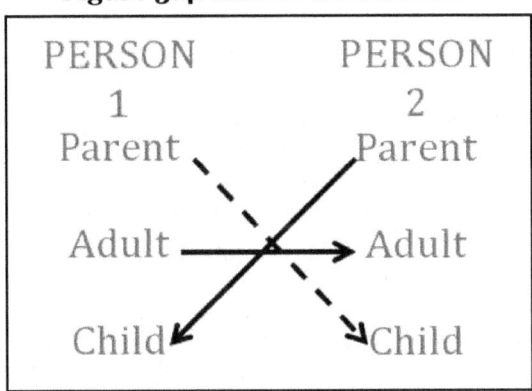

Building Personal Effectiveness and More Robust Relationships

The key to building personal effectiveness and more robust relationships is to create more *Complementary Transactions* from the constructive sides of all *Ego States*.

The most effective way to begin this process is to learn to engage the *Adult Ego State* in the other to rebalance the exchange deriving a mutually beneficial and supportive outcome. However, to do this in a sustainable way requires us to fully understand our patterns from the past and be willing to master them. It also requires us to non-judgementally gain insight into other people's patterns, especially our intimates. We need to know what triggers us and manage it not react to it.

One key skill that assists us to engage the *Adult Ego State* is *"Listening for Potential"* (David Rock). A summary is included as an Appendix to this chapter. For example when you find your defences aroused ask open ended questions that are enquiring and non-judgemental both in form and tone. Reflective and empathetic listening techniques can be employed from either the *Nurturing Parent* (provided there is no patronising) and the *Adult Ego States*. The NP can be very useful when the other is highly charged emotionally. Find ways to agree with parts of what is being said or at least validate feelings, before challenging the statement. Just be silent and listen intently to the other's perspective, genuinely looking for connections and a mutual intent. Find ways to apologise in an allowing not victimised way, even if it is only that there is a misunderstanding between you. When you sense the person might be ready, ask about possible alternatives or suggest some if they have none.

Focusing on Greater Good Outcomes

In any approach it is essential to be authentic and focus on the greater good outcome for each party. Approaches from a place of self-interest or avoidance will be quickly picked up by the *other's Little Professor* either unconsciously or consciously. Of course this only promotes more *Crossed and Hidden Transactions*.

Relationships are complex with no guarantees no matter how good your skills or authenticity.

The key is first understanding our own life strategy from the perspective of all three brains and neutralising it when it gets in the way of relationship connection and the outcomes we want. Our capability to step outside of ourselves, i.e. get out of our own way, while we are in an exchange and observe ourselves as we act is key to lifting not only the relationship but our personal effectivenss and satisfaction.

The first step to mastering transference is to understand and embrace the dynamics that bring it forward, learning to suspend our judgements on ourselves and others. That doesn't mean we become doormats and give up our standards. What it does imply is that we consciouly navigate our lives for a higher purpose beyond what we may have found in the past. We can free ourselves from our defences and live authetically and powerfully in integrity with our values, supporting ourselves and those around us. If we do this we will lead ourselves to live by the John-Roger's notion already mentioned in Chapter 1 and worth repeating here:

- Don't hurt yourself and don't hurt others
- Serve yourself so you have the strength to serve others
- Use everything for your upliftment learning and growth

Integrating my Personal Story

In my early years two people got me through some very difficult times. My mother, whilst emotive and sometimes temperamental, taught me to find humour in nearly every situation. We weren't allowed to watch the weather because it had the word depression in it; when things got really tough she went out and bought a laughing box and played it every time there was a fight in the house – nearly every day for many years in my teenage life. It was years later that I really came to appreciate Mum's natural capacity for joyful resilience and it inspires me every day even though she has now passed. She lived until she was 91 certainly not because of her physical health but her capacity to find humour in life. My paternal grandmother taught the power of unconditional love. She said I was her favourite grandson; I was her only grandson. I can't ever recall her criticising me in any way and I felt unbelievably peaceful just being around her. Although I have to say when my two children came along I lost my spot and gave it up gladly. These two people gave me access to my **Nurturing Parent** and **Adaptive Child** ego states very early in life and were vital to me later on when I had my own family.

My teenage life was a different story. Embracing, not suppressing the difficulties in my history, especially my teenage years, allowed me later to acknowledge the gifts they gave me. In this way, I learned to use my past as a vehicle for change and not remain stuck in old negative patterns. I learned over a long period to accept and let go.

In Chapter 2, I focused my personal story on my involvement with traditional incentivised ways of motivating ourselves and others. It was no accident that I found my career linked so much to reward and its relationship to achievement, as my personal history was steeped in reward and punishment – as a teenager it was mostly punishment. I felt highly criticised by my Dad – nothing was ever enough for him, and, to a lesser extent, my Mum. With her I felt guilt-tripped into doing things for her. I was in my middle 40s when I finally developed the courage to unpack the deeper patterns that had me live such a protected life avoiding criticism and punishment. I grew up with a then unconscious belief that "I am always going to get into trouble."

My **Rebellious Free Child** was well developed by the time I was 15 and definitely transferred into my early adult life, especially into my career. I recall one story where my Dad had promised to take me swimming three Sundays in a row and on each occasion, he reneged by sleeping in. I told him if he didn't take me I would smash his glasses and throw them over the balcony. He threatened that "Your life won't be worth living if you do." That didn't stop me. I trod on them to smash them and threw them over the balcony. He quickly got out of bed and chased me around the flat. He couldn't catch me. Needless to say, I didn't get to go swimming. On one level, I developed some healthy independence. On the other hand, my defiance of and lack of respect for authority had me struggle in my very early career to fit in.

I think my **Adaptive Child** didn't really arrive until my late 20s and even early 30s when I began to adopt a more cooperative approach to life. It was then that my career took off. I can thank Diane, my ex-wife, for showing me a different way of functioning. Her **Adaptive Child** was very well developed as was her **Nurturing Parent**. She showed me ways to integrate them into my own way of being. I became a better parent because of her. She had many similar traits to my paternal grandmother.

The deep critical patterns I had developed in my own childhood resurfaced with the birth of my first child, Mark; not in the early years but as he developed his own independence – funny about that! My **Critical Parent**, reminiscent of my own father and need for control battled with his **Rebellious Free Child** and his need to assert himself. On the other hand, my **Nurturing Parent** also had a strong voice in my head to support him and loved his spirit to challenge things. After losing Glen I think something deeply softened in me, and when Christopher came along I was transformed. His sensitive and natural loving energy made it difficult to even raise my voice to him. He just didn't need it. He was like his mother, naturally cooperative and nurturing. Mind you his **Free Child** took off a little later in his life but it didn't last long.

With some events in my life it may have been easy to retreat to victim consciousness and I can't deny there were periods, but something in me would not let me stay there. There had to be something better. My Dad contributed to this in two ways: I rebelled against his anger visited particularly on my mother and he often said: "There is no such word as can't." I first heard that when I was about 10. I told him: "Well fly now!"

From three years of age, my family squatted in a flat; for 20 years, we lived under the threat of eviction. It resulted in **transferring** an overcompensation strategy of high achievement (**Adaptive Child, Nurturing Parent** and **Adult Ego States**) to never face that again. Today the Longevity Bucket is fairly full and not a main driver but financial security still occupies my thoughts. I have faced my fears and have let go of nearly all residual concerns. Nonetheless in 69 years it hasn't completely left me. It doesn't run my day-to-day life, but I am still wary of financial setbacks. That protective driver to keep myself financially safe is still around when I need it.

My family of origin history included little education. Neither of my parents spent more than a year in high school although my mum ended up as a registered preschool teacher. She just had a way with very young children. I can thank my Dad's **Nurturing Parent** for ensuring I finished high school. Notwithstanding these good examples from them, my Dad's **Critical Parent** was visited on me. I can still hear his voice saying: "You're wrong John." I came to believe I wasn't very smart. In fact, I thought I was academically stupid. It later proved not to be the case but that wasn't until my early 40s when I finished my undergraduate degree in business. I had **transferred** the limiting belief of being wrong and not smart for 20 years into my adulthood even though I had a successful professional career already, without a degree. In 2016, I finally felt complete with the need for any more formal qualifications. I worked out I had studied for 20 of the last 30 years both academically and vocationally. I think my Knowledge Bucket is as full as it needs to be in this way. However, I don't believe my personal development and vocational efforts will stop in the foreseeable future. I believe in lifelong learning. These days learning fills up my Pleasure Bucket; well, most of the time! These efforts have been fundamental to developing my **Adult Ego State** and letting go of the hooks that gravitate into **Parent/Child dynamics**.

Together my learning and achievement compensation patterns covered up my vulnerability of self-doubt (hello Love Bucket and **Wounded Child**), built false confidence that got me validation and recognition (more filling of the Love Bucket!). As I presented myself to the world as a confident and directed (Power Bucket) human being I came to realise how important the Freedom Bucket was and is to me – "don't fence me in". Where did that **transference** come from? When I could walk, my mother put me on a leash; a common thing back then, but not just when we were going to the shops. When we were at the beach she attached a leash to a rope which was then staked into the ground and I could just reach the shore. Why would she do that? Because I just would not stop running into the water no matter what else she did. I remember her telling the story of being glared at by other parents and one day, having had enough of that, one person glared just one more time than she could tolerate and she said: "You keep chasing him into the water and try to stop him from drowning himself then!" Her own **Rebellious Child** and **Critical Parent** were alive and well in that transaction! Her **Nurturing Parent** was simply trying to keep me safe. But that's not how I felt about it. Give me my freedom was the unspoken cry. Later I was not allowed to have a push bike – it was too dangerous even though all the other kids had one. My Freedom Bucket kept being emptied. Eventually I bought a motor bike (**transference**) and I have already shared how that story ended. Today If I see a parent with a child on a leash it's all I can do not to go up to them and show them the scar on my left leg where it was nearly amputated and jointly operating from both a **Critical** and **Nurturing Parent** say; "This too could happen to your child if you keep him/her on that leash; leashes are for dogs, not for children!" Just a little residual transferred attachment to let go of!

The need for freedom was also driven by enforced emotional and physical responsibility at an early age. The combination of my Mum's message, "You can only play when all the chores are done." and "No, you can't have a push bike it's too dangerous." (so I bought the motor bike at 22) and my Dad's mantra, "There's no such word as can't." invoked my **Rebellious Child** that to this day will fight tooth and nail for my freedom. The bottom line became "Don't fence me in." (Freedom Bucket) and "Don't leave me out." (Love Bucket). These have become primary for me. The Pleasure Bucket loves to collude with the Freedom Bucket and enjoy the good things in life; my **Free Child** loves that. It's a foil for my freedom and sometimes it doesn't get a look in until all the work is done and other times my "Be Responsible" Protective Self gets overturned by my **Rebellious Child**. Hello **history repeating**! The patterns don't go away we just get better at managing them.

The conflict that emerged for me among my Pleaser, Be Responsible (both looking for validation aka filling the Love Bucket) and the **Rebel** as well as the Hedonist (looking to fill the Freedom and Pleasure Buckets) was no more present than when I finally decided to leave my marriage and explore the Authentic side of who I am, which included my sexuality. The fear of societal punishment (**Adaptive Child**) for such a choice, plus the pain it would create for my family, was juxtapositioned with a deep unhappiness (**Wounded Child**) that made me no good to anyone. I simply was unable to suppress this core part of me any longer. I took the selfish path and aimed as best I could (**Adult Ego State**) to minimise the pain for others. Authentically integrating my **Adult** and **Nurturing Parent** with my **Free**, **Adaptive** and **Wounded Child** had to prevail or we would all be miserable and that was a worse outcome as far as I was concerned. This decision began a new learning about what constitutes healthy selfishness (**Adult Ego State**) i.e. when on an aeroplane, we are told to put the mask on ourselves first so we can then put it on others; akin to John-Roger's philosophy of "take care of your yourself so that you have the strength to take care of others".

Phew! This seems a lot. But putting 69 years on a few pages is a challenge.

I mentioned John-Roger's approach to forgiveness in Chapter 1. It's worth taking a deeper look at it. I have repeatedly used his teachings to move me through and let go of the most difficult times (**Adult Ego State**). Here are some excerpts that might assist in your own approach:

- There are two layers of forgiveness: first, the person we judged (ourselves or another); and, second, ourselves for having judged in the first place.

    The technique? Simple. So simple, that some people doubt its effectiveness and don't try it. We urge you to try it.

    Say to yourself, "I forgive (name of the person, situation, or thing you judged, including yourself) for (the "transgression"). I forgive myself for judging (same person, situation or thing, including yourself) for (what you judged)."

    That's it. Simple but amazingly effective. You can say it out loud or say it to yourself. But, please, do say it. That's all there is to forgiveness. Simple but powerful. How powerful? Do five minutes of forgiveness. See what happens.

- Heal the memories. Forgive the past. Then forget it. Let it go. It is not worth remembering. None of it is worth remembering.

    What's worth experiencing and giving is the joy of this moment. Sound good?

And from www.msia.org/quotes when asked a question about forgiveness he suggests:

- Question: When I try to let go of my past and forgive, I get stuck in my thoughts about what happened instead. How do I really let go of all that stuff and go on with my life?

    John-Roger's response: Keep focusing on how you're progressing. Instead, we often keep referencing back to the last hurt, pain, anguish and upset. And guess where we are? Back at that. We can't cure it because it's in the past and we're already in our present and future, dealing with the past, and we can't do a thing with it. We've got to get it up to here and now, which we can do. Just by addressing it, we bring it present. Then we bring in the acceptance and the forgiveness. In that is the letting go. And then we must forget it and move on by bringing our focus, awareness and attention to right now, to what is before us to do.

For years, I have had these quotes taped to the inside of my bathroom cabinet and every morning they remind me to stay present in the moment make the best of it (**Adult Ego State**). Sometimes I falter, but these quotes by their presence pester me to keep going (**Nurturing Parent**) and as I have heard John-Roger say: *"What else are you going to do anyway?"*

I have learnt to forget my story in the sense that it doesn't hold me hostage to the past. I can *create, promote* and/or *allow* my future based on who I believe I have become. Having journalled and written about my history many times I've noticed a renewed sense of *neutrality* and *healing* that leads me to appreciate my life in all its ups and downs. I can move forward to whatever is next with gratitude, trepidation, resolve and resilience and simply *love it all* from a higher place (**the best of all Ego States**).

Questions I ask myself and suggest for you:

1. What patterns from the past are holding me back and are present in this situation?
2. What judgements on myself and others, especially my parents and significant others, might I still need to forgive?
3. What resistance (usually a limiting belief) is present to any forgiveness that might set me free?
4. What is before me to do next?

See the *Appendix – Companion Exercises to Support Your Understanding and Growth* for more ideas and questions to explore:

- Exercise 6: Reviewing Our Early Story, page 147
- Exercise 7: Mapping Current Transactions in Your Relationship(s), page 149

Also see the following, *Appendix – Listening for Potential*.

Appendix - Listening for Potential

A tool for developing the Adult Ego State

This excerpt points to how the brain functions in relation to listening, a key **Adult Ego State** skill essential for effective communication.
"We only hear what we listen for. We pay special attention to what we are expecting to see, hear, feel or taste... Prediction is not just one of the things the brain does. It is the primary function of the neocortex, and the foundation of intelligence." (David Rock, 2006)

In other words when we listen to people, unless we consciously listen in a certain way we will listen to prove our existing theories about this person. This is hardly the most effective way of transforming our own effectiveness and our relationships.

These seem to be the common approaches to listening. Check those that you might find you commonly find yourself doing.
- Listening for opportunities to sound intelligent
- Listening for a chance to seem funny
- Listening for how you can sound important
- Listening to get information you want
- Listening to external distractions such as other noises, music, etc
- Listening for what's going on with the other person
- Listening to your own thoughts and not listening at all
- Listening to see how you can help

- Listening to understand the problem
- Listening for how you can benefit

What is the most effective way to listen? The most common responses are:
- Listening for what people feel
- Listening for what the problem is or something similar

There is a new way to listen:
- Listen for people's potential
- Believe in another's potential completely
- Encourage and support others to be the best they can be, just in the way you listen without saying a word
- Listen to others as if they have all the tools they need to be successful and could simply benefit from exploring their thoughts and ideas out loud
- Listen for their intention i.e. what might they really want (which might be something they are not even aware of)
- Listen for their hopes and fears
- Listen for their deeper drivers and needs
- Listen for intellectual, emotional and spiritual needs and desires (what it means to them)
- Listen for what is not being said

Examples of explorative questions might be:
- What might be helpful here for you?
- Would you like assistance in thinking this through?
- How else can I support you?
- Do you have a sense of what you want to do and want to explore?
- What excites you about this?
- What challenges you about this?
- What does this all mean to you?
- What need does this highlight for you?
- How do you feel about this?

The assumption we make behind these questions is that people have the answers and we're just here to help them think.

If we find ourselves in judgement or in any way not neutral, we limit our listening capacity as we have our judgement linked to our own theory about the person or situation. This indicates potential *Crossed* or *Hidden Transactions* are at play and our history is being projected onto the other, transferred from the past.

"Listening for potential is a choice in every moment. By choosing to listen to people as successful, competent and able to resolve their own dilemmas, guess what's likely to happen? They often solve their own problems and get on with the job." (David Rock) – a great formula for *Complementary Transactions*.

Rock suggests that when people listen effectively they have turned off their mind chatter. They may see the other in a completely new way and even become intrigued or fascinated by what the other is saying. This brings us present in the moment and can contribute to enjoying listening to another.

This kind of listening is beyond "Empathic" and "Active" listening but does include these. It asks us to turn your "self" off to tune into the other so they can turn their 'self' on and realise the potential that lives inside them. The benefit to the listener in doing this is a sense of being in charge of oneself, not being governed by one's emotions that most likely come from the past. It is a discipline that actually fosters personal freedom rather than restricts it.

Chapter 4
Loving Ambiguity and the Unknown

It doesn't matter what happens to us in life; what matters is what we do with it!

The pace of change today makes adapting to it a necessary life skill. Never before have we faced such rapid and dramatic change and such a compelling need to change and learn. Technology is the primary driving force making our world more accessible and so much smaller. The social pressures to participate seem to have many of us overexposed to such things as cyber-bullying and personal celebrity unheard of in times past on such a scale.

Most of us are looking for order and stability to feel safe in the world. However, rapid change creates chaos in our lives. We then aim to create order and in turn are disturbed by yet another unpredicted event or indeed many, reverting again to chaos. In this way, we live in a "*chaordic*" world. If we are to function effectively in it we need to learn how to adapt to it. There are certain things we can't control or bring order to but we can be in charge of our response to continual change with the right skills and attitudes.

Our Chaordic World

In 1993 NASA researched the rate of change for the last 2000 years and predicted the future rate of change based on developments in the late 20th century (Figure 4.1).

Figure 4.1 shows the change rate began to incline faster than ever in the latter part of the 20th century. The prediction from 2014 was startling. Now that it is 2016 we would be hard pressed to challenge NASA's earlier predictions; indeed, we could argue they were understated.

In a slower linear world, we have time to think about cause and effect, using our minds to figure things out; not so in a world moving on a vertically accelerating curve, i.e. in a quantum world we don't have time to think in the same way. So, what can we draw on? How do we start to deal with change that enables us to cope with its pace? What does it take to continually manage it? Can we really manage it or simply adjust or adapt to it? Better yet, how might we willingly embrace and even love it?

A new way of thinking, requiring constant adjustment rather than systemically controlling each change, requires far greater self-trust and a different mindset. Being purposeful and positive in such a world asks us to transform old thinking and rely on our intuition more, i.e. operate from our hearts. It's a *"Chaordic"* process – waxing and waning between order and chaos.

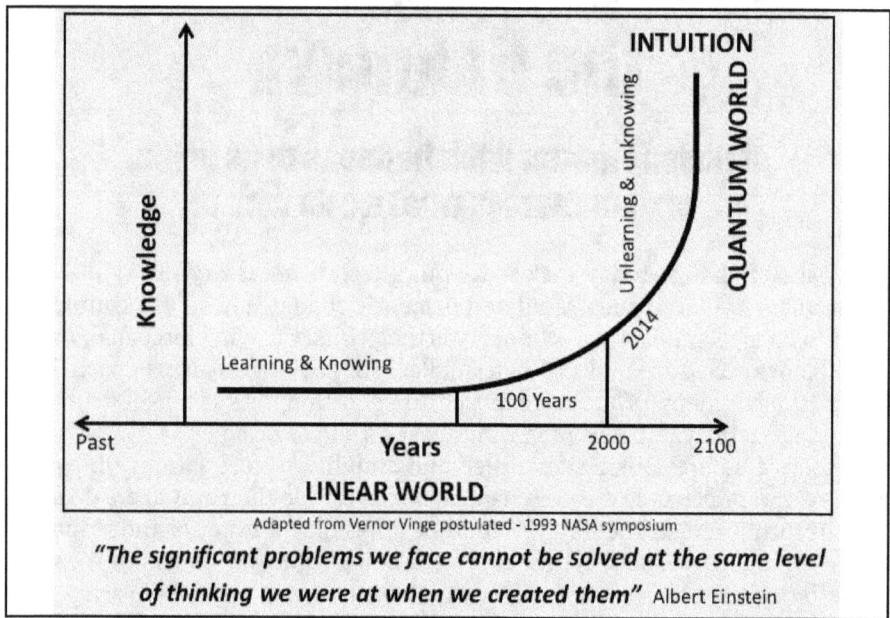

Figure 4.1: OUR CHAORDIC WORLD

Adapted from Vernor Vinge postulated - 1993 NASA symposium

"The significant problems we face cannot be solved at the same level of thinking we were at when we created them" Albert Einstein

Our capacity to develop a tolerance for and skill with ambiguity and loving the unknown becomes central to navigating such a world. It asks us to let go of that master addiction – our need to control or not be controlled.

Learning Cycles

Traditional learning cycles foster this addiction through "knowing". We can feel safe if we're in the know. A learning cycle begins with not knowing what we don't know, i.e. unconsciously unskilled; we then discover we know what we don't know, i.e. consciously unskilled; then we know we know as we become more skilled, i.e. consciously skilled; and finally, in this linear model, we simply just know, i.e. unconsciously skilled. It is here we feel in control.

A good example of how this works is learning to drive a car. We may have watched others drive a car with a measure of confidence. However, it's not until we sit behind the wheel for the first time and turn on the ignition that we discover what we didn't know (consciously unskilled); it's an "oh heck" experience, especially if we are learning on a manual gear shift. Once we know how to engage the accelerator, brake, steering wheel and build a little confidence we might feel we know we know (consciously skilled). Then we hit busy traffic or try backing into a curve or negotiating a hill start. Guess what? We revert to not knowing what we didn't know until we try it and then rediscovering what we didn't know. Each step or new experience deepens our learning and sense of control (or not) through knowing. When we receive our provisional licence, we are probably at the "we know we know" phase of learning to drive and then new experiences that build over time such as wet weather driving and nearly having an accident present opportunities to shift us to simply knowing how to drive. How many of us think about other things while driving? We listen to the radio or talk to the person in the passenger or back seat. Hopefully we are unconsciously skilled at driving to do this. These distractions would not be tolerated at the beginning of learning how to drive.

Beyond these levels, however, there is another learning opportunity: we know we don't know and it's okay. I call it *"comfortably unskilled"*. In this state we handle the unknown, trusting ourselves to find a way forward without feeling the need to control what is going on, but simply respond to what is presented in a calm, collected and thoughtful way. Instead of reacting (re-acting) based on past experience with worry or anxiousness we are *response-able* (able to respond) with a comfortable sense of confidence that we will find our way forward trusting our intuition to guide us.

A Quantum Approach

To be *comfortably unskilled* we need to let go of our need for order and control. The paradox of letting go of control is that we take charge of our responses and indeed are in control of ourselves and not run by outside unpredictable influences. Quantum theory labels these *"strange attractors"*. It is in these moments we can be creatively responsive rather than reactive. It's about granting permission for unexpected change, indeed expecting unexpected change, i.e. living on the edge of chaos. There's a phrase that goes *"If you are not living on the edge you are taking up too much space."* (source unknown).

Most of us feel confused when things become chaotic, wanting to remain within the knowing phases of the learning cycle. We feel that clarity brings more control. Ironically, clarity comes from knowing what we are confused about. We need confusion (chaos) to discover clarity, i.e. we need chaos to create order and we need order to deal with chaos. It's about living comfortably, chaordically, loving the opportunities of ambiguity. But how do we do that in a world moving as fast if not faster than NASA suggested in 1993?

Quantum science has evolved new theories of how to respond to a complex and an ever-changing world. A whole new language emerged with terms like autopoiesis, bifurcation, fractals, fuzzy logic, harmonious resonance, semiotic dynamics, strange attractors, virtuality of meaning, vortical emergence and others. It is not the intention to explore the detailed meaning of these terms, but a glossary of terms is appended at the end of this chapter for those interested. What is proposed is that when we master the concepts of the complexity and chaos theorists and allow any trepidation to be replaced by a renewed enthusiasm for one's life with the invigorating realisation that, "Ah! I am simply a *'fractal'* (a mirrored part of a whole – see glossary) of a larger structure." (see Figure 4. 2) *we know we don't know and it is okay!*

I have used the shape of a triangle to depict a fractal. Each triangle carries the same properties only the scale changes. That is the same for humans as individuals, groups, communities, countries and the world. For simplicity's sake I have merged groups, communities and countries as one triangle as their form is the same. Within each triangle, the symbol of a Russian babushka doll illustrates the human element of the *fractal*. An everyday example of the triangle/doll metaphor is that water is water whether it resides in our body, a bath or from the rain, in a lake or the ocean.

Figure 4.2: THE STRUCTURE (FRACTALS) OF THE HUMAN EXPERIENCE

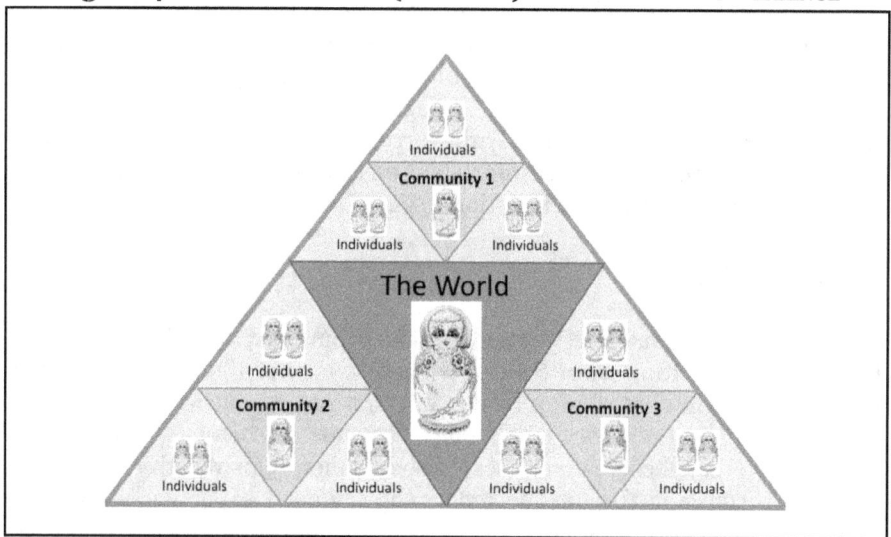

The Individual

A starting point is to unpack the *"fractality"* (structure or parts) at the individual level. Then we can better understand the broader *fractality* of a community, then a country and ultimately the world. We move from individual makeup – especially beliefs and values – to how they play out in family and group dynamics to community and country cultures to world views.

There are many ways of describing the parts of individuals. In Chapter 2, *"Embracing Ambiguity and Authenticity"* we used the iceberg to depict an individual's inner fractals. That image is repeated in Figure 4.3. The *fractal* we see above sea (see) level is behaviour and at the next level down we may just get a glimpse of the *fractals* of thoughts and attitudes. What are harder to detect are the lower levels. The preferred *fractal* in our culture is rational thought. The emotional fractal is often denied with scripts such as "Big boys don't cry."; in business – "Leave your feelings and emotions at the front gate."; "S/he wears their emotions on their sleeve." Things have changed with some of these mantras but oh so slowly. I'm reminded of the show *My Fair Lady* in the 1960s and the song *"Why Can't a Woman Be More Like a Man"*. The first line goes "Women are irrational, that's all there is to that. Their heads are full of cotton, hay and rags. They're nothing but exasperating, maddening and infuriating hags." Okay, the social inappropriateness of such language would be frowned upon and even illegal in certain settings. But, guess what? *My Fair Lady* is currently (2016) playing at the Sydney Opera House and directed by its original stage play star Julie Andrews. How much have we changed really when we are still intrigued by such concepts, albeit in a light-hearted musical? Do you think there are not people in the audience that still think these lines are true? If they do I'd guess they would be unlikely to say so in a public setting. Social *fractals* are slow to change suggesting that so too are individuals – until they pro-actively choose to.

Figure 4.3: INDIVIDUAL CONSCIOUS AND UNCONSCIOUS ECOLOGY (from Chapter 2)

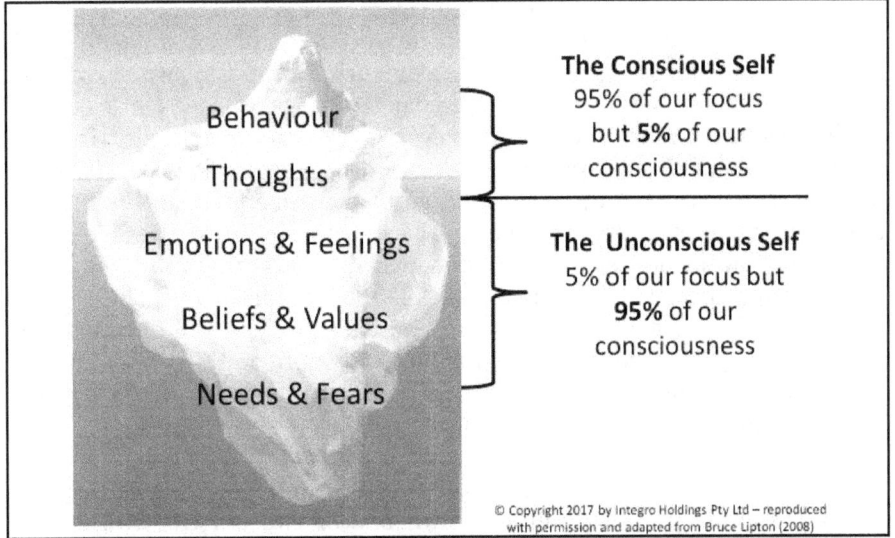

How these fractals unfold in each individual vary of course, by background and life approaches. Vladimir Dimitrov (2003) suggests that the "complex interplay of interactions" at the individual level is paradoxical and concerns the "interplay between physical, emotional, intellectual and spiritual fractals of human personality." Chapter 2, *"Embracing Vulnerability and Authenticity"* expands on this concept.

The Community

When we understand our own process, it supports insights into others. With collective understanding and acceptance, through exploring shared meaning, groups and communities are better able to respond to change that is thrust upon us.

The community *fractal* is a collection of individual *fractals*; the whole consists of wholes (Benoit Mandelbrot as cited by Vladimir Dimitrov, 2003) and only the scale changes. These individual *fractals* are constantly reacting to disturbance, perturbations and changes in varying ways. Individuals, groups and communities could always be at least on the *"edge of chaos"* or indeed constantly in chaos – *"the chaotic edge"*.

Dimitrov suggests that thoughts and feelings, ideas, emotions, aspirations, expectations, hopes and dreams cannot conform to pre-imposed order. I have certainly found this to be true in my previous corporate life. Most of my counselling clients are conforming with resistance, avoiding and/or rebelling against pre-imposed order in both their personal and work lives. Just think of the work life balance issue brought about by technology and the financial pressures of living in a demanding world. How do we even have a pre-imposed order in a world moving as fast as it is? One day's pre-imposed order is outdated the next. If you have young children in your life, what they're learning is outdated in the next hour – even minutes.

Evolving ourselves to a higher state of wisdom and being *uncomfortably skilled* to search for shared meaning, is a precursor to sustainably dealing with change. Adaption to and adoption of change may take place consciously at the behavioural, thought and perhaps even at the emotional levels. However, its sustainability is questionable unless we drop down below emotions and feelings (Figure 4.3) to the deeper layers of the iceberg – persevering with the discovery of unconscious beliefs, values, needs and fears. In Chapter 2 I suggested that the needs for control and inclusion plus the fears of failure and rejection appear to underpin nearly all other needs and fears. The patterns of these needs and fears emerge from negative experiences in our early lives (see Chapter 3, *"Taking Charge of the Past"* for more on this). We formulate limiting beliefs about ourselves and the world from these negative experiences. Try this small experiment by completing the following sentences:

- When I was very young (up to around 10 years old) my world was... (Describe your environment with one or two emotive adjectives –

positive or negative); so I was... (Describe yourself, i.e. how you reacted to your environment with one or two emotive adjectives – positive or negative).
- When I was a teenager (up to around 20 years old) my world was... (Describe your environment with one or two emotive adjectives – positive or negative); so I was... (Describe yourself, i.e. how you reacted to your environment with one or two emotive adjectives – positive or negative).

These two periods are critical to our development and inform how our patterns will unfold in later life unless we choose to interrupt those limiting patterns and choose new, constructive ones.

My examples of these two statements are:

- When I was very young my world was *fun* so I was *happy*.
- When I was a teenager my world was *angry* and *dangerous* so I was *reactive* and *protective*.

These beliefs about myself and my world spilled into my adult life formulating positive and negative emotions, thoughts and behaviours. I was to find happy, reactive and protective ways peppering my way of living. I had both positive and negative outcomes from these patterns and changing the negative outcomes meant reframing my beliefs (see Chapter 2 for more about reframing beliefs).

Dimitrov proposes that change only at the behavioural level is characterised by ever-growing stress and tension. He holds that a deeper transformative approach results in growth and creativity.

The bottom line is that order is short lived and emerging complexity leads to constantly changing situations. Our capacity to effectively move in and out of equilibrium and chaos is fundamental to living a happier and more joyful life; in other words, it is critical to develop our willingness and ability, i.e. become *comfortably unskilled* to learn to *"live chaordically"* and love ambiguity. The alternative is to retreat into rigidity and control. Rigidity and control arise to allay fears of failure, uncertainty, confusion and dealing with paradox and ambiguity. Embracing our fears is therefore essential if we are to handle chaordic situations with minimal stress and maximum effectiveness. For more about this read Susan Jeffers' (1987) *"Feel the Fear and Do It Anyway"* (see *Recommended Readings* in the *Appendix*).

Conventional linear (cause and effect) thinking does not account for underlying emergent drivers that exist in all of us to self-organise in changing circumstances. Dimitrov advances the notion that individuals are deeply and even unconsciously motivated by one or more of six core drivers: Longevity, Power, Knowledge, Freedom, Pleasure and Love. These core drivers are explored in Chapter 2, *"Embracing Vulnerability and Authenticity"*. They live at the emotions and feelings, beliefs and values, and needs and fears levels of the iceberg model. If any of these drops below an individual's equilibrium point their unconscious drivers will trump any conscious thought or behavioural effort which acts in opposition to those drivers. Further, Dimitrov distinguishes between "decision making" and "decision emergence" and how these six drivers play a role in both. He suggests that decision making imposed by pre-selected criteria is inefficient in complex environments; rather, emerging decisions are not imposed but free to surface and self-organise, adapting to changing circumstances and choosing the best of them. Powerfully, he declares that robots can live linearly in complex environments but humans cannot.

Personal Transformation in a Chaordic World

This perplexing dilemma yet again beckons us to attempt to clarify (bring some order to) the ambiguous and ever changing circumstances we find ourselves in, in everyday life.

I have identified some key elements (*strange attractors* and *fractals* – see glossary) that are frequently present in the transformational process of moving between order and chaos internally, in relationships and group settings.

People move in and out of orderly and chaotic situations in a circular way (Jonathon Rosenhead, 1998). What follows and is depicted in Figures 4.4, 4.5, 4.6 and 4.7 is a way of identifying how this functions in all of us. Order is broken when a disturbance or some disorientation occurs. At that point, we are on the "*edge of chaos*" as distinct from a "*chaotic edge*" which occurs at the point where disturbances are the norm, continuous and unpredictable. The extremes of order and chaos are on the perimeter of the circle in each figure. One may have to wonder if today's life is not in truth at the *chaotic edge*. The irony is that to make sense of the chaos we find ourselves in, we need to bring some sense of order or structure to it to help us understand the situation.

Figure 4.4 : Personal Transformation In A Chaordic World

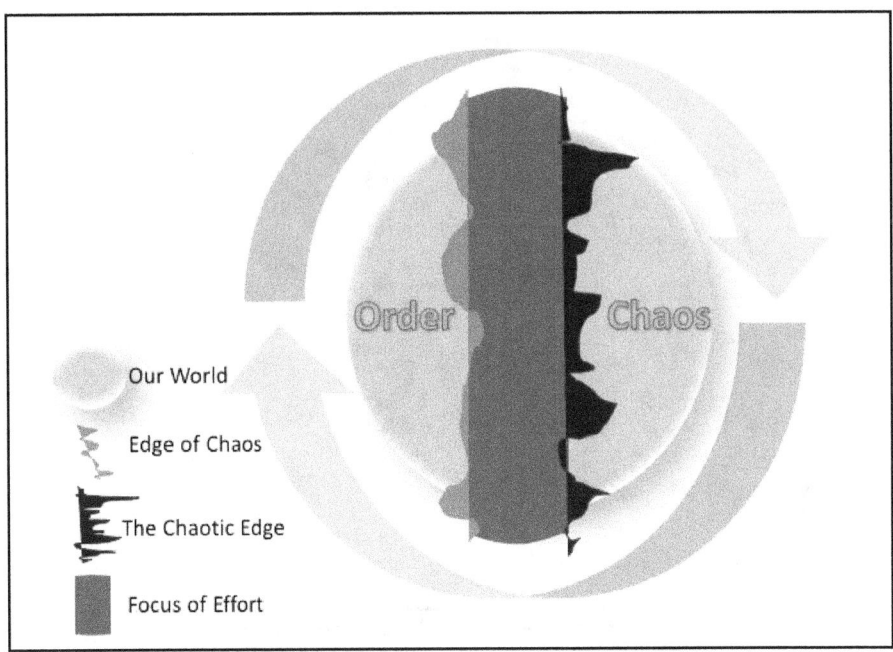

Figure 4.5: Yesterday's Ordered World

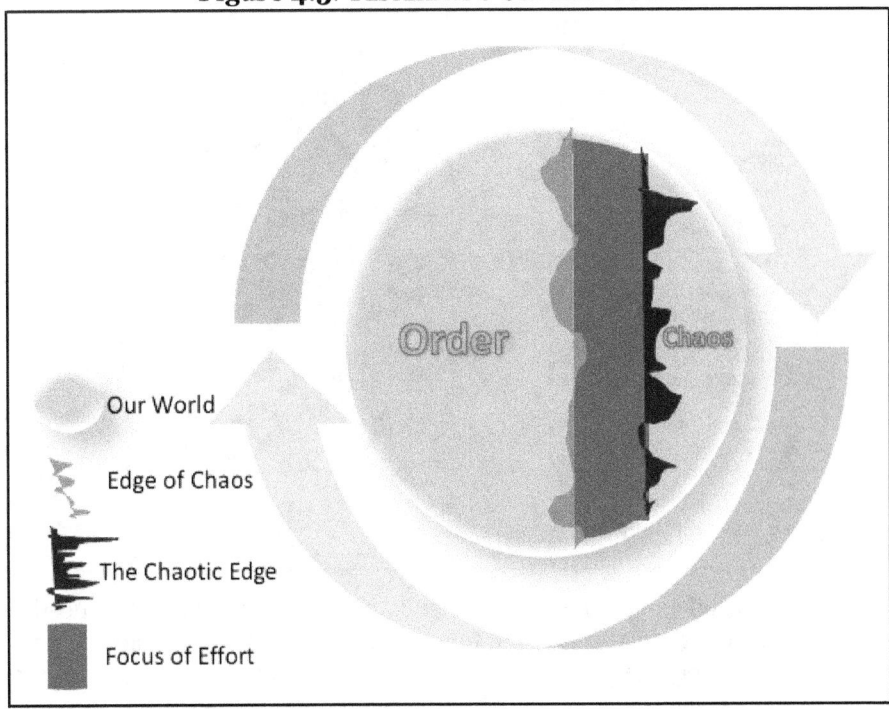

Figure 4.6: THE EMERGING CHAOTIC WORLD

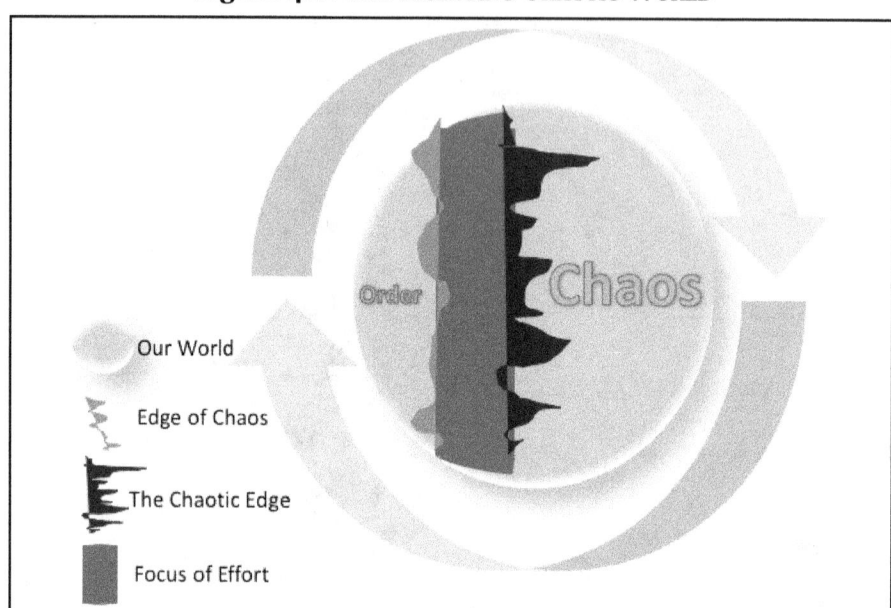

Figure 4.7: RESPONDING TO A CHAORDIC WORLD
(AKA - Loving Ambiguity)

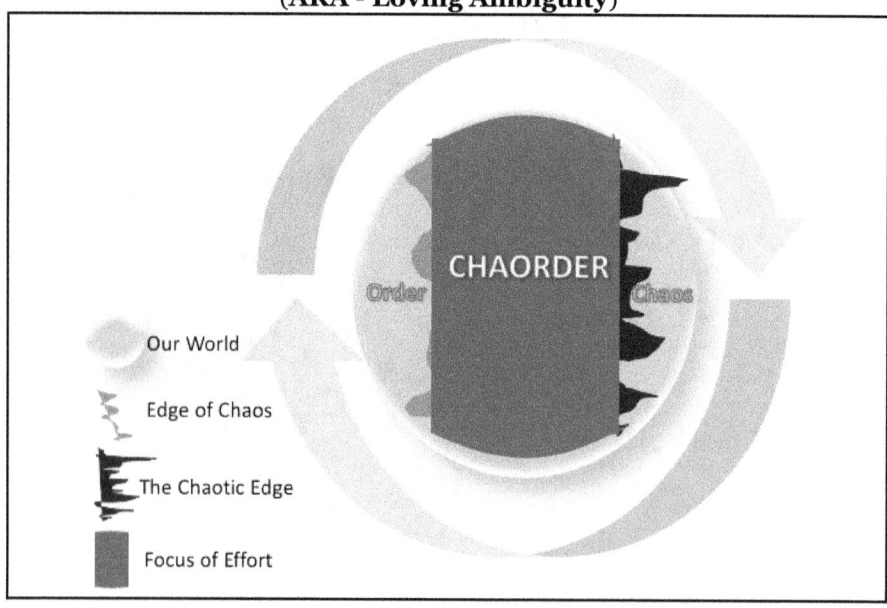

To function effectively, i.e. love ambiguity in a *"Chaordic World"* we need to understand what the attributes and tolerances are of order and chaos. Figures 4.8 and 4.9 outline these.

Figure 4.8: ATTRIBUTES OF A CHAORDIC WORLD

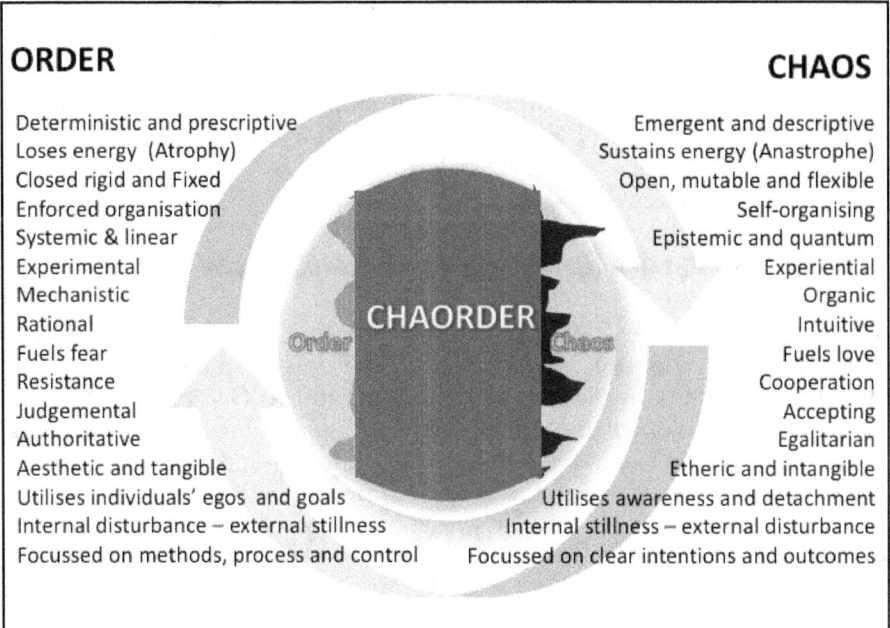

Figure 4.9: TOLERANCES FOR A CHAORDIC WORLD

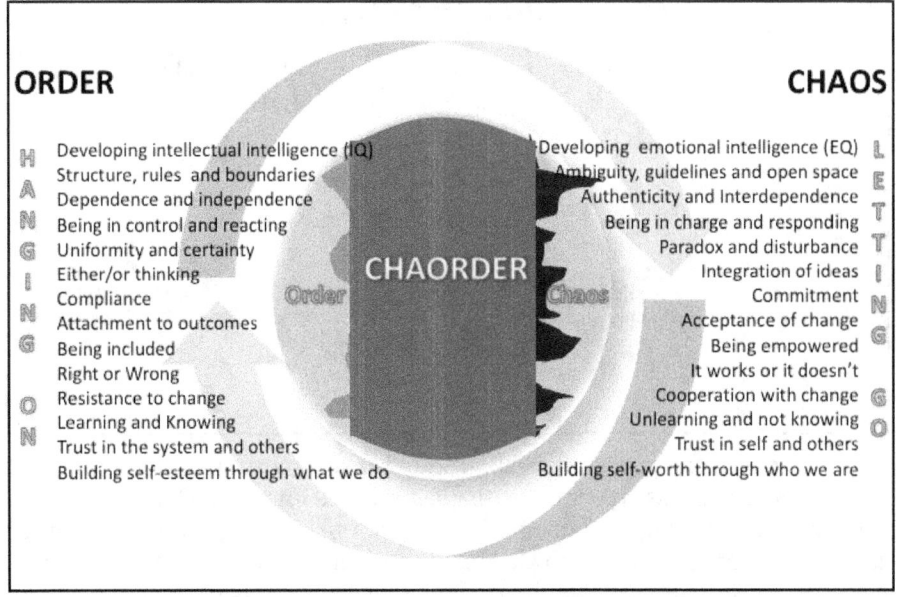

Understanding how we may operate in completely different ways provides insight to potentially unresolved conflicts. If, for example, one individual's behaviour indicates that they prefer an ordered environment and are decidedly uncomfortable not knowing or not being in control and another individual is comfortable in uncertain situations, then through this awareness they can better understand, accept and cooperate with one another. It enhances conflict resolution both within and between people.

Those who insist on keeping order in situations tend to "hang on" to opinions, ideas and control. Those who are willing to accept emerging changes and respond to them seem to be able to "let go" of entrenched attitudes, behaviours and moreover – fears.

Growing and Effective Functioning in a Chaordic World

Willingness to grow and learn is central to loving ambiguity. We don't grow in our comfort zone. Our *chaordic world* is asking more and more of us in this way. Figure 4.10 overlays the varying applications of learning required for different levels of order and chaos; data collection, information processing, awareness, applying knowledge in a given situation and the application of wisdom in unknown circumstances, i.e. *comfortably unskilled*.

Figure 4.10: TRANSFORMATIVE LEARNING

ORDER		CHAOS
Developing intellectual intelligence (IQ)	Developing	al intelligence (EQ)
Structure, rules and boundaries	Ambiguit	and open space
Dep...		dependence
Being i...	Wisdom	sponding
Uniformit...	Intuition	rbance
Either/or thi...	Knowledge	deas
Compliance	Awareness	nt
Attachmen'		ange
Being in	Data & Information	powered
Right		or it doesn't
R...		n with change
Learning and Knowing		and not knowing
Trust in the system and others		st in self and others
Building self-esteem through what we do	Building se...	ch through who we are

(Left side: HANGING ON; Right side: LETTING GO)

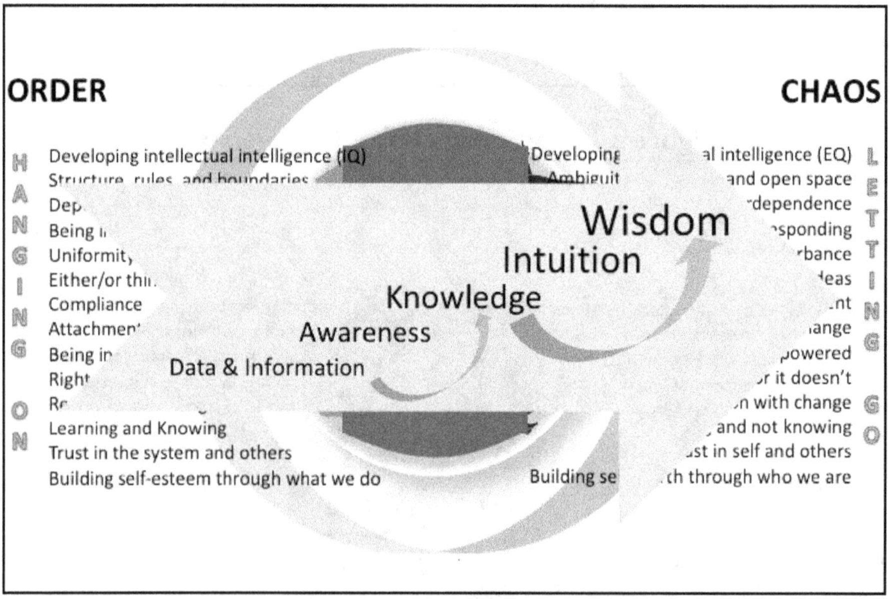

In effect, loving ambiguity is about the transformative learning process of raising consciousness across the entire iceberg (see Figure 4.11). It's about how we move from relying on data and information to creating certainty, through gathering awareness and knowledge, to utilising wisdom in ever changing, unknown situations. Essentially a reliance on wisdom is of greater effect in uncertainty and chaos where past information may serve only as a reference point.

Figure 4.11 - Ecology and Transformative Learning

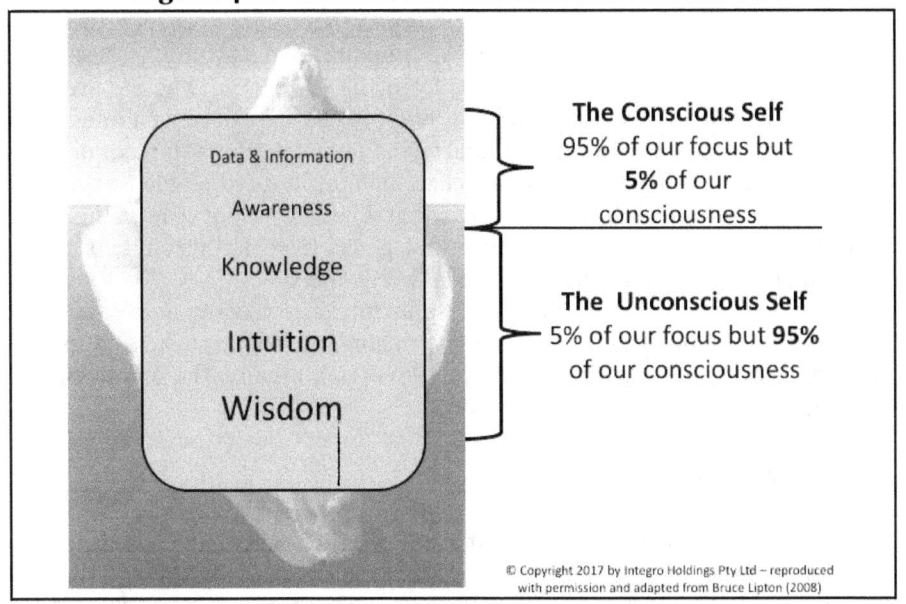

Laurent Daloz (1999) suggests that "growth can be understood as a series of transformations in how we make meaning... Thus as we grow; we develop new ways of knowing that can include more information and experience but make finer distinctions; ways that are ever more open to new learning but integrate and pull these learnings together in more comprehensive patterns." Imagine then how the transformative learning process that raises our consciousness might live across the spectrum of order and chaos (see Figure 4.10). By moving in and out of order and chaos, we build capacity to be more discerning, to see the world on its own terms and as others see it. We are continually able to understand its growing complexity, simultaneously making sense of it, whilst retaining our sense of meaning and respecting its diversity (Daloz). Perhaps this is a fine definition of "wisdom".

To embrace transformative learning and respond effectively to change in disturbed and unknown circumstances there is a need to accept that we know we don't know and it is okay (*comfortably unskilled*). This idea is reinforced by Bob Hodge and Vladimir Dimitrov (2003) who suggest that "Spirituality is an individual experience at the edge of chaos of the fractal inseparability of human life, which unfolds in harmony with the evolving universe." And "Acceptance is the first law of Spirit." (John-Roger). And "Security in life is learning to live with life's insecurities." (Wayne Dyer). And "To keep the process of knowing in a receptive and open state of creative chaos, out of which the emergence of new insights can be facilitated, lays the secret of a wise person." (Dimitrov 2003)

The indications are that when we have reached this level of understanding we can function most effectively in all circumstances. We can utilise order to make sense of things, create understanding, meaning and clarity without attachment to its rigidity. We can also embrace chaos with confidence, trusting our own and others' intuition. In short, our wisdom has a chance to shine. When wisdom shines we continually examine our own learning process at all levels to embrace and make meaning from the essence of who we are (our spirit). When we do this our capacity to adapt to change can be sustained from a place of inner self-worth rather than relying on what others think of us. This is the essence of more fully exploring change in our unpredictable world.

Acting out of fear is the enemy of wisdom. Living with our fears rather than in them is the essence of acting from a wise place. If we do this our capacity to move in and out of equilibrium is decidedly advanced.

Accessing wisdom is perhaps the personal integration of our needs and fears that moves us along a path of discovery, raising our consciousness in known and unknown situations; in essence just loving ambiguity, the unknown and the gifts of possibility they have for us.

Integrating My Personal Story

There are two aspects of my life that epitomise my experience in learning to love ambiguity and the unknown. I can't say I felt in a loving state all the way through them. It was the learnings and outcomes that have come from them that I love. As I look back on it all, it has given me so much to take forward into an **unknown future**.

Professionally, retrenchment in my late 40's took me on a journey I never anticipated. My father was in his own business for nearly all his life and it didn't work out well. We were always struggling for money. When young, I vowed I would create security in my life by working for others. I spent 10 years working for one of the most successful companies in the world in the 20th century. I had a stellar international career and it had all gone. I had also been separated for about three years from my marriage, family and the life I had built with them: my career in the form I had known it; no longer living with my children; and what I knew about relationships, had all disappeared. It felt **chaotic** and it was my launch pad into learning how to live **a chaordic life**.

Since that time (1996) I have spent only three years working for other companies, i.e. 17 years in my own business, of which five were in partnership with another. As Forrest Gump said in the movie, "My mother always said life is just like a box of chocolates; **you never know what you are going to get.**"

The idea of setting up my own business, Business Transformation Services (BTS Consulting), brought forward all the **uncertainties from my childhood**. I had walked away from my marriage with few resources, leaving the house mortgage free to my wife and children, to ensure my kids would never have to face the idea of not having a roof over their heads. I can acknowledge that whilst it was an altruistic thing to do, it was also borne out of guilt for choosing to leave. I was aiming to minimise the pain of our separation but also felt better about myself regarding how I was doing it. It taught me that altruistic acts have a selfish side as well.

During this time, I returned to study postgraduate courses in counselling, social ecology and psychology to build credentials operating in the organisational change, leadership and business strategy areas. Unlike my Dad, who found it difficult to work for others, I missed working for a large company and so to compensate, I began to network to build business but moreover to connect with people, a central tenet for me in living well and joyfully. Also unlike my Dad, I was successful at it. Although there were only two or three short lean times I found these really challenged me to keep learning to **accept what emerged** and **detach** myself from my expectations and still maintain hope and optimism. My old limiting beliefs from childhood also got some air time during these periods: "I'm not enough" – I think we all have this one but in different forms and one of mine is "I'm not smart enough"; "I'm going to get into trouble no matter what I do"; and the two big ones – "I'm not wanted" and "I'm not safe in the world". I had to move through all of these in deeper ways as I no longer had the external validation and recognition I had built up previously. I was in **unknown territory internally and externally**. Glad to say that all the personal development work I applied myself to paid off. *I must also* thank my first boss at DEC, Kevin for sending me to a program called Insight Seminars in 1986. His support and that choice were to form the foundation of a lifelong learning journey I am still on today.

On a personal level, in my late 30's and early 40s, I recognised I wasn't living authentically. I had done many years of personal development work and realised I had to come to terms with my sexuality if I was to be happy and indeed support my family to be happy. **This transition period had no map** that I was aware of to guide me. I was now working in the field of organisational change and the principles I was advocating I wasn't fully living.

I can't say I loved this time of my life but I was experiencing some freeing moments as I came to terms with the truth. All I had learned was to be put into practice now in ways I never imagined I would have to face. I had to face the hurt I was creating for my then wife, children and extended family. My Rescuer had to be broken through: The Persecutor of myself i.e. my inner critic, had to go; I needed to embrace my Victim to let the truth in and deal with all the socially unacceptable views about being gay I had accumulated over the years, i.e. break my own homophobia. **Many if not most old patterns had to be released to chart a new unknown path.**

In more recent times, I have worked with and presented to the Gay and Married Men's Association (GAMMA), supporting the coming out process for married men. I put the following ideas together (Figure 4.12) in my work with them as a map of the questions I needed to ask myself and to also assess how far along the path I have come. **Sometimes the only thing we can do in unknown circumstances is ask questions and trust that the solution will emerge.** Certainly, that has been my experience and what I suggest to others.

Figure 4.12: Navigating the Path

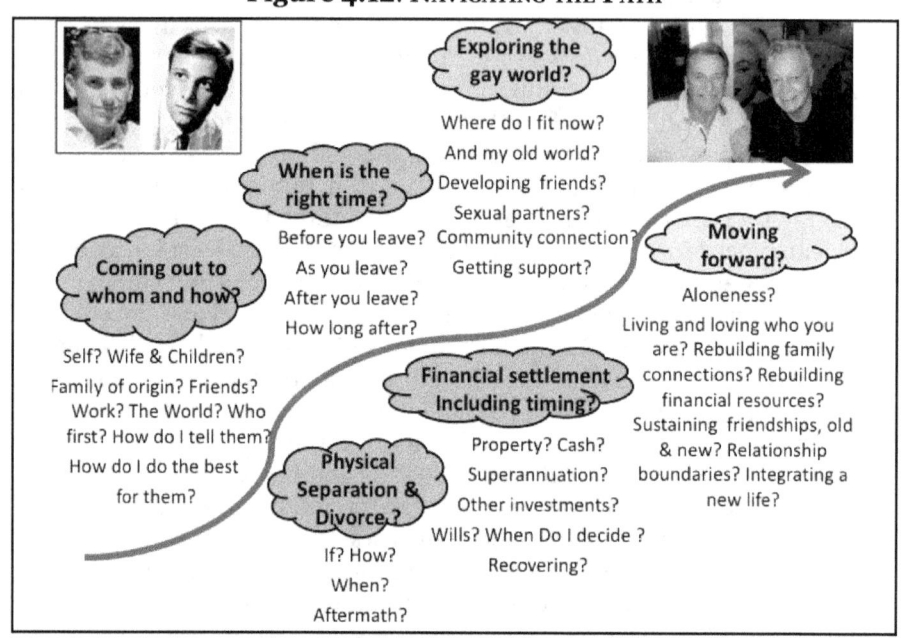

The coming out journey has certainly been characterised by **unknown and surprising events**. In 2015, I decided to submit my partner's and my story to Seniors' Week. We were one amongst 12 others selected from several hundred submitted to share our story at Sydney's Angel Place Recital Hall. It was like coming out a second time, though with more self-confidence and knowing who we were. It felt like a kind of closure to confusion and a **complete acceptance of all that had gone before and still not knowing what was before us** but knowing who we were on the inside made it matter less about what the external world said. As it represented a significant shift in **dealing with the unknown** I have repeated it here and I entitled it: GROWING WITH GRACE AND EASE IN OUR REFINING YEARS – 29TH MARCH 2015.

The collage of our lives is coloured with many challenges and blessings, some ordinary, some extraordinary. We are a couple in our refining, not our declining years; two men that are in our 20th year together at ages 67 and 65 with five straight sons between us – the Gaydy Bunch!

Between us the challenges of our collage are adoption, including finding Maxx's biological mother but with no permission to speak to, or see her; squatting as a child for the first 20 years of my life with eviction threats; life threatening car accident for Maxx and motor bike crash for me; through a windscreen head first and almost an amputated leg respectively; me experiencing family alcoholism, violence and suicide attempts; divorced parents on both sides, ourselves and some of our children; a full term stillborn child (it took me nine years to find his grave and have it named – that search changed the system as a result); leaving our children; parental loss early and later in life; strained family relationships at times; the death of long term close friends; retrenchment; business failure; financial loss from superannuation fraud; living with a mortgage in our mid 60s: stroke and spinal damage; not to mention coming out in our mid to late 40s and again in this way now. Just your everyday stuff eh!

Our blessings are varied and many; two solid marriages of 20 years to great women and the raising of five children; successful business lives for a long time – me in the professional services space internationally and Maxx in his own business; middle to upper middle socio economic lifestyles for the most part; generally managing health well with some hiccups; wonderfully supportive friends – our chosen family; between workable and wonderful relationships with our children; some amazing travel experiences around the world; a rich intimate life; cruising the harbour on our 27-foot Bayliner sports cruiser for many years and especially on New Year's Eve with our chosen family; a lifetime on the competition tennis court continues; belief in what's possible for us; and above all our commitment to ourselves and each other grows stronger every day. So how did we get here?

A willingness to keep adding to our collage and not be a victim to our setbacks; an attitude of gratitude with some pity partying along the way to keep us balanced and centred – we need both ends of a battery, positive and negative, to have it charged up; a sense of deep loving of life and for each other, notwithstanding societal opinions; the capacity to find a gift in everything; the willingness to dance with our inner demons (and there are many), individually and together; faith in our capacity to meet what is presented to us in life; there's a saying "You never get what you can't deal with, you always get what you need."; our add-on is – "It just mightn't be what you want at the time." – It's an attitude of mind; resilience to get up one more time than we fall; forgiveness of our judgements on ourselves and others (all judgements do is hold us hostage to our story).

Today we live in a modest three-bedroom renovated unit in a Sydney lower North Shore suburb which we bought 18 years ago for much less than it is worth today, still with a mortgage, offset by a part pension and a small income from one of us working part time. When we bought the unit, we had been together for eight months, had a difference of opinion, well actually an argument – a fight, one of many, which we resolved by buying a fixer upper place together, agreeing we would give the relationship 12 months and if it didn't work out, sell the place and make some money. We renovated the unit and agreed that if one of us disagreed with an item or inclusion the answer to it was "no" – the unit took us seven years to renovate! We are still here in our 20th year with a little help from counselling along the way. Well, maybe more than just a little help!

Maxx has had a recent health setback, a silent stroke two years ago and has had two serious spinal operations; a hip replacement is likely to follow (and has since happened) – par for the course for many people our age. I just keep running around the tennis court! But it shows after I've played – sometimes for days.

What we wish for is what we already have; each other, our children and their significant others and family, some amazing friends, a place we both love living in; knowing who we are and content with that, warts and all. Whilst Maxx has retired I am not intending to. Even though there is financial pressure to keep working I would anyway. It's about putting back as well. What we wish for others is that they know who they are and find inner contentment with themselves and their loved ones. Having it all is loving it all!

Setting ourselves up to create a new part of the collage every day is what it is about and sometimes that may be a challenge. The gift in that is we go on; for what else are we to do. It's in the "how" not the "if" that we can find our joy in each moment. Most of all an enduring sense of humour is needed. Thank you, Mum!

We are optimistic about our future and at the same time we can see some financial and potential health challenges ahead; but they are ahead, they are not here and now, so "enjoy the moment" is the mantra. What's that poem? "The past is history; the future is a mystery; now is the present which is why they call it a gift." (Source unknown)

Our vision of the future has us recovering from our financial setbacks – yes, we believe we still can even at this age, travelling, especially to the Mediterranean, visiting the USA where two of our sons live, putting back to support others in our community and exploring life to its fullest whatever it brings. "Life's a banquet and most poor fools are starving to death." – a quote by Aunty Mame.

Acceptance of what is and following our hearts is how we live our lives as it unfolds to the best of our ability. This poem I wrote some 25 years ago still applies today:

Learning to Accept – 16th July 1989

Acceptance is the walk of life
Wherever it may take you,

It's a free and wandering spirit
Whatever it may make you,

It's all the things you've learned
From your anger to your passion,

And it's all the things you've yearned
From your squalor to your fashion,

It's everything, it's nothing,
It's all your heart's desire,

It's a little and it's something,
It's the truth and it's not a liar,

And when you do the things you must
Learn from suspicion comes trust,

Acceptance is uncertainty
You'll not know where it leads you,

It's about taking a risk
And accepting the death that bleeds you,

Acceptance is freedom
From the restriction that tries to bind you,

It's an incredible awakening
From the sadness that will blind you,

It's a free flowing wondrous thing
That comes right from the heart,

It's all that you can imagine
And it's right here where I start.

Figure 4.13: GROWING OLD IN OUR REFINING YEARS

Questions I ask myself and suggest for you:

1. What am I scared or fearful of?
2. What or who am I judging (including myself)?
3. Are there any limiting patterns I have learned about myself that are holding me back?
4. Do these connect with the current situation?
5. What is my worst-case scenario?
6. What and/or who am I trying to control?
7. What is my tolerance for the unknown?
8. How can I handle my worst-case scenario if it were to arise?
9. Who or what can I trust right now?
10. What is for the greater good?
11. What does my intuition/authentic self tell me to do?
12. What do I still need to let go of?
    a. Continue the rounds of questions until you have let go or your next step (13) is to do something about letting go
    b. Once complete revisit the questions one last time to clear any residual resistance
13. What is my next step?

Learn to love it all!

See the *Appendix – Companion Exercises to Support Your Understanding and Growth* for more ideas and questions to explore:

- Exercise 8: Assess Your Focus on and Effectiveness with Order and Chaos, page 152

Also, see the appendix.

Appendix: Glossary of Terms

Autopoiesis: (from Maturana and Varela) "is a notion of a structure generated from within, maintaining both boundaries and relationships with whatever is to be taken as their 'context' or 'environment', evolving by 'co-drifting co-evolution' in which ever more complex structures self-organise." (Hodge & Dimitrov, 2003)

Bifurcation: A transition point of meaning where two or more thoughts or ideas converge. It may result in being "co-opted into an experience that is not theirs (or anyone else's) but which they act on as though it was." (Dimitrov & Hodge, 2003)

Detailed Complexity: "When a phenomenon involves a larger number of variables." (Fitzgerald, 2003)

Dynamic Complexity: "the ever-present condition of movement when the multitude of variables each refuses to sit still." (Fitzgerald, 2003)

Fractals: (from Mandelbrot) "represent similar patterns appearing at different levels (scales) of a complex structure. Each pattern is an image of the whole structure." (Dimitrov & Woog, 2003)

Fuzzy Logic: "is a conceptual framework for the systemic treatment of vagueness and uncertainty." (Woog, 2003)

Harmonious Resonance: when "the thoughts and feelings in the mental space of each individual spontaneously self-organise into coherent dynamic patterns." (Dimitrov, 2003) Swarm-like Dynamics)

Semiosis: "relates to human ability to establish meaningful connections (relations) between signs (things, events, phenomena, process) a priori seen as not interacting with each other." (Dimitrov & Woog, 2003)

Semiotic Dynamics: "relates to the changes in the meaning carried by signs and sign structures" (Dimitrov & Woog, 2003) and "explores the process of making sense of dynamical signs, that is, signs standing for objects (phenomena, events, processes), which constantly move, change, evolve and transform the scope of our perceptions." (Dimitrov, 2003, Strange Attractors of Meaning)

Soft Systems Methodology (SSM): "is a systematic inquiring process developed by Peter Checkland for analysis of poorly defined systems that have a strongly imbedded 'human element'. According to Checkland, "models in SSM are constructs which represent, from some explicit pure point of view, purposeful human activity."" (Dimitrov & Woog, 2003)

Strange Attractor: "islands of relative stability within the sea of chaos." (Dimitrov & Fell, 2003.) "A *strange attractor* by its nature, is dynamic, and it is in the dynamics and associated boundary conditions that the shape of the *strange attractor* may be found." (Woog, 2003)

Swarm-like Dynamics: (from Langton) "networks of agents capable to act autonomously and to produce higher level identities, such as the flocking behaviour of birds, the swarming behaviour of bees, the concourse of people, etc." (Dimitrov, 2003, Swarm-like Dynamic)

Virtual Systems Methodology (VSM): "applies virtual logic and operates with virtual meanings when exploring whirling complex dynamics of social systems." and "aims at discovery or creation of virtual connections between events, phenomena and processes embedded in social complexity." (Dimitrov & Woog, 2003)

Virtuality of Meaning: "the meaning of an expression simultaneously reflects the past, present and assumed futures of both individual and group experience." (Dimitrov & Woog, 2003)

Vortical Emergence: "seeks to describe the chaotic self-feeding nature of energy flows that emerge from human systems. Vorticity means the system is expansionary." (Woog, 2003)

Chapter 5
Unconditional Relating

We cannot see in others what is not true for ourselves!

Relationship Pathways

At the beginning of every relationship there is chemistry that determines whether we are attracted or repelled towards others. I have heard it said when you see "that person across a crowded room", run the other way. What at first looks attractive often does not turn out to be so. I'm not just talking about romantic or sexual relationships here. Friendships have chemistry of a different kind as do families. The essence is that something draws or distances us. Have you ever walked into a room full of strangers and something draws you towards someone or a small group and steers you clear of others? Chemistry! This is the beginning of a beautiful friendship, the relationship from hell and/or everything in between regardless of how the other person responds to us. We are mirrors of each other. When we look in the mirror we see things we like and things we don't like or wish were different. It's not actually what we see that matters; it's what we do with it. The figure below suggests how we might navigate our way through relationships and what it takes to have it all, whatever "all" is for you.

Figure 5.1: Relationship Pathway

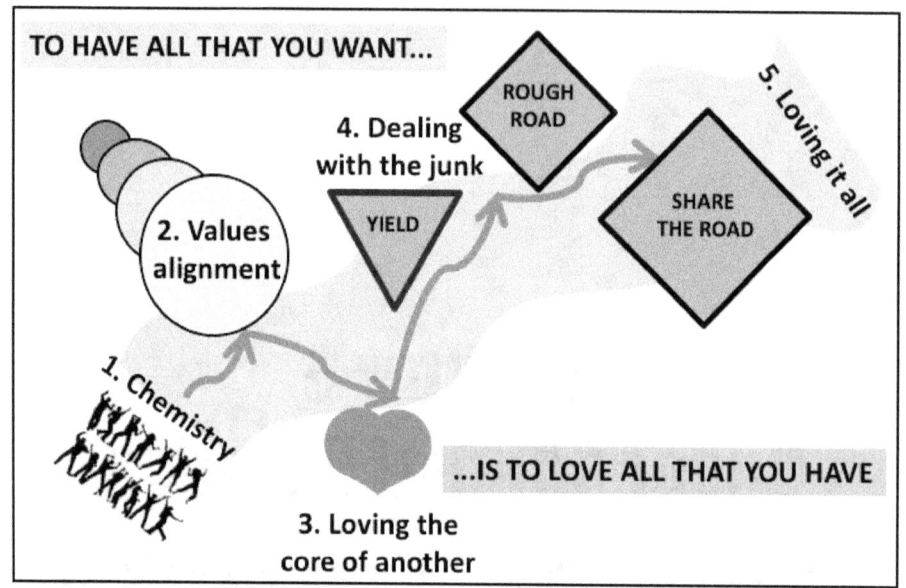

1. **Chemistry** Whilst chemistry is the beginning point of any relationship, it is not what will sustain the relationship. If the relationship starts out on a good note, we form what Hal and Sidra Stone (founders of a therapy modality called Voice Dialogue) call *"Positive Bonding Patterns"*. A *Positive Bonding Pattern* is not necessarily good; it just feels good when we are in it. It can blind us to others' less than desirable traits. The ultimate Positive Bonding Pattern is falling in love or the love for a newborn child – it's just perfect in every way; unless of course it's not! At some point one of the parties will act in a way that is a surprise to the other at best, and can become a downright irritation or serious disturbance at worst. Positive Bonding Patterns don't last. They are invariably interrupted by surprises, usually of an upsetting nature. At best Positive Bonding Patterns run out of steam.

All relationships develop *"Negative Bonding Patterns"*. They occur when negative judgements or fear come forward from either party. Sadly, many relationships fall blindly into these patterns as partners are ill-equipped to navigate this territory. Reflect on how much time you spend in the *Power/Control Triangle* (often called the *"Drama Triangle"*) described in Chapter 1, *"Living Freely"*. (You can do your own assessment of your relationships past and present there.)

A *Negative Bonding Pattern* isn't bad; it just doesn't feel good when we are in it. It is in fact the relationship teacher – indeed a gift for us to grow and expand. Of course, we seldom think of it that way. It is typically a trigger that initiates our need for control – the master addiction! John Gottman (2013) in his book *"The Seven Principles of Making Marriage Work"* proposes there are *"Four Horseman of the Apocalypse"* of a relationship that will ultimately bring it undone.

- Horseman # 1: *"Criticism"* is distinguished from a *"complaint"*. A complaint would be something like: "You said you were going to the dishes and you haven't and I am upset about it"; a criticism would be: "You never do the dishes" said in a harsh tone.
- Horseman # 2: *"Contempt"* is a sense of superiority over a partner and shows ongoing disrespect. It includes sarcasm, cynicism and aggressive humour. The intention is to demean the other and can often occur when criticism has not changed the other person. Trying to change the other person in a relationship, by the way, is a death sentence to it.
- Horseman # 3: *"Defensiveness"* where one partner constantly explains themselves and justifies actions to counteract criticism and even complaints. It can also include whingeing and staying in *victim* consciousness. Gottman suggests it's really just another way of blaming your partner.
- Houseman # 4: *"Stonewalling"* can emerge after the relationship has some longevity. One or both partners tune out. Behaviours include looking down and away, muffling sounds under one's breath, raised eyebrows without an accompanying response; overall a refusal to respond and acting as if one couldn't care less.

Negative Bonding Patterns ignite us and where we learn most in and about relationship. They are part of the fire we need to keep the relationship going. However, if they dominate the relationship with judgement and fear, they will ultimately kill the attraction that began the relationship.

Imagine if we had a battery with only a positive or negative charge; it simply has no spark. We need both polarities of the battery for it to work. When we put two batteries together, if we want them to turn the torch light on we don't place the positive ends facing each other or the negative ends together. We face the positive end of one battery toward the negative end of the other. The positive end charges the negative end and vice versa. Relationships are like that.

To better understand bonding patterns, it is useful to understand something about how each person develops *"Primary Selves"* to live by (Hal & Sidra Stone, 1989 *"Embracing Our Selves"*). These *"Selves"* are all the values we hold as important. For example, the standards we set, how we approach people, what our achievement focus is, how much personal time we allow ourselves. Each of the *Selves* we develop has an opposite part that we *"disown"* – our *"Disowned Selves"*. The book *"All I Really Need to Know I Learned in Kindergarten"* (Robert Fulghum, 1990) suggests that we develop our dominant personality types by the time we are seven years of age and neuroscience has since confirmed this. We try to push our *Disowned Selves* down and indeed it weighs us down and elevates the *Primary Selves*. We end up pretty early in life on a seesaw with an established and sometimes hard-wired *"Operating Ego"* i.e. a Primary and Disowned Selves system (see Figure 5.2 below). The *Power/Control* roles of *Persecutor*, *Victim* and *Rescuer* form part of this *Operating Ego* (See Chapter 1 – *"Living Freely"*)

Figure 5.2: OPERATING EGO – PRIMARY & DISOWNED SELVES

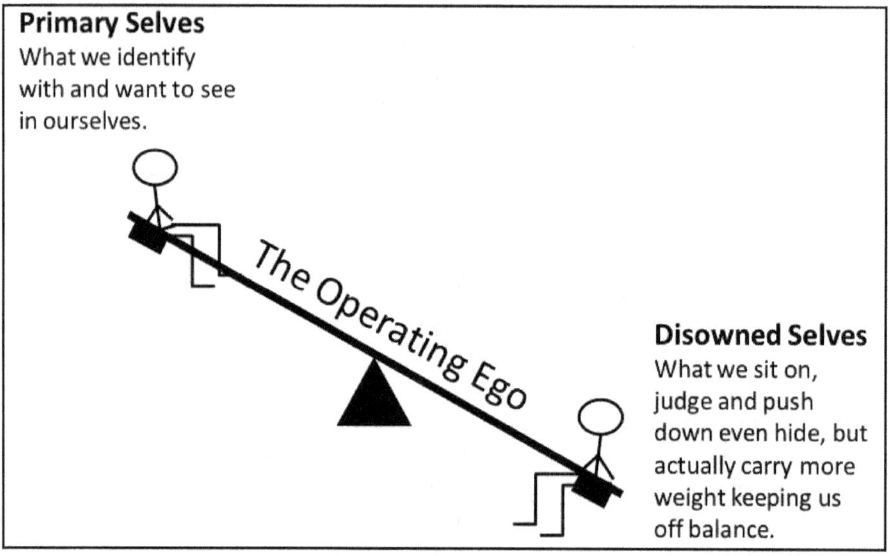

Primary Selves
What we identify with and want to see in ourselves.

The Operating Ego

Disowned Selves
What we sit on, judge and push down even hide, but actually carry more weight keeping us off balance.

The *Operating Ego* forms the basis of our values and beliefs, our judgements and very importantly, how we project these judgements onto others and transfer them from situation to situation. Accepting all our *selves* is a critical first step if we are to be truly happy and satisfied. Yes, both the parts we like and the parts we don't – the *Primary* and the *Disowned Selves*. When you look into the mirror at yourself, what is the chemistry like? Do you like what you see especially beyond the physical? Many of us aim to compensate for what we judge in ourselves through our relationships with others; it's a substitute for really learning about and loving all our *selves*.

What we see in others is true for ourselves. We tend to attract into our lives our *Disowned Selves* to the extent that we have disowned them. For example, if we have a primary focus on pleasing others and we push down allowing ourselves to be selfish (the opposite of pleasing others first) we are likely to attract people who have a selfish *Primary Self*. Not surprisingly, often our romantic partner may carry our disowned trait as *Primary*, i.e. our *Disowned Self* is frequently the other's *Primary Self*.

Typically, if we are prone to pleasing others we might judge others who we think are selfish as bad or wrong in some way. When we act selfishly and put ourselves first, the pleasing side of us is likely to judge us for being bad or wrong. We won't like what we see in the mirror whether the mirror is looking at ourselves or the mirror of what we see in another. Fundamentally if we have a charge on judging another for being selfish it's most likely we have not cleared judgements on our own past selfishness. Rather, we have buried those into our unconscious minds and every time we look into the mirror of selfishness up come the judgements. Carl Jung called this *"shadow boxing"* and it forms the chemistry of *Negative Bonding Patterns*.

The same can be said of *Positive Bonding Patterns*. Often, we may admire others for traits we don't feel we possess or have enough of. Falling in love with someone is mostly falling in love with traits we want for ourselves that we have disowned. Equally we need to claim these for ourselves and truly own our strengths rather than rely on others to supply them for us. The chemistry of *Positive Bonding Patterns* without awareness of what is happening will soon turn sour as that positive trait will also have its downside. After a while that part we were so attracted to can become the biggest irritation in the relationship. For example, *Pleasers* tend to help even when it is not wanted and exhaust themselves in the process. The selfish side wants us to stand up for ourselves and if we push that part down we may give away our power. What is required is to develop awareness about the many combinations of our *Primary/Disowned Selves* – our *Operating Ego*.

Hal and Sidra Stone have identified what they call archetypal *Primary/Disowned Selves* (Figure 5.3) as they are widely represented in the human condition. They permeate our society affecting how well we relate to others.

Figure 5.3: ARCHETYPICAL PRIMARY & DISOWNED SELVES

- Pusher/Procrastinator
- Perfectionist/Laissez Faire
- Pleaser/Selfish One
- Rational Mind/Emotional Self
- Judge/Compassionate Self
- Inner Critic/Authentic self
- Rulemaker/Rebel

What is key to understand is that none of these *Selves* are good or bad, right or wrong. Every part of us that we view as limiting wants something positive for us.

- The *"Pusher"* helps us achieve things; the downside is burn-out. The *"Procrastinator"* may want us to avoid conflict and have peace of mind; this can lead to living in resistance to what comes our way and ending up in the conflict we were trying to avoid. No peace in that!
- The *"Perfectionist"* sets standards; the downside is that it is never good enough. *"Laissez Faire"* wants us to relax; the drawback is we don't get enough done.
- The *"Pleaser"* wants connection with others; the problem is that we

give our power away to what other people want, making our own needs less important and disconnect from ourselves. The *"Selfish"* One wants to help us get our needs met; unfortunately, it can alienate people.
- The *"Rational Mind"* (for many people this is the hardest Primary Self to separate from) wants to figure things out; it lacks empathy for others. The *"Emotional Self"* wants to be acknowledged and gives us access to a whole range of positive emotions, e.g. enthusiasm, optimism; the trouble is that it can be reactive, impulsive, defensive and lack control.
- The *"Judge"* offers us discernment; the issue is overdone righteousness. The *"Compassionate One"* gives us access to loving; if overdone it is excusing without holding for accountability.
- The *"Inner Critic"* wants us to lift above our limitations; overdone it can kill our confidence. The *"Authentic Self"* helps us live our truth; it can create distance from others, especially those who are less aware of their own inner world.
- The *"Rulemaker"* helps us cooperate; it lacks innovation and the confidence to take risks. The *"Rebel"* wants adventure and independence; it can be opinionated and stubborn about personal wants and insensitive to others.

These caricatures are just some examples of the nature of our various *Selves*. They all contribute to charging our batteries and the chemistry of relationships. We need to learn to love them all for what they want for us and the energy they provide us. If we push them down we also push down the energy of their gifts and their positive intentions.

Neuroscience research has shown that we can add new wiring to our *Primary/Disowned Self System*. It's like having cable in our lounge room and we put a satellite on our roof. We don't need the cable anymore, but it can still provide what we want if we need it. How we do that is through awareness. It can be said that this forms the three basic skills to begin leading our Selves through our life – *awareness, awareness* and *awareness*!

When we are in our *Operating Ego* we react to life very often unconsciously, from the ingrained *Primary Self System* – we have a charge on things; we are not neutral. We operate out of *Persecutor, Rescuer,* and *Victim* – three classic *Selves* known as the *Power Triangle* (see Chapter 1, *"Living Freely"* for more); we are in judgement of some kind and that judgement drives us.

An example of transforming a *Primary Self* can be found in Thomas Crum's (1998) book *"The Magic of Conflict"*. He suggests a difference between *"perfection"* and *"discovery"* approaches to life. The former engages our *Operating Ego* with some not too desirable results. The latter builds on our conscious awareness to assist us to develop an *Aware Ego*. Awareness by itself is not enough to sustain changes we may wish to make that will improve our relationships (see Figure 5.4).

Figure 5.4: PERFECTION & DISCOVERY APPROACHES

When how we perceive ourselves and others....	
....is judged against	....is open to
PERFECTION we are driven by:	**DISCOVERY** we are motivated by:
• Right/wrong • Judgements • Failures • Unwillingness to risk • Anxiety • FRUSTRATION	• Enquiry/creativity • Acceptance • Learning • Willingness to risk • Excitement • FASCINATION

Does a discovery approach close off the search for excellence? Not at all! We start by acknowledging how we feel about a situation and then look at what we can learn, for better ways of doing things, for new doors that are opening in the future. Being willing to risk is more likely to achieve excellence than a model of perfection Which is limited by definition of what's right and how people ought to be.

Adapted by the Conflict Resolution Network from Thomas Crum – The Magic of Conflict

Beyond awareness we need to develop an *Aware Ego*. An Aware Ego is engaged when things that trigger our judgements and offend our values and beliefs are not reacted to defensively; i.e. there is no projection or transference. There is no energetic charge we have on the situation. We become curious. We are neutral about it. We move from *"this is right; this is wrong"* to a more neutral position of *"this works; this doesn't"*. We may have a flashing reaction to the trigger (perhaps a twinge somewhere in the body or a quick negative thought and a fleeting desire to react) but it is so quickly quelled it can even go unnoticed by others and we will have genuinely embraced and deflected the reaction ready to discover what is available for us to learn and grow from.

Some ways of developing an *Aware Ego*: we can authentically call out our initial reaction to the other by speaking up for ourselves. For example: "When I think about what has just happened, I notice I felt disturbed (defensive, resentful, angry, disappointed, etc.). What I am going to do about that is let it go and reflect on it later. I'd also like to ask you what your intention was behind the statement so I can better understand where you are coming from." This takes practice and does not guarantee that another will respond in the way we want. Inevitably, everything we say and do contribute to our relationship chemistry. Developing an *Aware Ego* to lift ourselves and our relationships is like learning an Asian language if you are a westerner or vice versa.

Instead of reacting from the *Operating Ego* we can process a situation internally and free it from our bodies. This takes even more practice, especially in up-close and personal relationships. A way to start this is to get curious with our *inner thoughts* and ask: "Mmm, I wonder what that was?" or "Here's that feeling again. I wonder where that comes from; when might I have experienced this before?" Another technique is to use inner self talk like "It's not critical now and I'll look into it when I have a quiet moment." We need to make sure we attend to this later with this technique and not let it slide. As we become more consciously skilled in identifying our defences we become aware of what we are aware of; it's called *"meta-awareness"*, i.e. we start noticing what we are noticing.

Figure 5.5: AWARE EGO – PRIMARY & DISOWNED SELVES

Awareness

Primary Self
•The parts we need to separate from

Disowned Self
•The parts we need to embrace

The Aware Ego

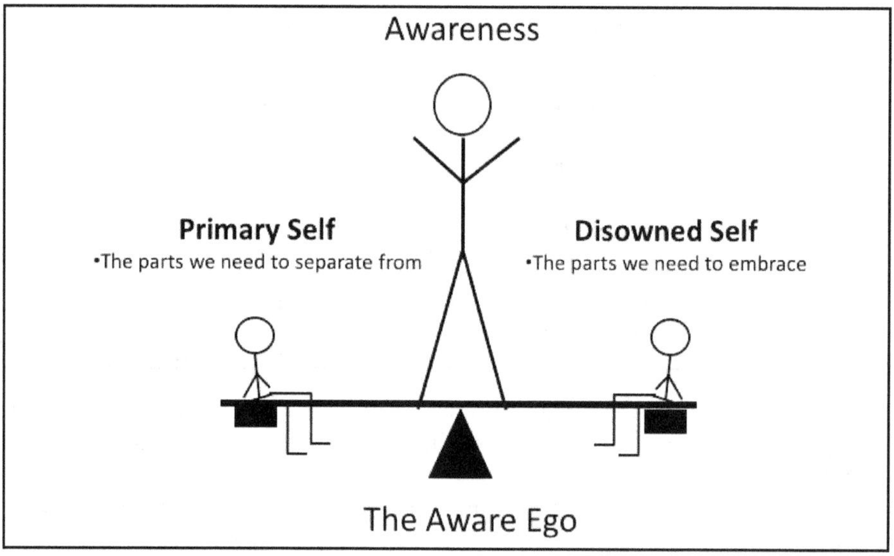

Figure 5.5 illustrates bringing our *Primary/Disowned Selves* into better balance; first though, we need to identify what we are aware of. All previous chapters and their companion exercises in the appendix can assist with this. Then we can create a strong foundation for an *Aware Ego,* separating but not surrendering *Primary* Selves and beginning to embrace our *Disowned Selves*.

There is no quick fix to this. It's about learning a new way to live and that seesaw can rock backwards and forwards quite a bit. As a child, have you ever been on a seesaw with someone and you're in the air and the other person on the ground decides to surprise you and simply gets off the seesaw? You come crashing down to the ground. *Disowned Selves* can be a bit cantankerous if pushed down for too long and decide to become *Primary*, crashing and burning a *Primary Self* once and for all. I heard a story about a fundamentalist Christian, a version of the *Rulemaker*, who ran his country's censorship system. In his mid-forties, he resigned his job and became one of the biggest pornographic filmmakers (*Disowned Rebel*) in the country. His instinctual *Disowned Self* had had enough of rules and piety and got off the seesaw and his instinctual energies became *Primary*. Perhaps not the most elegant strategy for growth and change! An *Aware Ego* can better manage such important life choices and empower us to navigate our life and our relationships far more effectively.

If you wish to know more about *Primary* and *Disowned Selves* I recommend reading *"Embracing Our Selves"* and *"Embracing Each Other"* by

Hal and Sidra Stone (1989). These concepts are a great foundation for building better and more rewarding relationships and ensuring we keep the chemistry alive in healthy ways. Healthy self-regulation is essential in forming healthy relationships and mostly we are taught little about that in our early years.

Notwithstanding our awareness levels, a necessary second step in the *Relationship Pathway* is to align and accommodate the values embedded in our *Primary/Disowned Selves System* with our partner, family, friends and colleagues.

The first step to doing this is being clear about the *values* we live by and how they match or at least can be accommodated with others. The values we live by are those that we espouse and act out; not just those we espouse. If our values are polarised within ourselves (we behave differently from what we say) and with others, relationships are not sustainable. Often, we mistakenly think our values are what we articulate. This is not always the case however. Our *true values*, often hidden, are indicated by how we behave, especially during conflict – those *Negative Bonding Patterns*. Our strategies for dealing with conflict will surface underlying and often *unconscious values* that are not evident when we first meet others. Moreover, if we are not living out our stated values, our dreams start to shatter. If we don't face this – yes, another look into the mirror at our *Selves*, we end up seeing another as our mirror, triggering our judgements and fears.

When we align and accommodate our values with those around us, we have a good chance of building strong foundations for the future with others – notwithstanding the bonding patterns that are present in the relationship. If the values are polarised no amount of remixing the chemicals will work. Indeed, deeper and divided values unattended to can become explosive or worse, implosive and potentially atomic. For example, what values does someone with a *Pleaser Primary Self* surrender to keep the peace? How long can they go on living someone else's values before they break? One core value I have observed in primary relationships that if not upheld will disturb, even fracture and break a relationship and that is not withholding from our partner. A truly robust relationship can handle anything, i.e. nothing is off the table for discussion and both parties fully trust that all challenges and issues as well as hopes and dreams will be brought forward. That doesn't mean it's easy. It's the relationships that can have the hardest of conversations that not just survive but thrive.

To understand our own value system, we need to notice our behaviour as if we are looking at someone else. What do we see? What values might be driving that behaviour? For example, if we say we value our family but we work long hours and hardly see them, an underlying stronger value might be earning money to create a sense of security. We may tell ourselves we are doing it for our family, but are we? Or we might be someone who on the surface values honesty but secretly takes home office supplies. In this instance, what we really value is a kind of entitlement. Spend some time looking at your own behaviour to learn what you *really* care about, being gentle and non-judgemental with yourself about what you discover. Use it to learn more about your relationships.

3. Loving the core of another

If two people or a group, are clear that their values can be accommodated the next step is to see into the core of the other, i.e. know who they truly are. When we look at a koala bear the adjectives that are most often used to describe them are cute and cuddly. They seem to soften our heart in some way. How do other people soften our heart? Who do we know them to be at their core and do we love that about them? If the answer is yes, we are ready for the next step in our *Relationship Pathway*. However, there is a catch. When we pick up a koala they can scratch, growl and even urinate on you, and they smell. Our *Positive Bonding Pattern* with our cute and cuddly koala just went south.

Hello *Negative Bonding Pattern*! Our first inclination, of course, is to separate from the koala and, if the experience is bad enough, never pick one up again. Invariably, though, most of us still see koalas as cute and cuddly and maybe we love them more from a distance depending on how much we love cute and cuddly. If we really really love cute and cuddly, we are likely to give it another go. Human relations are a bit like that.

What's the payoff and what's the price of engagement? If the love of another's core being is strong enough, we only need to decide that we are willing to work with what comes with their core, i.e. those annoying irritating parts that bring us back to our judgements and fears. I say only as if it is a single decision but it is much more than that; it's about whether this is a relationship we want and how much we are willing to take care of the relationship to make it work. If the relationship is governed by polarised values it will ultimately break down whether or not the two people physically stay together.

Many of us enter relationships to have them take care of us. Our decision to take care of the relationship asks us to own and be responsible for our part (our 100%) in it, regardless of what the other person does or does not do that suits us. There is our 100% and the other's 100%. There is the 100% of the relationship, of which each person owns 50% as their contribution to what is happening and the relationship outcomes. We can only ever change our part (our 100%) to affect our 50% in the relationship. Aiming to change the other's 100% in order for their contribution to be what we want is a pathway to separation. Change the part you have control over (your 100%); it will affect 50% of the relationship and, if the other does the same, a way forward can be found. It's worth repeating: look how you can take care of the relationship rather than have the relationship take care of you. The perfect relationship is not "finding the one", it is how we set each free to be who we are and finding a worthwhile connection with each other based on mutual values and boundaries that each respect and hold to.

When we accept the chemistry in our relationship and are sparked by it, whether positive or negative; have decided our values align and can be accommodated; have decided we love, like or respect the core of another and are willing to own our part in the success or otherwise of the relationship, we have answered the question that asks: "Am I in this relationship?" – the "*If*

Question". When we are 100% clear the answer is yes, we only need to ask "*how*" from there on in. If we are not 100% clear on a yes to the *If Question*, we need to go back to the previous steps until we can satisfy ourselves we are or are not in the relationship – 100% is a breeze; 99% can be a gale! It's kind of like being pregnant – you are or you are not. At this point, there is no 99%.

Relationships are not naturally linear. Maybe at some point we answered the *If Question* fully committing to it and then found out what we didn't know, bringing the *If Question* back up. It's often not until some water has gone under the bridge that we feel fully informed about a longer-term commitment. That usually occurs when *Negative Bonding Patterns* have surfaced and we haven't been able to resolve them. Sometimes we have stepped into a full commitment prematurely or something fundamental has changed, taking us back into the *If Question*.

4. Dealing with the junk
ROUGH ROAD
YIELD

Every relationship has a junk yard. It's how we navigate our way through it that is critical. "By the inch, it's a cinch; by the yard it's very very hard" (source unknown) as the saying goes. A yes to the *If Question* is a necessary precursor to navigating by the inch. Anything less like a "yes but" or a "maybe" will make the journey excruciating (see Chapter 5, "*Intentionality*" for more about commitment, especially Peter Senge's seven levels of commitment).

Climbing into and embracing what is not working in a relationship can require the strength of a lion, the skill of a micro surgeon and the resolve of an anthropologist who looks for what the ruins can tell us about our history. The junk can be found in the *Negative Bonding Patterns* that have evolved throughout the relationship – values misalignment, our judgements of ourselves and the other, our fears – have blinded us from continuing to see and love the core of our self and our partner. Outside assistance may be necessary depending on how deeply embedded and powerful the *Negative Bonding Patterns* are. Often the deeper they are the greater the learning. A friend of mine once told me that their mother was married to the same man four times. They were just all in different bodies. We tend to carry patterns from one relationship to another, especially if we are locked into *Operating Ego – Negative Bonding Patterns*.

Sustaining a relationship can sometimes feel almost impossible the longer it continues if *Operating Egos* are at the forefront. The result is most often a dependent or co-dependent, even toxic relationship that is based upon what the other does and characterised by undealt with issues leading to guilt and resentment; or an independent relationship where two people co-exist in a numbed-out state, not connecting with each other. These are relationships of convenience, begrudging compromise and a refusal to look in the mirror for fear of what might be revealed to us about ourselves. An *Aware Ego* and discovery approach on the other hand will make the journey more palatable and the "how" question easier to deal with. However, it is still likely to be a challenge. It comes back to that first step of *awareness, awareness,* and more *awareness* as we examine all reflections in the mirror ball of relationships. We are then better equipped to develop an interdependent relationship that allows for individuality and deep connection.

Essentially the willingness and courage to dig around in the junk yard is what will see us through to the fifth and final stage of the *Pathway*.

5. Loving it all   Perhaps this caption says it all. We may not like some of our behaviours or the behaviours of others, but we can love what those behaviours might want for us – their positive intentions. *Every behaviour has a positive intention* if only for the individual exhibiting it. It might simply be to keep ourselves safe, to protect ourselves in some way. That may not make the behaviour okay, but it might help to understand it. Once we have identified a positive intention in a limiting or harmful behaviour, we can find strategies to assist those positive intentions to be realised through more acceptable means. If we stay in right/wrong judgements or fears about the behaviour, we regress into the junkyard. Often this requires that we get out of our own way to love it all – perhaps the most challenging of all things to do in relationship with others.

Judgement and fear are the opposite of loving, not hate as one might think. In order to hate something, we must love something more. It informs our loving. Although staying in a hateful, resentful or angry, upset state either leads us to what we judge or fear and kills our relationships, or alternatively, to loving it all. It's a choice.

The question begs: "*Would you rather be right or happy?*" If we'd rather be right it's likely that our relationships will disconnect at some point. Access to building more rewarding relationships is limited by this, i.e. having the same relationships over and over again with different people. Once we've decided that we want a particular relationship, it might be useful to understand what characterises the relationship we have and the one we want. Figure 5.7 summarises the way relationships are likely to progress contingent very much on how we navigate the *Relationship Pathway* just explored.

Relationship Characteristics

Initially when we are attracted to another, especially in a serious potentially primary relationship *Positive Bonding Patterns* dominate. The judgements we carry are usually admiring and positive about the other. Our fear might be more about whether the relationship will last. Questioning is more exploratory than conclusive in its nature.

If it is not sustainable, the relationship will initially either disconnect or move into an unbalanced state. See Figures 5.6 and 5.7. Notice the degree of judgement and fear versus the amount of loving and connection that is present in each of the figures.

Figure 5.6: Building Relationships

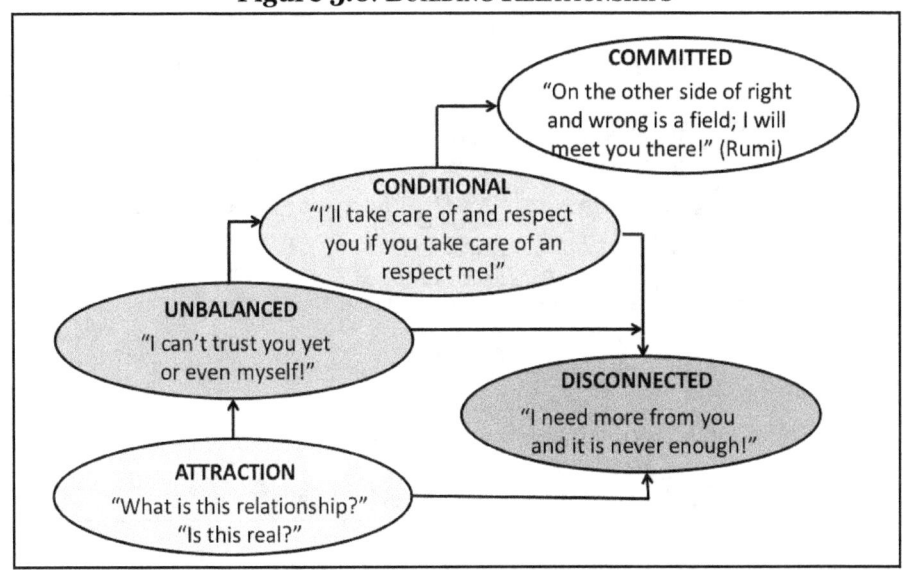

A "*Disconnected Relationship*" is most likely to feature two people relating from their unconscious *Operating Ego*. An "*Unbalanced Relationship*" is not necessarily characterised by only one of the members behaving from judgement and fear. It can flip from one person to the other. If it switches very frequently it is likely to regress to a *Disconnected Relationship*. If one of the parties, not necessarily the same person each time, can continually function from their *Aware Ego* and the first three steps of the *Relationship Pathway* are intact, the relationship has a better than even chance of progressing to the next stage – a "*Conditional Relationship*" (Figure 5.9).

Figure 5.7: Disconnected Relationship

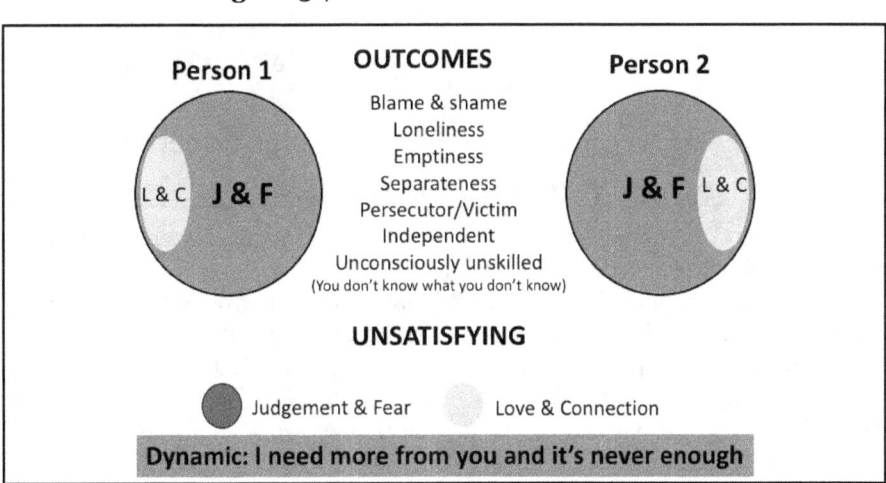

Figure 5.8: Unbalanced Relationship

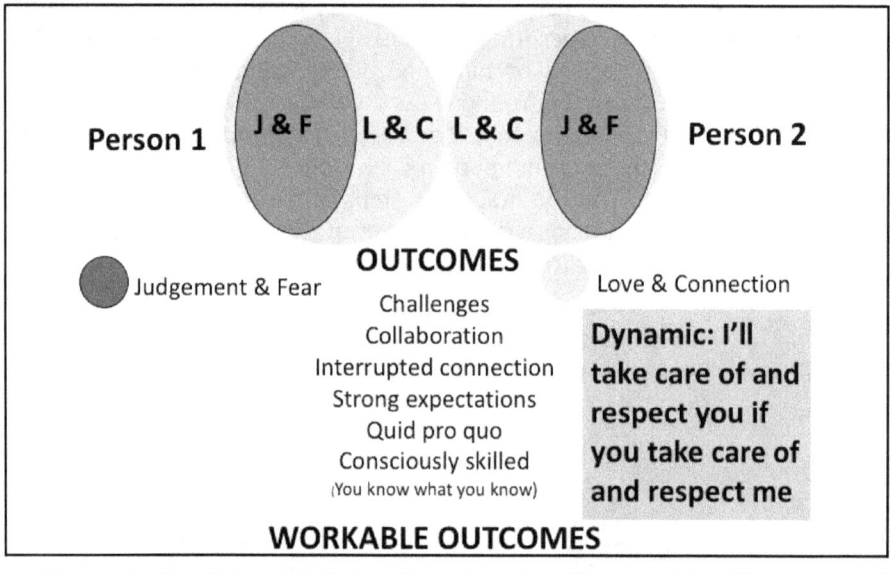

Figure 5.9: Conditional Relationship

Notice in *Conditional Relationships* there is still a considerable amount of judgement and fear matched by a good dose of loving and connection. This can be a confusing time in relationships and can regress to *Unbalanced* or even *Disconnected*, depending on where the members are on the *Relationship Pathway*.

If the relationship can grow through this phase to a fully "*Committed and Enduring Relationship*", it's because the *If Question* has been held up as a "yes", and the willingness to do the deeper work that can sustain the relationship is the focus.

Perhaps the two hardest things to be in life is a partner and parent, and it is likely the thing we are least educated in. We expect we should know how. Unfortunately and sadly, many of us are simply older children. Sounds harsh. Maybe. However, researcher Robert Keegan at Harvard University has developed a concept of *"stages of adult development"* which has shown that:

- 15% of adults do not grow beyond an *"Egocentric"* level naturally found in teenagers – "It's all about me!"
- Another 60% are what he named *"Socialised"* – "What do you think about me?" i.e. predicating their actions on how others react to them. It seems the *Operating Ego* is alive and well in our society.
- A further 24% are described as *"Independent"* – "I am true to my beliefs; I respect yours, but I may not necessarily agree or connect with them." Here we have the beginnings of an *Aware Ego* and the foundations of Keegan's next stage of development.
- *"Integral"* – "I am true to my beliefs; I respect yours and I'm interested in what we could create together that would be greater than what we could do separately." It's at this level that the *Aware Ego* takes hold opening the door to sustainable *Committed Relationships*. See Figure 5.10. Keegan proposes that only 1% of the population is centred at this level and adds that around 17% are on their way to it.
- The final stage he describes as *"Sacred"* – "How do we make the world a better place for our children and our children's children?" – he suggests 0.1% of the population are at this level – the Nelson Mandelas of this world.

The interesting thing about his model is that *"Integral/Sacred"* thinkers do not leave the less developed levels behind. They simply manage these levels in much more functional ways. They learn to love it all and therefore can and do have it all.

Judgement and fear are still present in a *committed relationship* and there is a merging of the two parties without a loss of identity. Deep interdependent connection paves the way to work through any residual junk yard experiences and resolves new ones along the way. It's a fallacy that being in a loving relationship in this way is always about being nice. It can be very challenging even once we have arrived here. At the same time, it is exciting as the batteries of each party are constantly re-charged to light the way forward, shining a torch on the whole relationship and its participants – it's good and not so great bits within and between the individuals. The *right/wrong game* transforms to the *this works/this doesn't* pastime. Parties are hard on the issue and soft on each other and lift together. We don't go up alone is the bottom line. (Figure 5.10)

Figure 5.10: COMMITTED RELATIONSHIP

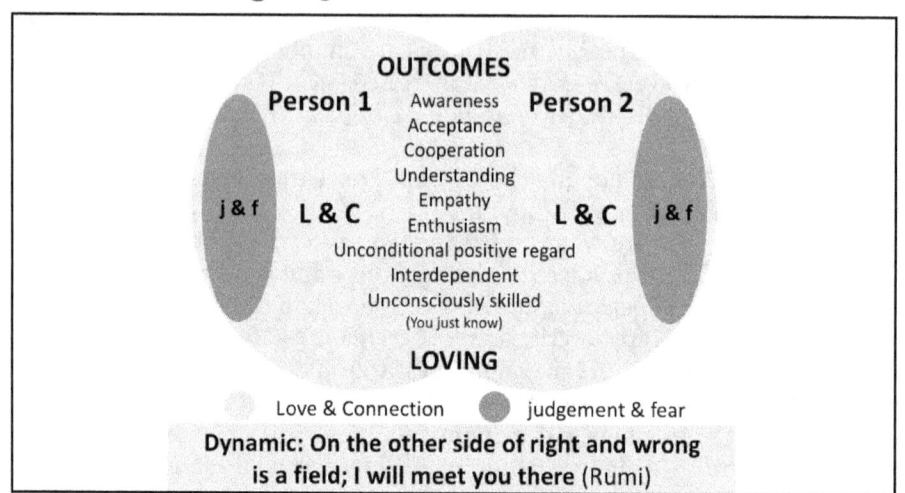

Unconditional loving of self and the other is made larger than the conflicts and disagreements that arise in a fully committed relationship. Partners turn towards each other in challenging times, especially when the conflicts trigger deeply held values; a search for understanding dominates differences and power struggles. There is an overriding sense of continuity in the relationship no matter what. You'll note that the first six attributes in this relationship are the same as the steps in Chapter 1, *"Living Freely"* – Figure 1.3, *"Building a Bridge to Freedom"*.

The question of *if* this is the relationship I want to be in is supplanted by "*how* do we do this relationship together". That does not mean to say that upset, anger, frustration, irritation and annoyance don't arise. These are overridden by an overarching sense of knowing who we each are in our hearts and we hold for loving that over everything else. There is permission for upset and difference but boundaries around how these are delivered are honoured to the best of each party's abilities; when boundaries are transgressed, there is room for remorse, regret and forgiveness. Each person owns their part and takes responsibility for their contribution to the dissonance without blame and shame, right or wrong. Each strive to own and live their *Authentic Selves* (Chapter 2, *"Embracing Vulnerability and Authenticity"* for more).

A plethora of literature exists about the construct of unconditional love, but many see it as an unreachable ideal, especially when experiencing trouble in their relationships. Dr Greg Baer calls it *"Real Love"* (www.realove.com). He challenges us to forego imitative or conditional love for it. In his research around addiction Dr Baer suggests that our parents taught us to feel loved when we are good and to feel unloved when we were bad or at least loved less. The patterns that emerge from this dichotomy are transferred into our adult relationships (Chapter 3, *"Taking Charge of the Past"* for more). My favourite quote from his work is *"With real love nothing else matters; without it nothing else is enough!"*

I have recommended a number of books on relationships in the Recommended Readings section of the Appendix and I think John-Roger says it best and poses that "spiritual loving is unconditional: 'I do love you and will love you no matter what.' In this form of loving there is fulfilment because there is no hidden agenda, just 100% positive expression. It is complete in itself because it is not dependent on the actions of the other person."

Integrating My Personal Story

Formulating and sustaining relationships is a lifelong quest for all of us. When we are very young we develop a relationship with relationship, i.e. how we experience what happens in them. It starts with our parents and family of origin, moving into relationships at school and our community. In our teenage years, our identity is being formed through our relationships with our peers; how we socialise ourselves and gain acceptance or not. By our early twenties, we either want to recreate what we have experienced, avoid it or rebel against it.

I mostly **rebelled** against what I had experienced. I wanted stability, deep understanding and caring. My now ex-wife Diane filled the bill and for 15 years we had all of that, at a certain level. The last five years were tenuous as underlying needs not being met on both sides had us slide strongly into a **Conditional Relationship**. I remember when I got married, I looked up to the heavens and said to myself: "I will make my marriage work no matter what." That was my rebellious relationship with relationship, i.e. my witnessing of my parents' relationship was characterised by how "madly in love" they were and how it could be deep affection and fun one day and World War 3 the next. Whilst I was determined to make it work no matter what, I didn't know what "the no matter what" was. I had a vision of a happy nuclear family in the traditional sense but it was to be shattered not by anyone else but from within me. My relationship was a **Conditional Relationship** – *"I'll take care of and respect you if you take of and respect me"*. It stopped working and began to slide to **Unbalanced** and ultimately **Disconnected**.

I left my marriage once at 15 years for four months and then again finally just before our 20th anniversary when I realised I genuinely couldn't celebrate it. Apart from losing Glen, the two times I left have to be the most painful two days of my life. I was about to turn my life upside down and inside out and the lives of my wife and children. My vision of the ultimate nuclear family was shattered. **Rebelling** against the model my parents delivered hadn't worked. The battle between my responsible **Rulemaker** and **Rebel**; and **Pleaser** and **Selfish** side was on.

As it happened, I had defined what I wanted next and guess what it was – with a woman. Again, a battle between my *Belonging* and *Independent Selves* was also on. I met an amazing lady and we explored a primary relationship for nearly two years. The **unconditional love** and **positive regard** was exceptional but it was not sustainable given my emerging sense of what I really wanted but was unprepared to face. Even though I had admitted to this lady that I was bisexual – at least I thought I was and it felt more palatable to declare that – I was still not at peace with my own homophobia. It wasn't the full truth. It ended as a primary relationship and after some healing we have remained in a deeply loving, incredibly close friendship and she has a great relationship with my partner. In fact, I can feel a bit ganged up on in a fun way when they are together. She is part of my chosen family.

Finally, I faced coming out and experienced a whole new perspective on relationship in the gay world. Like the straight world, every kind of relationship from **Disconnected**, **Unbalanced** through to **Conditional exists**. However, I had rarely experienced a fully **committed relationship** in the unconditional sense in that world or indeed in the straight world for that matter.

Three years after coming out I met my partner Maxx and for six years the relationship remained the same as most others, of course with its unique dynamics as well. All those issues I still hadn't cleared came home to roost. He too had been married and has three sons. Whilst our family values created a connection, two alpha males under the same roof certainly brought forward all the attributes off the four types of relationships described in this chapter and probably aspects of every other chapter.

With counselling assistance and a **wholehearted commitment** to building something lasting and fulfilling we have learned to set each other free to be who we are and agree boundaries that have us trust and feel genuinely and deeply loved. We have celebrated 20 years together. We are still going strong and we both see ourselves living out our years together. We have preserved our relationships with our sons and even our ex-wives. Beyond that, my ex-wife gets along well with Maxx, and I get along well with his ex-wife. We mostly see each other at family functions but if either of them needed us we would be on call and would likely offer without wanting to intrude. We have spent some Christmases and birthdays together. My youngest son got married in 2015 and he asked Maxx, his mother and me to speak at the wedding. We have had to work towards this over time but the caring we all have for each other's welfare has remained a centrepiece for us and them.

Maxx's and my relationship is not conventional. We have had to make up our own rules and employ all the concepts presented in this book to live life to its fullest. I am glad to say we are doing that, including making the best of our setbacks. Our intentions are clear. We have gone through all the stages of relationships described in this chapter including walking through the junkyard of our relationship. We both have a strong **Rescuer/Pleaser** energy that manifests in different ways; our **Persecutor/Perfectionist** can kick in when pushed too hard on a point of view and we can fall into **Victim/Inner Critic** when things have gone on for too long. Fortunately this last one is rare and usually related to something outside the relationship when it happens.

We have both different and shared interests, allowing each other to pursue personal time and concurrently sharing any misgivings about the balance of me and we time. Nothing is off the table for discussion. There are no withholds and our values align. We are **100% committed** as long as we both shall love!

In 2015, The Feed show from SBS Sydney interviewed Maxx and me about having been married, our coming out and our 20 year relationship. Here is the link if you're interested.

*http://www.sbs.com.au/yourlanguage/video/554462787504/
John-and-Max-The-Feed*

In addition, in January 2017, SBS asked me to comment on how relationships function today and whether the traditional romantic notions of love are relevant. An appendix at the end of this chapter outlines my responses and the published article is also included. You can also connect with the published article online.

http://www.sbs.com.au/topics/life/relationships/article/2017/02/01/stop-searching-your-happily-ever-after-fairy-tales-have-no-place-modern

Questions I ask myself and suggest for you

1. How does this situation classify the nature of my relationship(s)?
2. What emotions, feelings, beliefs, values, needs and fears are in play for myself and those involved?
3. What defences/*Protective Selves* are being triggered in me and potentially others involved?
4. How do any judgements I am running on others mirror truths about me?
5. How can I let the judgements on myself and others go?
6. Is this a one-off situation or a pattern (bonding pattern)?
7. What do I want?
8. What do others want?
9. Can I reconcile these?
10. What is the impact of any choices I might make on myself and others?
11. How might I deliver any hard or challenging messages to others in a loving way (hard on the issue, soft on the person)?
12. What is my next step?

See the *Appendix – Companion Exercises to Support Your Understanding and Growth* for more ideas and questions to explore:

- Exercise 9: Knowing Your Primary/Disowned Selves, page 158
- Exercise 10: Relationship Assessment, page 161
- Exercise 11: Your Relationship Current State, page 164
- Exercise 12: Relationship Sharing Exercise, page 165

Appendix - SBS Request for Comment - 23rd January 2017

The journalist from SBS, Shannon McKeogh wanted to write on the following and I was asked for comment.

I am exploring the idea that fairytales or idealistic romantic fantasies are detrimental to relationships, but I would <u>also like to explore how cultural diverse and interfaith relationships</u> fit/don't fit into these ideals and some practical tips to common problems.

See her article following my full response below.

My Response

1. **How can fairy tale ideas such as searching for a Prince Charming, or "the one" be disempowering to modern relationships? What damage can this cause?**

   Romantic love has us lose ourselves in the relationship and in the long term we forfeit our identity which is often tenuous in the first place. Enmeshed relationships that ride on romantic love in the long term can lead to co-dependence and even addictive patterns, which result in each person judging the other when their ideals are not met. When you think of a koala bear the adjectives typically used to describe them are cute and cuddly. When we 'fall in love' we typically do so with what we think are the 'cute and cuddly' parts of the other person e.g. their kindness, fun loving nature etc. But when you pick a koala bear up they scratch, growl, smell and may even urinate on you. When we are enmeshed in romantic love we ignore and even pretend not to notice the scratchy, growly parts of the other. Once we begin to discover these parts romantic love starts to sour.

As mentioned earlier a relationship is like a battery. It needs both a positive and negative end to charge it up. Falling in love is the ultimate 'positive bonding pattern' (charge) but whilst it is a euphoric feeling, by itself will not last. 'Negative bonding patterns' are needed to charge the relationship up. This is where we learn and grow. The problem is judgement and fears are what people retreat to and they are the antidotes to loving in the long haul.

I think that two of the hardest things to be in life are a parent and a partner, yet these roles are mostly learned from the models we are given and 85%+ of us come from dysfunctional families. When my clients arrive for their first session after asking them why they are here I ask how they feel about being here. Their responses are typically 'embarrassed', 'anxious', 'wished it hadn't come to this', and even 'I wish I didn't need to be here'. This resistance is ego driven wanting to solve it themselves and yet not equipped to do so. Often there is unwillingness to seek help until it may be too late. Very few seek help in the early stages of the relationship to better navigate it.

2. **Why do you believe these old-fashioned romantic ideals are still popular?**

Intimacy and passion (not just sexually) are key drivers in our lives. We are 'belonging' beings and the adrenalin rush of passion excites us. The endorphins that are fired up in a romantic relationship satisfy these two biochemical needs. Think about how much of our intake from movies and music is devoted to (romantic) love. It's almost as if we are brainwashed into thinking it is the entire answer and yet at some level we know it isn't. Maybe the challenge of finding and keeping these positive feelings keeps us going for it.

Relationships today are strewn with multiple distractions juxtapositioned with us seeking a 'sense of place' in the world. For a while romantic love gives us that sense of place.

I'm not convinced the ideal itself is old fashioned. We all need a spark in our lives. It's the view that it is the foundation model of a lasting and enriched relationship that is the problem. In a robust relationship that faces all of its aspects can revitalise romantic love as part of the relationship tenor and accept each other for all of who they are. If we only love the good bits of someone we live in a conditional world that is doomed to separation even if it is not a physical separation. Having it all is 'loving it all'.

3. **What impact do these expectations have on interfaith and culturally diverse relationships?**

What holds a relationship together or divides it are the underlying beliefs and values that each hold about themselves and the world. If one person wants to be a bank robber and the other an auditor those value systems are polarised and irreconcilable. Aligning or at least being able to accommodate each other's values is fundamental to a successful relationship.

I had one client living in Australia with a westernised approach to his life. His family still lived in a country where marriages were arranged or at least needed to be approved of by both sets of parents. He battled with his western views and an arranged marriage. He came to see me already married. In the end he was unable break from his natal cultural norms and reconciled his marriage was a lifelong commitment and chose to build from there. One has to wonder what the long term outcome might be from such a choice. If he is truly reconciled without resistance or resentment it may very auger well for him.

Marriage or a long term invested partnership may last over time and does for many. A question though is what level of enrichment applies to the relationship over time. Enrichment can take many forms and is rested in what that means for the individual; without it though our lives remain unfulfilled. Settling does not generally lead to genuine commitment.

4. **What are the main difficulties interfaith and culturally diverse relationships face?**

Reconciling values which requires us to move beyond judgements and into unconditional loving not only for the other person but their intimates as well.

5. **What can they do to overcome these problems?**

   Get support early to better understand underlying drivers and needs. We don't go up alone.

6. **Often we learn about relationships and love from modern fairytales (movies, TV, books, The Bachelor, etc). Where could people look for more realistic representations?**

   Four books come to mind:
   - The Nine Principles of Successful Marriages by John and Julie Gottman
   - Getting the Love You Want by Harville Hendrix and Helen Hunt
   - Really Relating by David Jansen and Margaret Newman
   - The Five Languages of Love by Gary Chapman

   See a relationship therapist early in the relationship or even before you are in a relationship to uncover your relationship with relationship i.e. what you think relationships should or should not be about.

7. **Why is real love/life better than a fairy tale?**

   - Embracing all of ourselves and who we are with without judgement is freeing
   - In a robust unconditionally loving relationship each person sets the other free to be themselves
   - Boundaries are agreed and kept from a base of aligned values and trust
   - Life is lived more consciously and purposefully and therefore enriched
   - Fear of losing the other does not run us or the relationship
   - We are freed from the shackles of an idealised world to embrace a potentially idyllic reality with all its flaws and gifts
   - We know happiness comes and goes but an overriding contentment brings peace and joy in the long run
   - We live from the inside out not the other way around i.e. we are less dependent on what the world brings to us but more concerned with how we respond effectively to what it presents
   - We have a sense of place that is interdependent and enriched, not independent or co-dependent

Chapter 6
Intentionality

Intentions are the results we get, not the goals we set!

Diving into Resistance

I have witnessed myself, my family, friends, clients and acquaintances at some time or another sabotaging, often unconsciously, our desires and success through unclear intentions. I've been told for years I have a book in me, and when it comes to sitting down and writing it, I have balked. So, what is my intention really? If I set a goal to write a book from this place of uncertainty will it ever get completed? I suspect not if my underlying, unseen, unconscious intention doesn't line up with it. So, what might that be and how do I uncover it?

First, I have to have the courage to take a dive into my unconscious mind especially if I think I won't like what I find.

My uncertainty is associated with a fear. We might argue I lack information and that may be true; but so what if I don't have the information? What's that book? *"Feel the Fear and Do It Anyway"* (Susan Jeffers, 1987). Lack of information can create fear as much as knowing something bad is likely to happen. Fear of the unknown can intrude into our everyday lives. We learn more about ourselves by embracing the fear of the unknown. We can turn uncertainty into self-trust. A breakthrough is to be curious in the unknown and stay the course (see Chapter 4, *"Loving Ambiguity and the Unknown"*). Go fishing, even deep see diving to discover what the fear is about. Some examples in writing my book could be:

- I might not write well (self-doubt and skill deficiencies)

- No one will be interested in what I have to say (Ah! Rejection! Now we are getting warm)
- What I have to say may not be of value (Unworthiness! Even warmer)
- My sometimes circular and technical communication style may lead to being misunderstood and then criticised (Exclusion! Getting hot)
- Putting myself out there may expose me in some public way that attracts ridicule or judgement. It may expose things about me I'd rather keep private (Shame! The ultimate devastation and likely a bottom line)

So, being uncertain about writing a book (my goal) is tainted by my self-doubt, potential rejection, a sense of unworthiness, fear of exclusion and shame. Quite a catch on this fishing trip!

I, like most of us, want to avoid such uncomfortable emotions. The irony is that unless I embrace all of these attributes, in fact even love them, uncertainty rules over the goal of writing a book and it simply won't happen. This chapter and others are steps towards that goal. Protecting me from shame becomes the unconscious (until now) intention that supersedes the goal of writing a book – if I let it.

Why would I want to love:

- Self-doubt
- Fear of rejection
- Unworthiness
- Exclusion
- Shame

They all want something for me and are the keys to my unconscious intentions. You may recall from Chapter 2, "*Embracing Vulnerability and Authenticity*" neuroscientist Bruce Lipton (2008, "*The Biology of Belief*") tells us that when there is a battle between the unconscious and the conscious, the unconscious will always win; a good reason to know what all these parts want for me. What's the *positive intention* of each? Yes, they each have one.

- Self-doubt; Hmm. Humility might be something it is seeking – nice quality eh!
- Fear of rejection and exclusion (Okay two at a time – they are running mates); to belong might be the intention here.
- Unworthiness; more humility? What about a deeper one here? "If I'm humble I'll be loved". How Australian is that? That tall poppy syndrome has a way of creeping in, doesn't it? The fish are running hot today.
- Shame; what could possibly be positive about that? Shame and guilt help us course correct. They provide direction for a higher vibration in life. Perhaps the *positive intention* of shame is for us to be noble. Do I want to be noble? Well yes, actually.

So, what if my intention is to write a book about manifesting what we want in life and I do that with humility, loving myself and others and a sense of belonging to something greater? I think I'll water this tall poppy with those qualities.

Sounds pretty good, and yet I notice my energy remained tainted for some time with the limitations I've just declared. Okay, looks like I need to find out more on the next fishing trip.

My father, now passed, loved fishing and used to take me. I loathed it. Perhaps I am a fisherman of a different kind – I'm fishing for the human spirit. Juxtapositioned to all these doubts I am reminded how my dad also used to say incessantly "there is no such word as 'can't'!" Thanks for that gift, Dad. I'm on my way to the word "can". If you are reading this, I did break through the patterns described here.

Defining clear and workable intentions

We might say what's in a word? Does it matter if I use the word "*intention*", or "*goal*", or "*objective*", etc to describe what I want? Well in general discourse, perhaps not. However, to define our purpose and meaning in life, it is sometimes useful to play with semantics in order to differentiate points of reference.

Groups and individuals in organisations find it commonplace to talk about goals. By a *goal* we are referring here to a *quantifiable outcome* that can be measured over time and/or as an amount of something. A simple example might be 15% profit on revenue for the next three years or at a personal level to own my home by the time I am 40 years old.

Organisations are renowned for setting goals of this nature which are most often driven by business owners or shareholder demands and often a stretch to achieve them. It is the classic approach to organisation planning. It is focused on behavioural change, if required, to achieve a stated goal. What this approach *fails to examine* are the *inner often unconscious and perhaps even oppositional inner intentions* of the individuals that make up the organisation.

On a personal level this concept of unexamined inner intentions trumps stated outer goals if they are conflicting. For example, how many smokers have said on New Year's Eve they'll give up smoking only to find they are back smoking within weeks, months and even years? Something deeper has trumped their desire (goal) to stop smoking – pleasure, calmness, stress relief, relaxation?

Aligning inner intentions with stated outer goals is essential for any sustainable growth or change effort at either an individual or group level. This means taking that deep see dive into our unconscious to know what lies beneath and out of sight. Bruce Lipton suggests the unconscious mind is a million times more powerful than our conscious mind. Whilst we have free will, if we remain unaware of what is going in our unconscious, it will rule us (see Figure 6.1).

The significance of Lipton's work cannot be overstated in relation to the impact his ideas have on how we have been taught to live our lives – envisioning a future, setting goals and measuring ourselves against these aspirations founded on conscious thought. He proposes this can be completely out of touch with unconscious programming.

Unconscious intentions are not goals to be reached or gotten beyond. They stem from our values, beliefs, needs and fears that form core drivers inside of us. For example, if an employee is given a goal that they don't believe in and they have a high need to please their boss and fear exclusion and rejection, the likelihood of them saying yes to the goal in the moment is high. However, as they begin to implement what needs to be done and find their disbelief about its achievement is confirmed, they may avoid discussing it or offer excuses to appease the boss. Because of their fear, they are unable to be honest with themselves or their boss. Their real inner intention is to be included and that becomes more important than negotiating an authentic, mutually agreed, at least on the surface, goal. As mentioned before, Lipton and other neuroscience researchers have shown us that when there is a battle between the unconscious (inner world) and the conscious (outer world) the unconscious will always win.

Figure 6.1: THE BIOLOGY OF BELIEFS – NEW SCIENCE OF EPIGENTICS

- Our response to our environment, not our genes, dictates how our cells will behave – it is our perceptions of life that shape our biology
- The physical body can be affected by the immaterial mind
  - Thought 'energy' can activate or inhibit a cell's function, producing proteins via the mechanics of constructive and destructive interference
- Our beliefs control our bodies, our minds and thus our lives
- Positive thoughts have a profound effect on behaviour and genes but *only* when in harmony with sub-conscious programming
- The unconscious mind is a repository of stimulus response tapes – habits playing the same signals over and over again – represents 95% of our consciousness and a million times more powerful than our conscious mind
- The conscious mind offers us free will, meaning we are not victims of our programming and genetics but masters of our fate
- To pull that off however you have to be fully conscious lest the programming take over

On the other hand, if our inner world (our intentions) matches our stated outer goals we can achieve miraculous outcomes. If our intentions are clear and workable then the method will show up. Workable means our chosen intentions are 51% believable, i.e. we need to have a major shareholding in them. To live with *"intentionality"* we need to bring conscious awareness to unconscious intentions whether they are limiting or expansive. That is to say – aligning our inner and outer worlds will have the greatest chance of getting us what we want. It is critical therefore to minimise limiting intentions and expand those that lift us. Miraculous outcomes can be achieved. What's that phrase, "Careful what you ask for, you just might get it!" (source unknown). Ultimately, we will manifest what we focus on based on our inner intentions.

So how do we navigate our way through to ensuring our inner intentions and outer goals are aligned? Figure 6.2 represents an *"Intention Map"*, a process map of how to do this. What follows assists us to understand not only the process required but also enables a deeper understanding of the patterns that expand us and those limiting ones that keep us stuck. Each part of the map is explored.

Figure 6.2: INTENTION MAP

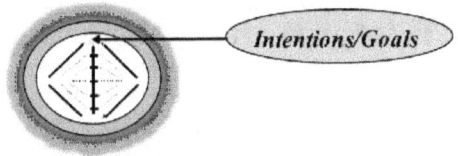

Uncovering Our Inner Intentions & Testing Alignment with Our Outer Goals

If I have a goal to be President of the United States and I am writing this paper here and now in Australia, there are several barriers, issues, challenges and tasks I need to complete to get there. These are represented by the vertical line with crossed horizontal lines above *"Now"* leading to *"Intentions/Goals"*. In this example:

- I need to move to the USA
- Get a green card and permanent residence
- Get into a political party

- Change the American constitution to allow non-native born Americans to be elected
- Get pre-selected by my party
- Win a presidential election
- And a squillion other things

That may be clear in my mind, but is it workable, i.e. 51% believable? Obviously not. We can go so far as to say that it is delusional. What if, however, I go for Prime Minister of Australia? How many barriers did I just remove? I still have several things to achieve, for example:

- Join a party
- Get known
- Get elected
- Move to Canberra
- Etc, etc, etc!

Still not workable! How about Premier of NSW – I don't have to move from Sydney. What about Mayor of my local council? Alderman of my local council? I don't have to move house. Handing out ballot forms on election day? I only have to walk down the street.

- What in this series of goals is a walk in the park that I wouldn't really have much investment in and maybe not even bother with?
- What is a goal that might panic me into doing nothing?
- What is a stretch that has a challenge I am willing to sign up for (51% believable and therefore workable), I am clear I want and will make a priority?

No matter the size of the goal, no one goal is better than another. It is what the individual desires that is important. One person's mayor of their local council is another person's President of the United States.

Once I have decided my goal, I need to uncover my inner intentions and pressure-test them for alignment with that goal, i.e. lean in and see if I hold true to what I have decided. The question to be asked here is "What experience am I looking for?" It might be I want power, influence, status or prestige – or to make a difference. These intentions might easily be found in my conscious mind. However, if I do not unearth my unconscious fears these are very likely to overcome my desires and goals. For example, if I choose to become Premier of NSW and I don't acknowledge a lack of confidence; or perhaps I am worried my family will suffer because I am unable to spend as much time with them, the misalignment that will come from that will ultimately undermine my original goal.

As so much of our consciousness is out of our awareness (95%), how do we really know when we are fully aligned consciously and unconsciously. In the end, it's our intuition that will tell us, if we are paying attention to it. Have you ever known when you have made a heartfelt decision you knew you would hold to no matter what? Ever made a decision that came from a wilfulness that pushed through and something told you to stop and you didn't? Ever not made a decision you wished you had as it would have worked out but fear stopped you? What can you learn about how you function from each of these situations? (See Chapter 2, *"Embracing Vulnerability and Authenticity"* for more on living authentically.)

In the end, it is the level of commitment we give to dealing with both our unconscious intentions and conscious goals that will see us through. Peter Senge (2006) in his book *"The Fifth Discipline"* suggests the following levels of engagement (Figure 6.3) as a way of evaluating just how engaged we are in whatever we choose to envision. Levels 6 and 7 are the most likely to have our unconscious intentions aligned with our conscious goals.

Figure 6.3: ENGAGEMENT & COMMITMENT LEVELS

1. APATHY: Neither for nor against the vision. No interest., No energy. "**Is it five o'clock yet?**"

2. NONCOMPLIANCE: Does not see benefits of vision and will not do what's expected. "**I won't do it; you can't make me.**"

3. GRUDGING COMPLIANCE: Does not see the benefits of the vision. But, also does not want to lose job. Does enough of what's expected because he has to, but also **lets it be known that s/he is not really on board.**

4. FORMAL COMPLIANCE: On the whole, sees the benefits of the vision. **Does what's expected and no more.** "Pretty good soldier."

5. GENUINE COMPLIANCE: Sees the benefits of the vision. **Does everything expected and more**. Follows the letter of the law." "Good soldiers."

6. ENROLLMENT: Wants it. **Will do whatever can be done within the "spirit of the law."**

7. COMMITMENT: Wants it. **Will make it happen.** Creates whatever "laws" (structures) are needed.

Extract from "The Fifth Discipline", by Peter Senge (2006)

Level 6, *"Enrollment"* approaches conscious/unconscious alignment. Level 7, *"Commitment"* is a pretty sound indicator we have fully aligned our inner intentions and outer goals. John-Roger puts it another way, "Don't make agreements you can't keep and keep all agreements you make." This asks for a level of integrity that will challenge most of us. Nonetheless it causes us to be clear on what we want if we live by it.

Does that mean we are stuck in the choices we make once we have made them? No! As new information emerges renegotiation with ourselves and others is always an option. Be careful here because if renegotiation becomes the norm the spirit of clear intention is broken. I commenced an undergraduate degree in my late thirties already having a demanding international executive role, renovating a house, married with two young children, and playing competition tennis three times a week. What was I thinking? The degree was an outer goal with the inner intention of attaining credibility and, at a deeper level, societal acceptance, with an associated fear of not feeling smart enough. After 18 months of study I decided something had to give. I renegotiated with myself to take 18 months off the study and some of my friends felt I would not return. I paid no attention to that and was clear that I was renegotiating my time window. I returned at the scheduled time and completed the undergraduate degree. My intention was clear, workable (Level 7) and could be renegotiated without compromise to the ultimate outcome. I felt stronger in my resolve than anything that might interfere with that completion and gained my intention of credibility.

What it takes to stay the course can be found in our beliefs about ourselves and the attitudes they lead to about our choices.

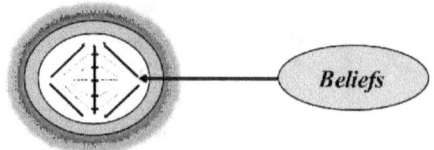

Knowing Our Unconscious Beliefs

Beliefs are formed very early in life and often core beliefs are embedded into our consciousness and begin to manifest as attitudes and related behaviours by the time we are seven years of age. (see Figure 6.1) As we live through our early years, our behaviour gets rewarded and criticised, and we begin to determine what works for us and what doesn't. If I learnt to push my way around the sand pit and got what I wanted, then it is very possible I'll develop a set of beliefs that have me push and drive later on in life. For example, "To get what I want I have to control and win". If I learnt that being polite and accommodating got me praise, then I am likely to develop beliefs that serve that outcome. For example, "If I do the right thing I'll be rewarded and accepted."

As repeated successes or avoidance of pain occur when we behave in accordance with these developing beliefs they become unconscious and ultimately form habitual behaviours. They become our deep-seated truths about life – life scripts (see Chapter 2, *"Embracing Vulnerability and Authenticity"*).

Naturally they will be challenged as alternative situations and environments present themselves in our lives. Once a belief becomes an unconscious habit it will be harder to shake. Even if we adapt, if it is an unconscious truth by age six or seven, we will retreat to behaving in accordance with it, especially under stress. It's as if we have become *"hard-wired"* to it.

Many beliefs remain in our unconscious. They are simply hard held even hard-wired truths that need no attention from our conscious mind.

These unconscious beliefs become our drivers and form a *"life strategy"*. They have *positive intentions* to give us control, prevent failure, have us included and not rejected (See Chapter 2, *"Embracing Vulnerability and Authenticity"*). This then is how we frame our consciousness.

Whether beliefs are limiting or expanding we will hold onto them tightly as truths and keys to our well-being and success.

"Limiting beliefs" are those that do not bring us the results that we want. They can be found in the negative self-talk when we experience failure of some sort. They can also be found in the negative judgements we hold on others. For example, a *limiting belief* I held on myself about going to university in my late thirties can be found in my entry into high school. I was placed in trades classes because my father was an upholsterer and I was classified as not "academically" smart, even dumb. Whilst I did matriculate to university level upon leaving, the shame of repeating a year at school when I was 15 stayed with me and my unconscious belief remained: "I'm not smart enough to go to university." I needed to embrace and move beyond this belief to stay the course lest my intention remained to think I was stupid and give up the goal.

These *limiting beliefs* all have *positive intentions*. What could possibly be positive about continuing to think I am stupid or not smart enough? Well, what if it keeps me from failing at something I don't think I can do? Alternatively and paradoxically, it could become a motivator to prove people wrong and ultimately myself wrong. These were the *payoffs* for holding the limitation. The challenge becomes how not to fail (AKA succeed), motivate myself and meet my goal at the same time. This requires a more expansive antidote to my fear of failure.

"Expanding beliefs" are those that build our confidence to handle ever-changing circumstances. They can be found in what we feel when we have success or feel complete with something. They can also be found in the positive qualities we see in others that we acknowledge in ourselves. In addition, we can re-shape limiting beliefs into expanding ones holding the *positive intention of the limiting belief.*

Affirmations have been a popular modern practice for some time now. The problem with affirmations by themselves is that they do not account for the unconscious fight back that occurs when it tries to stamp out its comparable limitation; when we stamp out a limitation we will also stamp out its *positive intention* unless we are fully aware of it. Searching for the *positive intention* in a limitation, often hard to uncover, is key to holding and sustaining new belief systems. Otherwise, it's like sitting on a beach ball in a swimming pool trying to negate the limitation, while it keeps popping back up to sabotage our achievement.

The process for converting a *limiting belief* to an expanding one is about bringing the *limiting belief* into our conscious awareness, uncovering its *positive intention* and reframing the limitation into expansion (Figure 6.4).

In the example I have given, an *expanding belief* that supports my desire to succeed and prevent failure might be "My innate intelligence and wisdom guide me to the success I am seeking".

An *expanding belief* can feel like a lie at first. One process I have found useful (proposed by John-Roger) is to repeat the *expanding belief* ten times a day for 33 days in a row. If a day is missed then begin again until 33 days in a row is reached. It's an approach to create a new neural pathway to access when challenges and old reference points present themselves. Another process I have seen work is a Buddhist one: 70 X 7; for seven days, write out the *expanding belief* 70 times and follow it with "oh no I'm not because..." At some point, we run out of "oh no I'm not" and keep going until the 70 X 7 is completed. If our intention is clear on deciding to do one of these exercises or any other process we will complete it (Senge – Level 7); if not then we had another intention. In that case do some more fishing; preferably at a deep see level.

Figure 6.4: REFRAMING BELIEFS

Beliefs	Examples
Limiting Belief	1. I'm not powerful enough 2. I'm not good enough 3. I'm not important
Positive Intention (AKA Payoff)	1. I keep safe 2. Keeps me from falling 3. I get to stay comfortable
Expanding Belief	1. I am empowered and wise 2. I stand for what I believe 3. I am strong and flexible

When *limiting* or *expanding beliefs* are out of our awareness, we react unconsciously to given situations. An *expanding belief* in one situation can become a *limiting belief* in another. For example, when healing from a relationship breakup, the belief "I am healthy and whole standing on my own" may be helpful. That same belief may limit us in a situation where it might be important to ask for support from others.

Bringing unconscious beliefs into awareness is critical in complex environments. It could be said we need to move from the *"information age"* to the *"consciousness age"* as events move faster and faster and more and more unknowns are presented to us (see Chapter 4, *"Loving Ambiguity and the Unknown"*). Very often early beliefs are inadequate to meet new complex circumstances.

If we truly want more for ourselves in life, then we are obliged to become more conscious about the belief systems we hold and especially to understand how those beliefs either have limited or expanded us. Moreover, it is important to examine how past beliefs that used to expand us may be limiting in new territory and circumstances. To continue to expand and grow, we need to accept that new life strategies and belief systems are continually required.

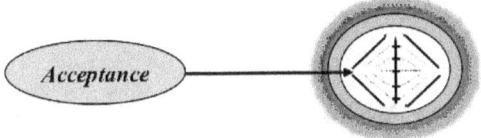

Moving into Acceptance

"*Acceptance of it is what it is*" is a necessary state to embrace to move through past hurts, sadness, pain, fear, anger or disturbance of any kind. This is not to say *acceptance* equals begrudging compliance. Any compliance that contains a skerrick of upset, judgement or limiting emotion is not *acceptance* as it is meant here. This is where a state of "*neutrality*" is found. Not always easy, of course, but necessary to move forward and renew.

In previous chapters, acceptance, neutrality and forgiveness are explored. The key is to surrender judgements. These ideas are so fundamental to sustainable desired change they are worth repeating here.

Residual negativity of any kind is a cue to return to awareness and repeat any questions that might assist us to uncover what it is that is disturbing us. It's like peeling an onion – layer within layer within layer – to find the source and core of what is preventing the *neutrality* needed to set ourselves free. If we experience ourselves challenged to let go then we might ponder how our resistance may be keeping us stuck: "*What we resist we are stuck with*".

One strategy among a number that can assist moving into acceptance is *forgiveness*. Challenging maybe; but often very necessary. We may not be able to forgive the behaviour and if we can so much the better, but we can forgive ourselves for the judgements we might be holding on ourselves and/or others. Start with "I forgive myself for judging myself for (insert your judgement, e.g. being angry)" and/or "I forgive myself for judging another (insert name) for (insert judgement, e.g. ignoring me)." We can keep repeating this over and over with either the same or additional judgements until we feel a sense of completion and our energy begins to settle. This is an indication that we are finding some neutrality in the situation. It can take time and practice. Fake it until you make it – even *faith* it until you make it!"

The challenge is how to surrender our judgements for something greater. Judgements, connected to our deeper beliefs and how they are upheld or not, trigger us into a reaction – think about it: "re – action"; repeating the same action over and over again (and expecting a different result is what Einstein said was the definition of insanity); all based on a belief we are holding onto. Better to be responsible (response-able), i.e. able to respond from that neutral place of freedom from our bias, emotions and upset.

With respect to intentions, acceptance is about the extent to which we embrace without judgement of ourselves, others, the world, God, etc:

- The intentions and goals we have set for ourselves
- The support, challenges, issues that may go with those intentions
- The beliefs and attitudes we hold in relation to all that
- How present we are in the here and now

Using the political aspiration from earlier: let's say I've decided I want to be premier of New South Wales and it is 51% believable for me to achieve that; the first issue might be to join a political party or create my own. I decide joining a political party is the best way to go as creating my own party would reduce the believability of my intention for me. The next challenge would be to get known and position myself as a potential leader of that party; then I need to be nominated for leadership roles; elected leader by the party and eventually elected into office by the public. If, for example, I have judgements on the political system, the available political parties' integrity, policies or individuals, this may diminish my resolve or reduce my listening capability. If I have any doubts (judgements) on myself to achieve this it will inhibit my seeking support. These all need to be brought into awareness as they are as much if not more a part of the issues and challenges I face as are those that are external to me.

By judgements I am not referring to neutral evaluation or discernment; rather I am referring to being judgemental and having an emotional charge on it that disturbs me in some way. These judgements will surface when circumstances do not line up with my belief system and the word *should* becomes part of my self-talk: "I should(n't)", s/he should(n't), they should(n't), etc. The suggestion is "*no shoulding*" on yourself or anyone else. This is not to say we completely give over our beliefs and values but that we accept without an emotional charge that others have a different view. Here is a metaphor that illustrates this idea. Suppose two people are on opposite sides of a room and between them is a huge ball. Person One can see one side of the ball and it is red. Person Two can see the other side of the ball which is white. When asked "What colour is the ball?" Person Two says: "White." Person One says: "No it's not; it's red." Person Two replies: "No it's not; it's white." They go back and forth on this for a while and get frustrated and angry with each other. It takes one of them to give up the frustration and the judgement, to move around and look from the other's perspective, to see that the ball is both red and white. If each holds onto their belief that they are right and the other wrong, they are stuck.

The sort of acceptance I am advocating is one that requires detachment (See Chapter 2, "*Embracing Vulnerability and Authenticity*") but not disconnection from our judgements. We must become the "*neutral observers of our judgements*". This, in my experience, is one of the biggest challenges of all. Certainly, in my life it has been one of my hardest life lessons, if not the hardest.

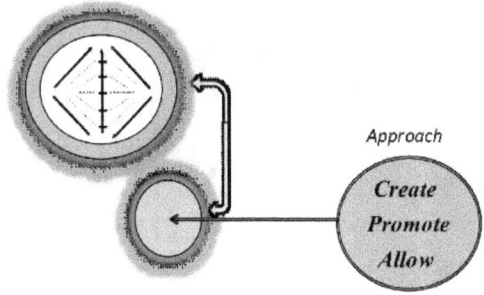

Adopting an Attitude of Create, Promote and Allow

An attitude of "*we create, promote and allow everything in our lives*" is going to optimise the realisation of our intentions and goals. The alternative is to fall perilously into the quicksand of judgement, wanting to overpower others (*Persecutor*), thinking we can fix what is in the way (*Rescuer*) or feeling overwhelmed by it all (*Victim*). (See Chapter 1, "*Living Freely*")

Chapter 1, "*Living Freely*" explores in detail how to hold for greater possibilities in all challenging situations that erode our capacity to manifest our intentions and goals. Figure 6.5 from "*Living Freely*" outlines the steps required to move beyond the roles of *Persecutor, Rescuer, Victim* (the *Operating Ego*) and embrace our expanded capacity to believe we are able to *create, promote,* and *allow* everything in our lives. This is not to imply that there are not many circumstances where we are unable to control situations, for example, natural disasters and other people's behaviour. What is important is our response to our circumstances. We can always *create, promote* and *allow* our response. As stated previously, it doesn't so much matter what happens to us in life; what matters is how we respond to what happens to us.

Figure 6.5: BUILDING A BRIDGE TO FREEDOM (from Chapter 1)

![Bridge diagram with Awareness, Acceptance, Cooperation, Understanding, Empathy, Enthusiasm, Loving arrow above, spanning from Operating Ego to Aware Ego, with Bungee Zone: "If we don't go within we go without" Neale Walshe (1995)]

Awareness as mentioned is the beginning point of raising our consciousness. *Acceptance* is that essential step to opening our hearts and minds to new possibilities and moving beyond the past. Cooperation with what is happening is *acceptance* in action (John-Roger) and about removing our resistance to find new ways to work with what is. It is then that understanding can emerge with new insights; rather than get on top of things we need to stand under them to understand it. As we find our compassion in what has been presented we can then empathise with the past and our present state. Empathy leads to enthusiasm for the illuminating new purpose of *loving it all* (see Chapter 2, "*Living Freely*").

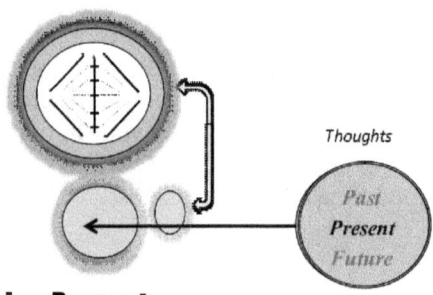

Being Present

This phrase from earlier bears repeating here: "The past is history; the future a mystery; now is the present, which is why they call it a gift" (source unknown).

When our thoughts are negatively in the past they generate *guilt* or *resentment*. Guilt is anger at self and rather than continually feel that, we can be present enough to use it to change and course correct. Re-quoting Deepak Chopra from earlier: resentment is like taking poison and expecting the other person to die.

When our thoughts are negatively in the future they generate *"future worry"* and even anxiety. We fear the past will be repeated. What's that acronym for fear? *False Expectations Appearing Real*. They are false because they haven't happened yet; expectant because our limiting beliefs hold us in the past; appearing real because our emotionality about them is projected into the future.

Living in the present is perhaps one of the most challenging things we find to do or should I say to *"be"*. Much has been written about mindfulness as the world tries to make sense of ever-increasing and discontinuous change. The changes we face as a society are challenging us individually to stay evermore present.

Our defences have a much greater chance of surfacing when we are under pressure and the less time we have to respond to life, the more pressure we feel. The chances of retreating into past *guilt* and/or *resentment* are multiplied, especially if we haven't focused on building awareness and moving beyond our limitations. Without raised consciousness we are more likely to project our past negatively into the future by worrying about what might happen.

Being mindfully in *"the now"* rebalances us from moment to moment, preparing us to approach the next moment from a place of *"What can I create, promote and allow from where I am right here, right now?"*

Figure 6.6 (from Chapter 4, *"Loving Ambiguity and the Unknown"*) describes just how important this is as the rate of change was predicted by NASA in 1993 to go vertical in 2014.

Figure 6.6: OUR CHAORDIC WORLD (from Chapter 4)

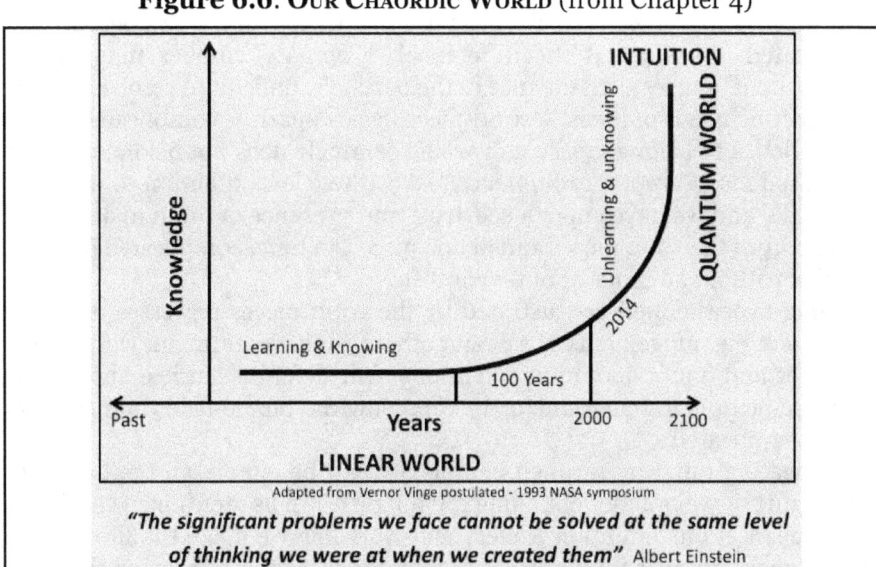

We are taught to seek structure and form to feel safe. We are not taught high tolerance for ambiguity. However, this tolerance is exactly what is required in a life filled with rapid and unpredictable change. Trusting our intuition in the unknown becomes an essential capability when circumstances challenge the intentions and goals we have set ourselves. Order is temporary and chaos is intermittent; chaordic competency, the capacity to successfully navigate both, sustains us to stay focused and be present (see Chapter 4, "*Loving Ambiguity and Authenticity*"). This brings us all the way back to self-trust as the vehicle that underpins our hopes and dreams, the heartfelt quality of our intentions and goals.

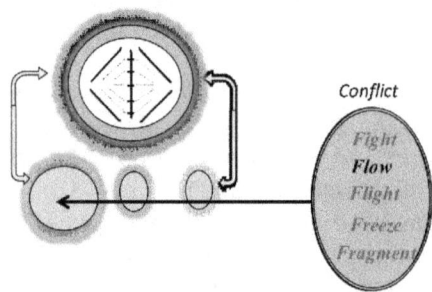

Flowing with the Moment – Giving Way with Inner Ease

If life isn't complex enough with what I have already described, dealing with conflict in our lives, not to mention within ourselves, is an ongoing phenomenon.

It may be complex but as we master our life's journey it can become less complicated. So, what is the difference? "*Complex*" implies many parts; "*complicated*" suggests dissonance of the parts, i.e. difficult to resolve because of competing needs or ideas. A 1000-piece jigsaw puzzle is complicated at first as what looks to belong, doesn't, or what seemingly does not belong might. If our attitude is "*I create, promote, allow*" with a clear intention to complete the puzzle, and we have enough self-trust and presence of mind to accept the complexity of the 1000 pieces and fit one piece at a time, complicated becomes complex without an inner or outer conflict.

Being overwhelmed or frustrated by the 1000 pieces regresses us to our limitations, e.g. judgements of self and others, guilt, resentment, worry about outcomes and doubt about our intentions. Our defences surface and act out from *Persecutor*, *Rescuer* and/or *Victim*. Now the puzzle is beyond complex and is complicated.

Navigating our way through complexity can be simple and still may be challenging, if we practice chunking the puzzle down as mentioned earlier. By that I mean, if our intention is clear and workable we make the first barrier or challenge the next intention, then look for what the barrier or challenge is to that and so on. If we give up on the puzzle of life then we have another intention we may not yet be conscious of. Understanding this moves us beyond the conflict of complicated to the simplicity of complex.

Fight and *flight* are *instinctual* responses to when we are threatened. They are survival attributes to stay safe when in physical danger. In emotionally conflicted situations however, we may not feel we can either fight back or flee from the situation without a worse outcome than staying in it. It's here where we are likely to *"freeze"*, i.e. we want to fight back, we want to leave but feel we can do neither. For example, staying in an unhappy marriage for the children; wanting to tell your boss off or argue with them but simply acquiescing with their demands and staying in the job. If we *freeze* long enough we eventually *"fragment"*, i.e. begin to crack.

Another option is to *"flow"* with what is going on at the time. There is a subtle distinction between *"give way"*, *"give in"* and *"give up"*. Giving in can take the form of compliance and yet withholding one's true opinions. It is most often *associated with flight*. Giving up is similar, but the opinions are put on the table and have been overridden. Often *giving up* is after *fight*. Giving way is done with internal ease. It is accepting the circumstances at the behavioural, thought and emotional levels – *flow*. The test is found in our physiology. *"Lose your mind and gain your senses"* (Wayne Dyer, 2004). If our body (senses) is tight and tense we are in *fight* or *flight*. If it is relaxed it is more likely to be *flow*.

It is useful to understand the dynamics of conflict to know when we are not in the *flow* of complexity, but rather in the *fight* and/or *flight* of complicated. *Fight, flight, freeze* and *fragment* can be more or less present depending on the level of conflict experienced. The Conflict Resolution Network has an effective way of looking at levels of conflict (Figure 6.7).

Figure 6.7: Levels of Conflict

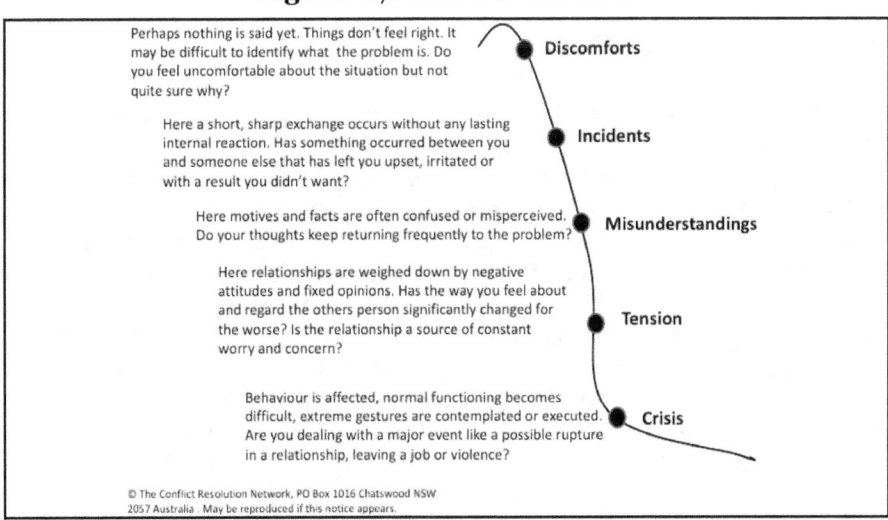

Understanding that a discomfort to us may indeed be a crisis to another can move us off our judgements, enabling empathy and *flow* to arrive. Every behaviour has a *positive intention* for the person exhibiting it. That doesn't make the behaviour okay from our perspective but it may help explain another's actions and give the space to achieve their intention that doesn't compromise our own values. Even the worst of behaviours are aimed at keeping a person safe in their own mind. This enters into the realm of our social ecology and what is okay and not okay in various cultures (see Chapter 2, "*Embracing Vulnerability and Authenticity*" and Chapter 7, "*Sacred Living*").

At an individual level extracting ourselves from our inner and outer conflicts to go with the *flow* with what is, energises us to keep going towards our intentions and goals. This will connect us back into our beliefs, our attitude and our thoughts and ultimately how resolved we are to go for what we truly want until we get it.

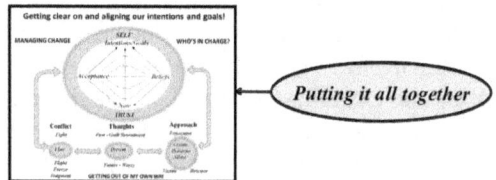

Mapping where we are placed on the map can assist in unpacking our patterns. The suggested questions at the end of this chapter can reveal much about your limitations and strengths in getting what you want in life.

I found it useful in challenging times to revisit the map time and time again and, as I have, some deep patterns have repeatedly emerged. Hopefully my story below may help you unravel your own patterns for greater self-understanding.

Integrating My Personal Story

Now that the jigsaw is complete, how can these ideas become a practical way of approaching life?

The first step is to understand our limiting patterns. For example, **a big pattern of mine** is to bite off more than I can chew, i.e. I choose too many **intentions** and **goals**. I don't accept that I can't do it all and push my way through the **barriers** and **challenges**. I tend to adopt the **Rescuer** role (AKA "St Francis of Assist You") and believe I can fix it all. I am more prone to fall into **future worry** and become anxious about how much I have chosen to do. I then **fight** my way through it with stress and anxiety. What a classic burn-out strategy that has certainly caused me strife. Being aware that I'm moving towards it is fundamental to re-negotiating with myself about how much is possible. Fortunately, I have a lot of self-trust to eventually self-regulate and stop and smell the roses rather than the rosé (wine). Lol!

I've learned over time that, when my **inner intentions** are in **conflict** with my **outer goals**, the results are not good. Conversely, when my awareness of my **inner intentions matches my goals**, the results are fulfilling. For example, at 23, when I set the **goal** to motor bike ride to Gunnedah, some 400 kilometres, to attend a tennis tournament, I paid little attention to a nagging fear about my competence to make the ride. Whilst a part of the accident was circumstantial, more experience and competence may have prevented the worst of it. And at 45, when my **goal** was to attend a 36-day professional facilitation training program in the USA, and my **inner intention** of advancing my credibility and confidence in this field was aligned and clear, I processed fears of job loss, financial setbacks and disapproval by my company (Digital Equipment Corporation (DEC)). I made the decision and attended with both time and financial support from my company. Surprisingly, after the event, I was made employee of the year mentioned earlier. The $20,000 of company shares more than took care of the costs.

I developed the **Intention Map** in 1991 when I was asked by the same company to talk to some people in Boston. They were about to manage the first retrenchment program the company had undertaken in its 38 years in business. I asked these leaders how they thought about what was to happen and drew the map on a white board as the conversation unfolded. The map was to catapult my career in international consulting and I have used it in various environments ever since.

The personal change process within the organisational change efforts became fundamental to successful change efforts. Traditional behavioural models had proved ineffective and remain so today in affecting strategic change, business process re-engineering, total quality management (TQM), leadership and team effectiveness, outsourcing, technology changes and restructuring. This map was successfully used across all these dimensions, including establishing two major telecommunications companies in Australia and restructuring a significant number of large organisations, including the one I worked for.

It was a foundation model to develop the strategy for the 2000 Sydney Olympics producing unprecedented results, and adopted in my work with the Australian Olympic Diving Team in the late 1990s. The work with this team was published in the Sydney Morning Herald and, in 2000, Australia achieved its first diving medal. The total quality management program for my company at the time was awarded 2nd place in the Australian Quality Awards. My work was published in the British Transformation Journal and in a book reviewing business re-engineering and change processes around the world (Nick Obolensky, "*Practical Business Re-engineering*"). Since those days, two books published on renewable energy development have utilised the ideas from this map to promote personal change to effect organisational and community change (John O'Brien, 2009, "*Opportunities Beyond Carbon*" and, in 2015, "*Visions 2100*").

On a deep personal level the map found its place in my coming out process. For years, my **goal** of anchoring myself in my family and its traditional life was juxtapositioned with the **authenticity challenges** I faced about my sexuality. Eventually my **inner intention** to live an integrous life won out. My pattern of pushing through to achieve my **goals**, a positive set of **beliefs** and attitudes, **not accepting** I couldn't conquer something, **rescuing** anything that needed fixing, **guilt** about doing the wrong thing, **future worry** about what might happen and **fighting** it all internally at last just hit a wall. The map helped me identify what was going on and, eventually, I decided to navigate my way out of it. In 1999, I wrote the following – having finally resolved the internal war I had waged on myself for so many years.

From Pride to Dignity: one man's journey to freedom

The human spirit yearns for wholeness and integration. Yet it must find it through separation and individuality. This paradox can be no truer than it is for gay and lesbian folk. We not only have to separate from our family rules to re-integrate with them; we are also obliged to separate from society's rules to find ourselves.

The gay world has had some success in turning shame into pride, but are we yet as a group within society seen to have dignity, which may very well be the first step to having it. The irony is that being seen to have dignity helps you achieve it.

Finding dignity in us requires unconditional acceptance of ourselves, free of our own and others' homophobia.

If we are to achieve dignity as a group, each individual must find it in themselves. We can't demand society treat us with dignity, whilst we remain unwilling to do the inner work to be dignified.

"In-your-face pride" alone creates attention, separation and conditional acceptance, but not societal integration and an ability to live in a dignified open way in our broader society.

Many may argue we don't need that; we have our own supportive world. This in itself is a separatist approach and splits the energy of gay and lesbian individuals who work in the "straight" world and may predominantly socialise in the "gay" world (this may have changed since 1999 when I wrote this).

Whether it is "gay/straight/transgender", "black/white", "Asian/Caucasian", "male/female", "Catholic/Protestant", "Hindu/Muslim", or "Christian/Jewish", any of these divisions retard our society from uplifting our consciousness to acceptance, cooperation and compassion. These three things are essential precursors to unconditional love.

My journey mirrors many who have attempted individuation and integration, either consciously or unconsciously and of course my journey also has its differences.

Today (1999) I am a happy and gay man, once upon a time and maybe still seen as a contradiction in terms. This has not always been the case. It took me almost 52 years to get here. It wasn't until I was 52 that I accepted my first dinner invitation to a corporate executive dinner with my partner. I'm sure this was not a first in the world but it was a first for me.

Any event that causes us to be freer publicly with both pride and dignity is our individual step forward. It is those individual steps forward that challenge our own openness, cause us to face our fears of rejection and exclusion and help us come to terms with our orientation. This then leads us to self-acceptance, wholeness and dignity in our world; a step forward for anyone no matter their sexual orientation.

Notwithstanding the rhetoric about "is it nature or nurture" that causes us to be the way we are, fighting what we are because of a need for societal acceptance is a waste of energy in my experience. Being gay to me is simply the same as being left handed. It is what it is.

In 50 years, after a 20-year marriage to a caring nurturing woman, where we bore two fantastic sons, a subsequent beautiful relationship with yet another wonderful woman and a deep commitment to this traditional life, I was unable to exorcise the energy that in the end clearly defined my sexuality; I no longer want to. I have found the most complete life and love I want and need with a truly wonderful man, who coincidentally has come from a similar background to myself.

I've come to understand that our sexuality defines "what" we are, not "who" we are. "Who" we are is our character and values. Our character and values are not defined by our sexuality. Dignity belongs to all of us. The further we move toward dignity, the further we move away from shame. The further we move away from shame the worthier we become and, as we become whole, others pick up on it and want that dignity themselves.

I had begun to answer life's questions from a higher place and continue to do that today as best I can.

Whenever setting new intentions I start with small experiments, i.e. set small intentions and goals that will set me up for success and notice what I am noticing about the patterns that show up. "By the inch, it's a cinch, by the yard it is very very hard" (source unknown).

Questions I ask myself and suggest for you:

1. Am I clear on my inner intentions and outer goals?
2. Do they align?
3. What attitudes and beliefs support me to achieve these and what will block me?
4. Have I considered all that goes with the choice I have made (issues, barriers, tasks, steps, opportunities, risks)?
5. How much do I accept what I have chosen?
6. How much do I accept everything that goes with my choice?
7. If my answers are wavering on any of the above questions what might I be resisting?
8. What is my level of self-trust (do I trust myself enough to know I will commit to my choice)?

9. Am I fully in a place to create, promote and/or allow what I have chosen?
10. If not, what role(s) in the Power/Control triangle am I likely to retreat to if there are unanticipated challenges; Persecutor, Rescuer or Victim?
11. Am I fully present or am I finding myself thinking negatively about the past (guilt/resentment) or the future (worry)?
12. Am I ready to flow with any conflict that might arise?
13. If not, what is my fall-back position that could undermine my intentions/goals (fight, flight, freeze/fragment)?
14. If I find any answers to the above are less than resolute, what pattern might I fall into that historically has limited me?
15. What will I do about that?
16. Am I ready – yes or no/maybe?

Recycle through this process until you are clear and know you can and will 100% deal with what goes with any choices you make.

I find it's easier to align an inner intention with an outer personal goal as I generally have control over that. I can choose to lower the *goal* or up my commitment to a new *intention*. However, if I am unable to align my inner intentions with others' goals, that presents greater challenges. How do I remain authentic and in integrity in such circumstances, where, for example, I may be faced with presenting others with what they don't want to hear? Alternatively, how do I move to *acceptance* and adjust my *intention* to meet others' *goals*? If there is an element of compromise in these choices, I keep looking until alignment can be struck, else I expect a rocky road.

Freeing myself to live authentically (see Chapter 2, "*Embracing Vulnerability and Authenticity*") will generally manifest more than I imagine if I am willing to look inside and be open and honest with myself. My final test for alignment with myself is to ask:

17. What is my immediate next step to align my inner and outer worlds?

See the *Appendix – Companion Exercises to Support Your Understanding and Growth* for more ideas and questions to explore:

- Exercise 13: Setting Personal Intentions and Goals, page 167
- Exercise 14: Aligning your personal intentions with those around you, page 167

Chapter 7
Sacred Living

Asking higher order questions leads us to greater good results and joy!

Filling Our Pot of Gold

Think of everything you have in your life, material and non-material, as a pot of gold. Does it need to be continually topped up? And if so, why? Material focus alone, while essential for survival, will keep us caught in the never-ending loop of "cash up and spend" what's in the pot. What we fill our pot of gold with must be beyond material gain if it is to be continually replenished.

The greater pot of gold is a focus on something more than ourselves:

- A sense of personal mastery to own our authentic selves
- Sustainable stellar commitment about what we want to create
- Robust, challenging and joyful relationships that disintegrate blockages and enable new pathways
- Aligning our personal purpose with those we impact and how others impact us
- Ruthlessly focused on surrendering our judgements to the higher ground of unconditional acceptance, positive regard and loving for ourselves and others
- Saying no to whoever or whatever challenges these intentions
- Persevering to get up one more time than we fall
- Consistently standing for what we want but not against anything or anyone

This last one can often be the biggest challenge and requires a deep understanding of ourselves and others. That is not to say we agree with others but that we are incredibly discerning about what we choose to participate in and with whom.

Filling our pot of gold with all these things is no small journey and not for the faint of heart. Living from our hearts – not our emotions or minds alone but the best of both together – is foundational to living a truly joyful and contented life regardless of what has or will happen to us. It doesn't matter so much what happens to us – rather it matters what we do with it. Focusing on the greater good for and beyond ourselves requires endurance to see something really worthwhile through and adds meaning to our lives, fostering the contentment, joy and peace central to a fulfilling and sacred life.

Sacred Living Defined

What is "sacred living"? Does the word sacred have a place in your life? What does sacred mean to you? What are you dedicated to and who or what do you revere?

If you think about these questions and imagine who or what in your life is most sacred to you it may provide an insight into how sacred living might apply to you. Many of us name our family members, very close friends, our children or our home. What about our life purpose? Are you on track with that or are you compliantly and perhaps resentfully meeting the needs of others – your employer, business, family, friends and yes, your partner. What meaning do you derive from all of this whether you have a defined personal purpose or not?

What sacred means to us, consciously or unconsciously, is what drives everything we do. How can you make what is sacred to you a part of what is sacred to others and how can you understand what is sacred to others and add meaning to their lives as well as you own?

These questions and ideas are not commonly in our thoughts in today's fast moving world; indeed, they can intimidate many of us and/or be dismissed as "soft" or esoteric aspects of life.

To live a sacred life, we need to focus on a greater good; but what is that? It's more than "win win" (I win/you win). It's even more than "win, win, win" (I win/you win/we win). It's not even about winning as sometimes that is not even possible. The greater good is a search for what we each revere and are dedicated to, i.e. that which is sacred to us. It's about unwaveringly finding a way to optimise the best for all in anything that affects us and others no matter how dire, small or big the circumstances; it's about staying in the question long enough to find that solution; it's about integrity over expedience; it's about declaring what is authentic and real for each of us, then stepping up to it. It is about holding a win, win, win intention even when a win, win, win outcome may not be possible. This is not for the fainthearted. Satisfying ourselves is one thing. Satisfying all around us is another.

Thinking Holistically

"Either/or" thinking is most often the classic reaction to any dilemmas that arise. An either/or response is frequently invested in self-preservation, recognition, romancing an ideal, power and influence, and in what others think about us – inclusion and the capacity to participate. This thinking limits our capability to sustain efforts to achieve what we truly want and, beyond that, make a difference big or small in our world.

Ken Wilbur (2001), in his book *"A Brief History of Everything"* and in his research, boiled everything down to four components: what is inside of us; what is external to us; what is individually focused; what is collectively focused (Figure 7.1). From here he developed his four-quadrant framework: Quadrant 1 (Q1) – who I am; Quadrant 2 (Q2) – what I do; Quadrant 3 (Q3) – who we are; Quadrant 4 (Q4) – what we do.

Typically, these factors are focused on separately with attempts to linearly connect them leading to either/or thinking. For example, we might decide to do something together (Q4); we may consider the relationships we have and how that will work (Q3); we are likely to assess our capability to carry out what is decided (Q2); we might check-in with how we feel about it (Q1). This simple example may be approached differently by different people, i.e. there is no set order to the sequence. However outcomes (Q4) are often a conscious and primary focus followed by an assessment of our capability (Q2) to achieve them. These two quadrants are easy to see and focusing entirely on them means we can miss unseen and challenging aspects in our relationships (Q3), e.g. unspoken or hidden judgements, and in ourselves (Q1), e.g. unacknowledged fears or negative feelings and beliefs.

In previous chapters I have cited Bruce Lipton's work, *"The Biology of Beliefs"*. He has shown that 95% of what is going on for us is unconscious, i.e. unseen. The linear either/or approach described above misses so much that our reactions to the world often take us off track from our original decision or choice (see Chapter 5, *"Intentionality"*). This can disempower us as we re-act over and over using the same behaviour patterns we originally created to protect ourselves. For example, "silent agreements" – those things we agree not to talk about like "Dad or Mum are drinking too much"; "The boss is a bully"; "We don't talk about religion or politics at the dinner table"; "If we get asked to dinner we must take something"; whilst some can be socially acceptable others can undermine our choices. If unattended to they can have us bounce between Quadrants 1 and 2, trying to compensate for them and actually empty our pot of gold, if not tangibly then intangibly, i.e. we get left feeling empty and scared (Q1) and with unsatisfactory relationships (Q3).

What is required to counteract this linear approach is an ability to spiral around all four quadrants concurrently in a non-linear way; in full awareness of what is going on that is readily seen and what is emerging unconsciously. This takes courage to face ourselves and our conflicts across all four quadrants (see Chapter 4, *"Loving Ambiguity and the Unknown"* to expand on how to do this).

Figure 7.1: The Social Ecology Of Life

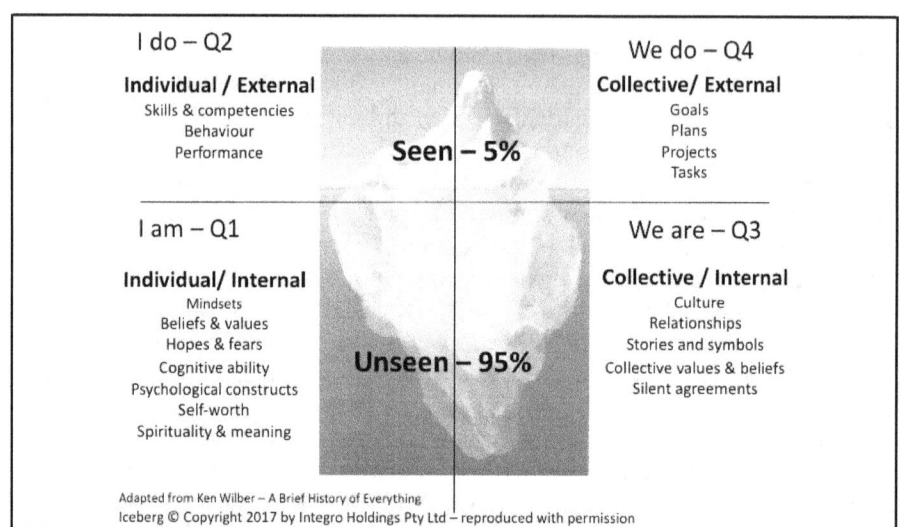

Adapted from Ken Wilber – A Brief History of Everything
Iceberg © Copyright 2017 by Integro Holdings Pty Ltd – reproduced with permission

A Quadrant 2 capability or skill to live comfortably with ambiguity is an essential ingredient of a *sacred* rather than a *scared* life. We will stay in the question longer, trusting the greater good answer will emerge; we will find ourselves responding more authentically to life; we will have a sense that we have and will have created, promoted and allowed our outcomes in some way rather than retreating into protective and defensive postures; our intentions and goals will more likely be realised; our past will simply be that – not being triggered by it or regressing into it; we will trust our capacity to be present in the moment and allow our intuition to guide us. It is likely we will ask more questions as we become more and more curious about the possibilities of trusting ourselves to live sacredly.

Asking the Right Questions

Our lives are defined by the questions we ask about how we fill our pot of gold; not, at least initially, by the capability to tactically solve complex problems. Many aim to answer how to solve a problem before it is fully defined. Whilst it creates a sense of "getting on with it", the method may not be solving the right or broader issue. For example, in Australia, with indigenous affairs we have continued to ask: "How can we ensure equal living, health, educational and work opportunities for indigenous communities?"

A higher level and more strategic (versus tactical) question is: "How can we support all Australians to be free from harm, find joy, happiness and meaning for themselves in a land that provides fair and equal opportunities for all?" We can then look at the specifics within the broader question and decide how much priority within the broader question is required for the more specific one. There may be different approaches for various communities within this last broader question, but only addressing one of those communities can lead to separatism and an "us and them" culture. What follows are unresolved conflicts, unhappy people and a pot of gold with far less than what is possible even in the material sense.

So, what might be some of the questions that can be asked to lift our horizons for all involved, have us believe in ourselves more, fulfil our lives more meaningfully and sustain us through difficult times?

The following sets of questions indicate the level of focus they are likely to evoke:

Figure 7.2: Life's Questions

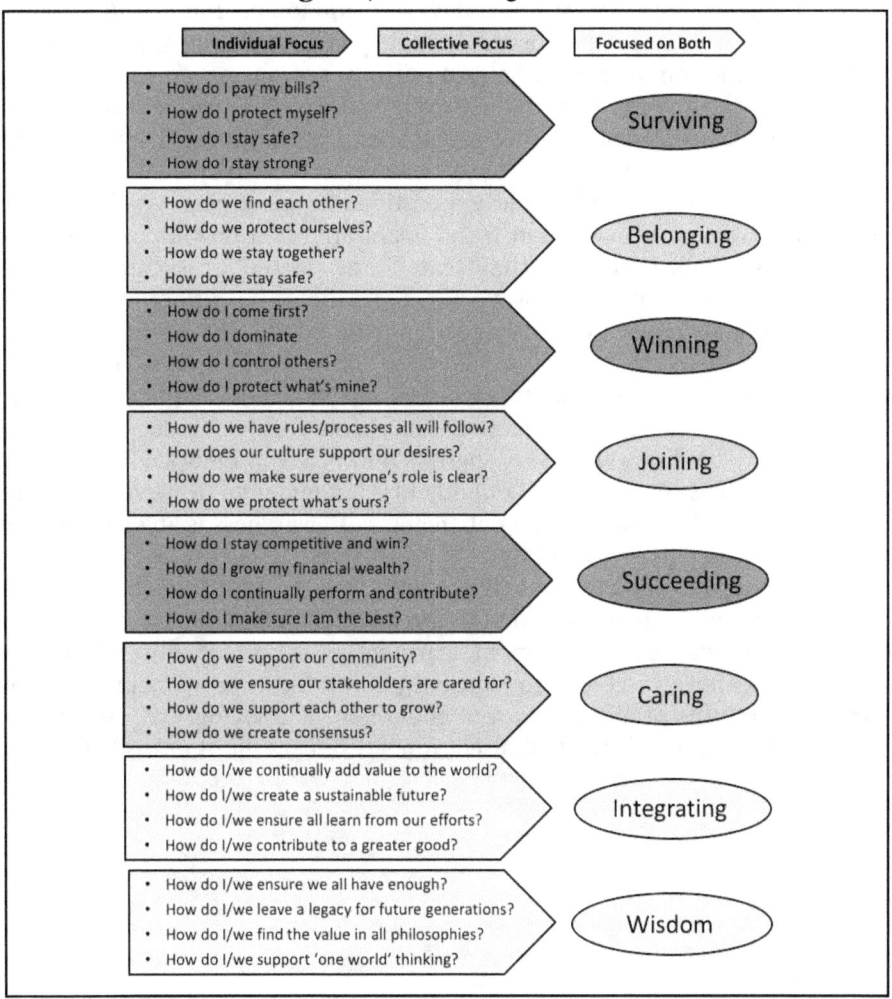

Adapted from the work of Clare Graves, edited by Cowan and Todorovic - Never Ending Quest (2005); Beck & Cowan – Spiral Dynamics (1996)

All the questions asked above are legitimate and necessary in certain circumstances. The question is how far we are prepared to lift toward wisdom. Of course, just asking the right questions is only the beginning. Our social ecology (layers of collective consciousness) requires a complete makeover and new wiring to sustain a lift that keeps us aiming at a sacred level.

To stay on a sacred path, it takes courage to face those parts of us we have long pushed down, those negative and limiting thoughts that become unconscious patterns and hold us back. Every time we hold a judgement about someone or something, become scared or fearful or operate from some defensive posture we create interference and resistance to a greater good path.

Do a little exercise over the next day or so and log the number of negative thoughts you have and every positive thought you have. Perhaps ask a friend to do the same and compare notes. Imagine if the two of you represent the average approach to life and multiply the net result (positive − negative thoughts) by the number of people you know or in the organisation you work for. You now have a barometer on the social ecology you are exposed to.

We are unable to ask higher level questions for the greater good while we focus on lower order needs and fears. Fears are often unconscious and get triggered by events. It's curious that "scared" and "sacred" are composed of the same letters. It just might be how you look at it that is the difference.

According to Louis Cozolino (2014) in his book *"The Neuroscience of Relationships"* we are neurologically programmed to predict how others are thinking to ease our anxiety. He adds that in the developing brain self-awareness lags behind the projections that come from concern with others. Moreover, he confirms that a willingness and effort to embrace the anxiety created from these projections about others is fundamental to alleviating it. He powerfully says, "Expanding and enhancing self-awareness is an evolutionary frontier that stretches ahead of us."

How we make choices from the events that we find ourselves in with awareness of our own contribution to the creation, promotion or allowing of them is at the core of our upliftment, learning, growth and results. Where you find yourself above and below in Figure 7.3 may indicate how you are doing at living a sacred life of meaning, joy, contentment and loving. "If you can't go within you go without" (Neale Walsch, 1996, *"Conversations with God"*).

Figure 7.3: GOING WITHIN TO AVOID GOING WITHOUT

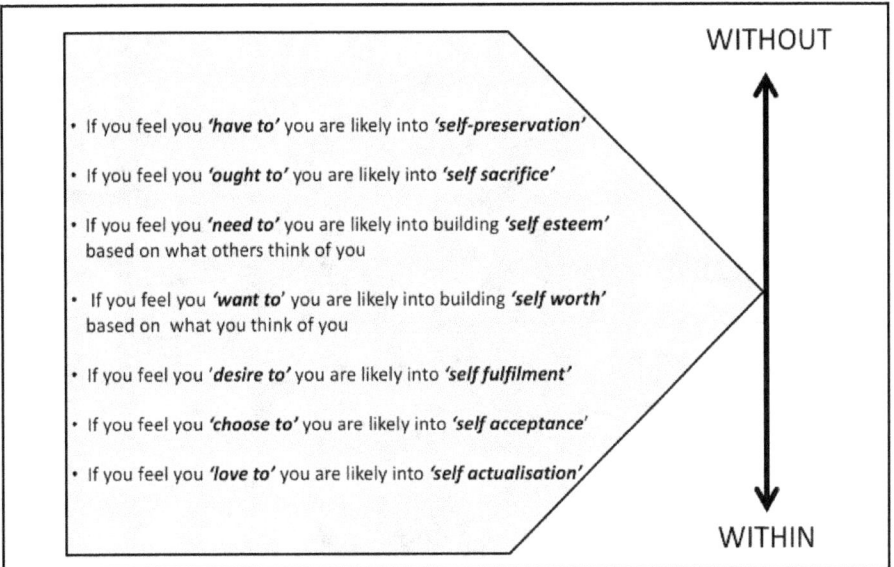

How Beliefs and Intentions Define Our Levels of Sacred Living

The following figures map a path to sacred living and complement the questions posed earlier in this chapter. Take the time to review each figure and take note of the limiting and expanding beliefs, as well as the intentions put forward for each of them. We can then begin to identify the beliefs and intentions that represent how we live our lives. We will find our beliefs are spread across several levels or some may strike a strong chord in one or two neighbouring levels. We can then think about the level of satisfaction, contentment and joy we experience in our life. We may hold beliefs in life beyond the examples provided for each level. The challenge is how we lift and expand our beliefs to higher levels of consciousness to create more satisfaction, contentment and joy. A process to explore how you might be positioned on the following levels is available in the Companion Exercise section at the end of the book.

Figure 7.4: Sacred Living

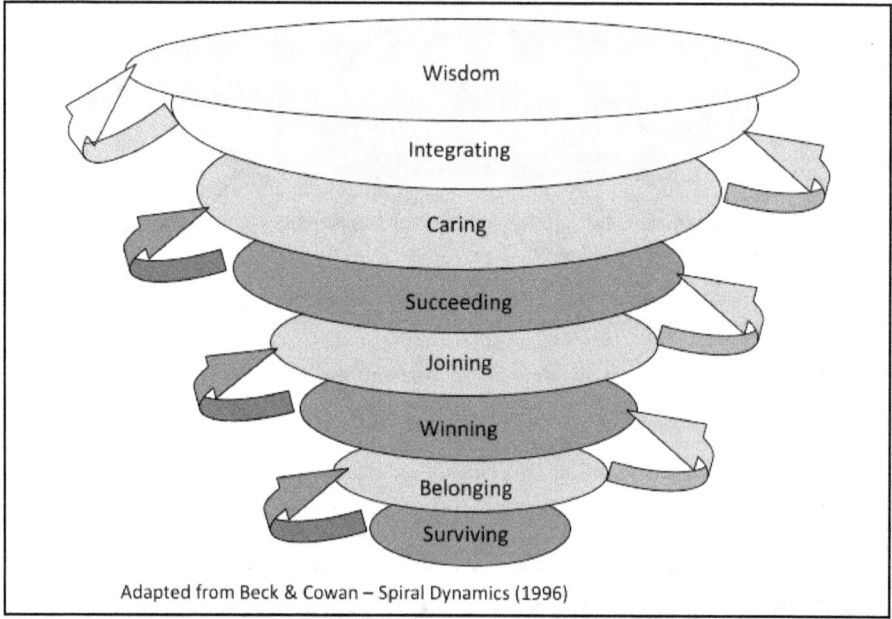

Adapted from Beck & Cowan – Spiral Dynamics (1996)

Figure 7.5: Surviving

Individual Focus

- **Limiting beliefs**
  - I must stand alone
  - I must be wary
  - I must move

- **Intentions**
  - To pay my bills
  - To protect myself
  - To stay safe
  - To stay strong

- **Expanding beliefs**
  - I can take care of myself
  - I am strong
  - I am vigilant

- **Essence**
  - Independence

Figure 7.6: BELONGING

Collective Focus	

• **Limiting beliefs**
  - I must belong
  - I must obey
  - I must submit
	• **Intentions**
	  - To be included
	  - To protect the group
	  - To stay together
	  - To ensure the group is safe

• **Expanding beliefs**
  - I am connected
  - I am accepted
  - I am safe
	• **Essence**
	  - Ritualistic

Figure 7.7: WINNING

Individual Focus	

• **Limiting beliefs**
  - I will be overpowered
  - I must win
  - I must dominate
	• **Intentions**
	  - To be first
	  - To dominate
	  - To control others
	  - To protect what's mine

• **Expanding beliefs**
  - I am powerful
  - I can win
  - I am in control
	• **Essence**
	  - Exploitative

Figure 7.8: JOINING

Collective Focus	
• **Limiting beliefs** - I must conform or comply - I must follow the rules - If you are not with me you are against me	• **Intentions** - To have rules and processes all will follow - To have a culture that supports our desires - To make sure everyone's role is clear - To protect what's ours
• **Expanding beliefs** - I am supported - I know what is important to me - I am of value	• **Essence** - Conforming

Figure 7.9: SUCCEEDING

Individual Focus	
• **Limiting beliefs** - I must have more than enough - I must be competitive - I must be seen to be successful	• **Intentions** - To stay competitive and win - To grow my financial wealth - To perform - To be the best
• **Expanding beliefs** - I am skilled, confident and successful - I have the resources to be successful - I know how to thrive	• **Essence** - Material gain

Figure 7.10: CARING

Collective Focus

- **Limiting beliefs**
  - I must take care of everyone
  - If I don't show care I will be rejected
  - I can never do enough for others

- **Intentions**
  - To support our community and the earth
  - To ensure all stakeholders are cared for
  - To support each other to grow
  - To create consensus

- **Expanding beliefs**
  - I am a loving, caring human being
  - I support my community
  - I know how to value people

- **Essence**
  - Humanitarian

Figure 7.11: INTEGRATING

Focused on the Individual and the Collective

- **Limiting beliefs**
  - I can't hold to my integrity in all situations
  - It's too hard for me to always be ahead of the game
  - I am not big enough alone to do this

- **Intentions**
  - To continually add value to the world
  - To create a sustainable future
  - To ensure we all learn from our efforts
  - To contribute to a greater good

- **Expanding beliefs**
  - I am strategic
  - I add value
  - I believe in myself

- **Essence**
  - Systemic flex flow

Figure 7.12: WISDOM

Focused on the Individual and the Collective	

• **Limiting beliefs**
  - What I have to sacrifice is too great
  - I can't change the world
  - It's too hard for me to stay loving
	• **Intentions**
	  - To leave a legacy for future generations
	  - To ensure we all have enough
	  - To find the value in all philosophies
	  - To support 'one world' higher thinking

• **Expanding beliefs**
  - I am whole
  - My loving lifts others
  - I am intuitive and wise
	• **Essence**
	  - Sacred living

I've come to learn that what is sacred to me are the deeper greater good beliefs I hold for, especially through difficult times. How much I waver from these depends on how much I engage with my fears, that is, how scared I am. Who would think that simply switching two letters could make such a difference to one's well-being – from scared to sacred!

The key to living sacredly is to stay in the questions long enough to allow a solution to emerge at a level that best serves ourselves and others. Sometimes not everyone may receive what they want. In these situations, the best we can do is to hold for the best for all long enough to optimise the overall outcome. We can never know for sure if a choice is right or wrong, good or bad. In the end, we need to trust our intuition independent of personal agendas and sometimes despite conflicting or even contrary information. The effectiveness of our intuition is governed by our levels of conscious awareness; our conscious awareness is governed by the beliefs and intentions in which we are anchored. Sacred living is about never intentionally bringing harm to ourselves or others. In this way, we can be sacred at all levels of consciousness. It just depends on our willingness to grow and build our lives for a greater good.

Integrating My Personal Story

My early life post World War II was quite **ritualistic**. I felt I **belonged**, although at three years of age, squatting in a flat up the road from my grandmother's house was to later influence my beliefs about **survival**. For the first three years of my life I lived with my grandmother, grandfather, mother, father, uncle, aunty and cousin in a two-bedroom house in Bondi. I can recall the day at three years old when my father loaded up my sister's cot and drove up the street for us to move into our new home; well not so new. It was an old mansion (about 100 years) converted to flats. We paid £2.46 ($4.45) rent per week for the 20 years we were there and later given squatters rights.

The first 10 to 11 years of my life were almost **tribal**. Lots of kids in the street; billycarts, cricket and other games, dogs and families all recovering from aspects of their experiences during the Second World War. The family **rituals**, too, were consistent – for example a baked dinner for the family every Sunday at Nan's; afternoon teas at her place were also very common.

Whilst for 10 or so years, these were pretty good, I have one stark memory that was to influence me for most of my life and keep me focused on **survival** for probably longer than I needed – early beliefs have an awesome power. My mother used to tell me that "When the meter man came round to read the meter, tell him your last name is Ritchie, not Harradine, as otherwise we will be evicted." As our family income was also very sporadic (my Dad was a self-employed upholsterer and Mum paid very little as a pre-school teaching assistant), so our alternatives were very limited. This was a source of family tension and was later to have a big impact in my teenage years when my parents' marriage ran into major challenges. The tribe began to fall apart.

My response from about 12 years old was coloured by strong independence and **rebellion** against my father who began to display dysfunctional **dominant** traits as a reaction to his own inner struggles. My teenage years were the worst time of my life even though spotted with some good times; the only thing that was predictable was the unpredictability of it. The home front descended into volatility. The combination of alcohol, PTSD and financial strain were at the core of it. My parents', especially my Dad's, inability to manage their lives had a profound effect on all of us. This was true for my Dad who at some level knew the trauma he was creating but couldn't admit it. I must say though, despite it all, they were good people in their hearts and I could see that. My Mum's inability to deal with life was mostly about her inability to deal with Dad. I adopted the protector role of both my mother and my sister as best I could.

My late teens saw my tennis take off and I got pretty good. At around 17, I did okay relative to my expectations in the NSW Championships. However, having resolved to be different than my parents, my **anger** had to go somewhere. The tennis court is where it showed up instead of striking out at others – having witnessed so much pain resulting from that. I developed some confidence from this and, when I suggested to my coach I mightn't need so much more coaching ,he fed back some of the wisest words I have ever heard: "Well, John, there's no good practicing your mistakes," inferring I had more to learn and was he right with this prophecy.

I also discovered two new **tribes**. The tennis club became my home away from home. I made a circle of friends that changed my life and have continued to develop friends through tennis my whole life. My sense of **belonging** has been a central theme in my life that has both limited and expanded me.

The second **tribe** I locked onto was my best mate Brian's family. Talk about **conventionality**! I'd say the most stable environment I have ever been exposed to. I spent most weekends and often weeknights at their home. I witnessed a completely different way of living. I **joined** them every chance I got, even boarded with them for a while in my late teens after I started working. Their lives were so predictable – including on a daily basis. I called Brian's parents DG and Mrs G. Here's the routine: Monday to Friday DG would be up at 4.00 am in summer and 4.30 am in winter. He would spend 30 minutes reading the morning paper and some time in his vegetable garden until 6.00 am, when he would get ready for work (he was a banker!) and precisely at 7.00 am would head off to work in the city. From Monday to Thursday he would return home exactly at 6.00 pm when dinner would be served within the next hour. After dinner, he would go into his room and work on his stamp collection until precisely 9.30 pm, when he would emerge, go to the kitchen and put the kettle on. He would head back to his room to continue working on his stamp collection and on the way through would announce: "I've just put the kettle on in case anyone wants a cup of tea." That was a signal for Mrs G to get up and go make the tea, which we would all have together before going to bed. On Friday night DG would come home exactly at 9.00 pm, having had some drinks with his work colleagues.

This was my peaceful escape from the chaos of my own home. I embraced it as often as I could. I can't ever recall a cross word between Mr and Mrs G (as I referred to them collectively). Brian has remained a lifelong friend and we were each other's best man at our weddings. He is still married after 45 years following in his parents' footsteps. I remember the times with him and his family with the greatest affection and gratitude.

My parents permanently separated when I was 21 after some short-term separations during my teenage years. It was not an easy separation – in fact it was traumatic and my father was **AVO'd** (Anti-Violence Order) through it. Things began to calm down between them when I was about 23 just before I was to get married.

The attachment I had to stability, **conventionality** and tennis was to attract me to my now ex-wife, Diane. She was a tennis player and also came from a stable family, though she had suffered the trauma of losing her father from motor neurone when she was nine years old. She was an only child but with a large extended family (19 cousins) who also demonstrated a deep connection to each other. Another new tribe was to arrive. I loved Diane's caring and attention to me, and I felt the same about her. It was not unlike how my grandmother had treated me. I felt a sense of place with her, in her family, with our tennis friends and life and so we got married as you did back then. I was 24 and she was 18. We were engaged for a year and married for 19 years. We were to have three children, Mark, Glen (still-born) and Christopher. These were happy years until about the last five of them. Di didn't change, but I did. Inevitable I suspect, given our backgrounds.

I'm glad to say I was able to shed the legacy of my volatile family, except for a time on the tennis court – a constant source of stress for Di. Also, my first son Mark was very independent and could act out in ways that triggered me to yell at him until I learned not to. I did chase him around the trampoline, which we laugh about today, but certainly it scared him when he was little. I regret that. I never wanted to scare my children as I was frightened by upheaval and threats in my childhood. I was also pretty, well, very defiant. Thanks, Mum! I fully **joined** with this **conventional** life and saw this as my life's future for many years. Overall, we parented well together. Sometimes I struggled to balance the **dominating** theme in my own family with the **cooperative** and **compliant** themes in Diane's, but together we made it work for a long time. Life was good! I look back with love and gratitude to Di for elevating me out of a history that many people repeat in their adult life. I got lucky!

It was not to last, however. During this time, my **career** took off and our **financial situation** felt more secure. I was experiencing a lot of **success** on this front and really loving it. I finally went to university when I was 38. So, balancing competing demands of study, house renovation, raising two children, playing competition tennis, began to take its toll. At some level, all this activity was allowing me to escape facing some underlying personal needs I was not prepared to declare. Now that I had satisfied the **survival**, **belonging**, **winning**, **joining**, and **success** conditions of my life, I had room to pay attention to my individuality and authenticity at a core level.

I could no longer use external conditions to fight off my inner battle with my sexuality. I finally had to face the vulnerability of a choice between remaining in a life that I could no longer find deep personal inner happiness in and deciding to take the unknown path of ultimately "coming out" as gay. I noticed I was becoming angrier with my life and felt trapped. I couldn't seem to shake it.

The beginning of coming to terms with this was when I was about 35. Diane was on a girls' night out. The kids were asleep and I was watching TV when a movie came on called "Making Love" with Harry Hamlin and Kate Jackson. It was about a married man who becomes attracted to men and the process he goes through to come to terms with it. I saw myself on the screen and I was mortified by it. The following night we were watching TV when the kids had gone to bed and I quietly turned the TV off and said: "We need to talk." It just came out: "I'm attracted to men and I don't know what to do about it." At a similar point in the movie, Kate Jackson went ballistic and started slapping her husband and accusing him of all sorts of things, so I had no idea what to expect from Diane. Contrary to the movie, Diane came over knelt beside me to comfort me and asked what did I want to do with it? I said I didn't know and we both cried. The **caring** from her blew me away and made my decision to leave even harder. At least I wasn't bottling it up anymore and some relief was achieved. I suspect it may have provided some understanding for Di about my restlessness. For me it explained some surfacing frustration and expression of anger towards Di which produced a lot of guilt in me. She really didn't deserve it. I think we were both confused about what to do with this information.

We persevered for a couple of years and I left in my early 40s for about four months to explore this underlying drive I couldn't seem to quell. I was still pretty confused and undecided and returned to the **conventional family** life. We stayed together for another four or so years, bought a house with a tennis court; something I always had wanted to do but Di had resisted. Interestingly she initiated the purchase. Both of us were trying to seal a commitment to each other with a **material** commitment to a way of living that had initially brought us together. Ultimately it didn't work, although it tempered our time together for a while.

Whilst many may judge my choice as selfish, I had to decide what was the most **caring**, in the broadest sense, right thing to do for a **greater good**. I wasn't consciously thinking this way at the time. It was more an unconscious knowing coupled with fear of getting it wrong. Staying with my **family** meant I would continue to become **emotionally unavailable** to them; leaving meant **dealing with the unknown** and creating **enormous pain** in the short term but with the **possibility of recovering** from that.

I finally left and separated on 10th January 1992. I was 45 years old. Leaving then and the time some five years earlier were the most painful days in my life, along with the loss of Glen. Witnessing the upset and pain I had created for my children and my wife was excruciating for all of us, but this time there was no turning back. I set out on a **new path** with all its **emotional downsides**, **unknowns**, **financial** and **career** implications, but also a renewed sense of **authenticity** that was now available to me.

The next few years saw some ups and downs in work and relationships. Not surprising, really. When we settled our divorce, I wanted to make sure the children and my now ex-wife were safe as I had a strong earning capacity and felt I could recover financially on my own. We sold the tennis court and it paid for the mortgage. I left the house ownership to Di. There were a couple of motives in this: I never wanted my children to experience **not having a roof over their heads**; I wanted Diane to feel **safe**; and I carried a lot of **guilt** for choosing to leave. At the time, none of these reasons consciously occurred to me. I just felt it was the **right** thing to do.

I entered a relationship with another woman who today is part of my **chosen family**. We have become such great friends and we went through a lot together for a couple of years. She witnessed, **supported** and was hurt by my coming out. She named me her "off-white knight". I am ever grateful for her generosity of **spirit** and **unconditional loving**. I remained very unsettled during this time exploring a life I never expected to be part of. My **career** continued to improve thankfully. **She**, some **very supportive close friends of long standing** and my **career** probably saved me from a meltdown – although there were a few close calls.

Three years later, on New Year's Eve, 31st December 1995, I met Maxx. I had been living alone for over two years – again, something I never imagined doing but needed to do to come to terms with how I was going to live this new life. In fact, two weeks before I met him, I deliberately spent ten days on my own, believing I would never again form a primary relationship. I had found the gay world incredibly non-committal, save perhaps the last best opportunity available to them. My **judgements** on this world were running amuck and retarded the shedding of my own **homophobia**. I had decided to let the idea of a primary relationship go and now felt, whilst not my preference, I **fully accepted** I could live a more solitary life – a big step for me.

Interestingly, having let all this go, on New Year's Eve I was introduced to Maxx at a New Year's Eve party in Annandale, Sydney. He, too, had children (3) and had been out for as long as I was. We agreed to meet a few weeks later and the rest is history. I did discover, though, that he and his wife nearly bought the house and tennis court my ex-wife and I had bought; his mother-in-law played on the court every Monday for 30 years, including the four years I was there; he and his **family** came every **Boxing Day** (the day after **Christmas Day**) to play on our court after we had headed off on our regular camping trip to the North Coast of NSW.

Back then our next-door neighbour's daughter became very close to Christopher. She turned out to be a good friend of Maxx's eldest son at school; Diane and Mark coached Maxx's niece and nephew tennis; they also had a junior competition team registered on our court; later Diane was to extend the house after we sold the tennis court. Maxx's brother-in-law did the extensions. At one point my ex mother-in-law and Maxx's ex-father-in-law were standing in the backyard during renovations and were lamenting Maxx's second son seriously burning his arm. Neither had any idea we had come out nor indeed that we were in a relationship.

It's amazing what occurs when **we let go and let God** as they say, whatever you believe God to be. Eight months after meeting Maxx we had a huge **fight** (one of many in our first eight months and beyond into our 7th year). Later Maxx came over to my place and said: "What we need to do is **pool our resources, buy a place**, give it 12 months and if it doesn't work out we will have **at least made some money**." My response was: "You've got to be kidding. We do nothing but **fight**!" Well, we did it and are in the same place 20 years later. Oh, and the fighting has stopped, replaced by an amazingly **loving relationship**; one I never thought possible (see the YouTube link in Chapter 6 for more if you're interested).

I was **retrenched** about three months after we met, and it brought forward **survival** thoughts like no other time in my life. My childhood history re-surfaced. I was still supporting my two sons in American colleges on part tennis scholarships, so life was not cheap. I was 48 years old. I was to discover **ageism** was alive and well in the employment market. Not only my **survival** instincts were triggered, but also where did I **belong** now? A colleague and I tried consulting for 12 months and secured a couple of assignments, but I found it too **isolating**. Connections saw me find a role as Director of Organisation Consulting at one of the **big four accounting firms**. It was the most **toxic work environment** I had ever experienced, although I had some incredibly **successful outcomes** focused on **leadership transformation**. I realised I had been spoilt by 10 years with an amazingly **caring** organisation for its people. The founder and CEO of 125,000 people was a **Quaker**. Six months into the role I decided to resign without anything to take its place, although I contracted back for some months to complete an assignment with a major Queensland government department.

I returned to my education and completed my Graduate Diploma in Counselling. Parallel to these events, I had been involved in the personal development field for 10 years; attending, volunteering and training as a facilitator. In 1993, I attended a 36-day program in the USA. It was the fourth and final leg of the series. I had been introduced **to the teachings of John-Roger** in 1986 by my boss and the philosophy of **personal transformation** and **unconditional acceptance and love** had been percolating through my veins ever since. Thank God! Without the learnings, I can't imagine how I would have coped. This work and now having a counselling credential had me park the idea of eventually transitioning out of the business world into a counselling and psychotherapeutic vocation. It was to become my plan B if I was unable to secure work in the corporate world. **Being employed** by others was not to be until December 2005. I set out to build a consulting practice. Again, it had me revisit the sporadic nature of my father's business. I had registered the name Business Transformation Services Pty Ltd (BTS Consulting) just after I was retrenched. Perhaps my **intuition** knew what was coming. During this time, I was **successful** but also with a few periods where my **survival** issues resurfaced.

I continued my personal development work as well as gaining a Masters of Applied Science in **Social Ecology**. I also advanced my **spiritual pursuits**, completing a vocational **Masters in Spiritual Science** and the course work in a **Doctorate in Spiritual Science** (treatise pending) with the **Peace Theological Seminary**.

My limiting belief of not being smart enough in my teenage years was certainly challenged by these **achievements**. I recall at 15 years old I asked to see my father's psychiatrist at Concord Repatriation Hospital in Sydney. She asked me how things were for me. My response was: "My dad blames us for his problems, but deep down he blames himself and he can't face the truth about what he has done." She said: "Where did you learn to understand that? You should be a psychologist when you grow up." My inner response was: "I'm not smart enough." So, I skirted around pure psychology all my life, but my passion for understanding the human condition has never wavered.

In 2013, I finally made the break from corporate life to set up a full-time counselling and psychotherapy practice. As **serendipity** or perhaps even **spirit** would have it, I met a psychiatrist some two years earlier on a cruise in the Mediterranean. Another year later we met again on a similar cruise in the Mediterranean. We got to talking and it turns out his practice was some 500 metres from where I live. When he heard I was considering setting up a practice, he offered me a room five minute's walk from where I live. We became good friends as well as colleagues.

It seems my plan B intention was clear. When I began the practice, I decided it was time to face my academic nemesis from 15 years of age and commenced a Graduate Diploma in Psychology. It is done! Something energetically was complete for me when I finished. Curiously, my first assignment was a real **challenge**. Mark the psychiatrist generously offered any **assistance** I might need, so I asked for some advice. He was walking through some ideas and I just blocked. Frustrated I uttered: "Oh, I am so stupid." That old limiting belief came rushing up from my unconscious in that moment. Our "stuff" doesn't go away – we just can get better at managing it. Guess what the assignment was? "Nature and Nurture have been the subject of debate over the last 100 years; discuss in relation to Intelligence." Argh! The light bulb went on, I unblocked and I was away.

The overriding learnings for me in life are that: there are no accidents; some things are both meant to be and not to be; sometimes the best thing that can happen is to not get what I think I want. John-Roger's teaching that "the place is already prepared, we just have to find our way there" rings in my ears every day. That place for me is peace, love and joy. I continue to head for it with all its twists, turns and curves. I simply aim to get up one more time than I fall, enjoy the ride, even the tough times, to the best of my awareness. It all has gifts and from there we can love it all.

I trust your own journey is travelled with as much **grace** and **ease** as you can muster and my encouragement is to be **gentle** and **soft** on yourself and others, **hard** on issues that block your progress and resolve to **use everything for your upliftment, learning and growth.**

The Questions I ask Myself and Suggest for You:

1. What questions in this chapter are relevant to me?
2. What beliefs (limiting and expanding) and intentions resonate with me?
3. What limitations and strengths in my thinking might I have unearthed that either block or enable what I want?
4. What does this all mean for me?
    a. What prices will I and those I care about pay?
    b. What is my positive intention?
    c. What payoff am I hoping for?
    d. What is larger – the price or the payoff?
5. What chapters or other resources might I need to refer to that could assist my intent and choices, minimise my fears (scared-ness) and allow me to live sacredly?
6. What might be the impact of any choice I make on others?
    a. How does the impact challenge and/or support my choice?
    b. How can I best attend to the impact?
    c. What greater good can I hold for?
7. What is my next step?
8. How do I feel about it all, right here and now?
9. If I'm not comfortable, what do I need to review to keep lifting my conscious awareness and move forward?

See the *Appendix – Companion Exercises to Support Your Understanding and Growth* for more ideas and questions to explore:

- Exercise 15: Exploring Your Sacred Living Journey, page 169
- Exercise 16: Your Quest(s), page 177

Appendix: Companion Exercises to Support Your Understanding and Growth

Chapter 1: Living Freely

The way I recommend you do these exercises is that you buy a small notebook and use it to respond to the questions in each exercise. Redoing the exercises or even just reflecting on them later can also assist you to identify how much progress you are making.

Exercise 1: Letting go of the Power/Control Triangle

- If you find yourself playing the Persecutor, Rescuer or Victim, make a mental note of any judgements (shoulds); just acknowledge them and see if you can let the judgement(s) go using the following steps
- Think about what you can do to move out of the role into at least considering other possibilities and the experience of freedom that can come with that
- "Lose your mind; gain your senses" (Wayne Dyer, *"You'll See It When You Believe It"*): get in touch with how your body is reacting; It might feel tight, tense, tingly, butterflies perhaps even nausea can show up
- Notice where most of your reactions show up in your body
- If you experience an emotional charge see if you can quieten

it before expressing any concerns about what is happening with others or yourself
- Breathe!
- Take it slow as you build your skill: "slower is faster" (Peter Senge, "*The Fifth Discipline*")
- After an interaction with someone that didn't go well, ask yourself the following questions:
    - Did you rescue and try to fix things, perhaps with the result that others felt smothered (Rescuer)?
    - Did you judge others and make them wrong (Persecutor)?
    - Did you feel disempowered or even helpless (Victim)?
    - Notice how your body felt from anyone of these three roles
- Practice forgiving yourself for any judgements you are holding
    - They hold you hostage
- Keep repeating the exercise until your body feels free of any tenseness or upset
    - Fake it until you make it the faith it until you make it

Exercise 2: Moving to the Possibility/Freedom Triangle

- Ask yourself "What can I promote, create and/or allow in the situation from Exercise 1?"
    - Try out some of the behaviours in Figure 1 below

Figure A.1: FROM POWER/CONTROL TO POSSIBILITY/FREEDOM

Persecutor ⟶ Creator
(Add your own ideas)
- Listen to others to uncover their needs
- Offer constructive feedback
- Suspend judgements, blame and criticism
- Act to include others in decisions
- Show respect and validate all needs
- Encourage sharing ideas, expertise and information
- Acknowledge and share your own ideas, needs and concerns

Adapted from Eric Berne (Games People Play), Helena Cornelius & Shoshanna Faire (Everyone Can Win), Hal & Sidra Stone (Embracing Our Selves) and John Roger (Do It – Get Off Your Buts)

Aware Ego

Rescuer ⟶ Promoter
(Add your own ideas)
- Clarify your own needs
- State needs assertively
- Ask questions to check how much help is appropriate
- Assist those playing Persecutor and Victim to listen to each other
- Ask questions to explore others perspectives
- Discuss consequences of persisting with current behaviours
- Support others to develop strategies for effective problem solving

Victim ⟶ Allower
(Add your own ideas)
- Assertively state your own intentions, needs and perspectives
- Actively seek appropriate support and assistance
- Acknowledge others needs
- Ask questions to explore others needs and look for similarities
- Avoid blaming yourself and others
- Reduce any unstated, expectations or demands on others
- Check and state what you really want
- Choose and act on realistic options

- As you explore the questions below if judgement, fear or disturbance of any kind emerges go back to the beginning to aim to clear them before you move to the next question
- As you engage with some of the above behaviours what awareness is present for you about you?
    - Notice any resistance, concern or fear that may present itself in trying something new, especially when any judgements trigger the temptation to retreat to Persecutor ("they should or should not" – "they are not okay but I am"), Rescuer ("How can I fix this?" – "I need to help this person or the situation") or Victim ("I can't do this" – "No one is here to help me")
- How can you accept (without judgement) the situation and yourself as you are?
- What can you do to cooperate with what is going on?
- What understandings are emerging for you?
- Who or what can you empathise with in this situation?
- What can you be enthusiastic about in this situation?
- How can you love what is going on in this situation?
    - Hint – look for the gift in it
- Revisit the ideas in Figure A.1 and retest your engagement with the behaviours you have chosen or test if alternative ones may be appropriate. Keep repeating the above cycle until you feel willingness to risk the change you want to make.

Chapter 2: Embracing Our Vulnerability and Authenticity

Exercise 3: Exploring Your Protective Selves

- What triggers your defences?
    - Think about who or what upsets you, including your own behaviour and thoughts
    - Think about the "should" and the judgements that may arise
    - What protective/defensive patterns do you employ?
    - Think about how you might criticise, control, withdraw from or aim to rescue situations
- What are the emotions and feelings that are present for you?
    - Look for the ones that are not obvious
    - What might be underneath the obvious ones such as anger, frustration, guilt, resentment, disappointment?
    - Typically, the core feelings are related to fear, sadness, pain or hurt
    - This is where our vulnerability truly starts to kick in
- Where does this feeling reside in your body?
    - It could be facial tension, a tight chest, a painful stomach, etc.
- What might you now see as the vulnerability you are aiming to protect?
- When can you recall first experiencing the deeper feelings that are present for you now?
    - Notice if your bodily experience changes as you think about this
- What conscious or unconscious belief or value may have evolved for you that has initiated your protective strategy?
    - For example: "If I don't do it nobody else will"; "I'm not good enough to do things on my own"; "If I am always polite people will like me"
- What do you imagine these beliefs and the vulnerability you have identified want for you?
- How does any awareness you now have inform how you developed a protective pattern to cope with the vulnerability that has come forward?
- What has been the payoff or positive intention of acting out this protective pattern?
    - This could be connected or the same as what you imagine your beliefs and vulnerability want for you
- What might be the price you are now paying or even have paid in the past for continually acting out this pattern?
- As you think about this does the current price of the pattern outweigh the payoff from the past or the other way around?
- What is your intention at this time?
    - To keep doing what you have been doing?
    - To change and grow from what you are now aware of?

- If you state your intention is to change and grow, what is both the price and payoff for that change?
  - Is it bigger than the price or payoff from the past?
- Now what's your choice and if it is still to change, how can you build your Authentic Self and sustainably live from there?

Exercise 4: Reframing Beliefs

- Review the following figure from Chapter 2, Embracing Vulnerability and Authenticity to refresh your understanding of the power of beliefs.

Figure A.2: INDIVIDUAL ECOLOGY & BELIEFS (from Chapter 2)

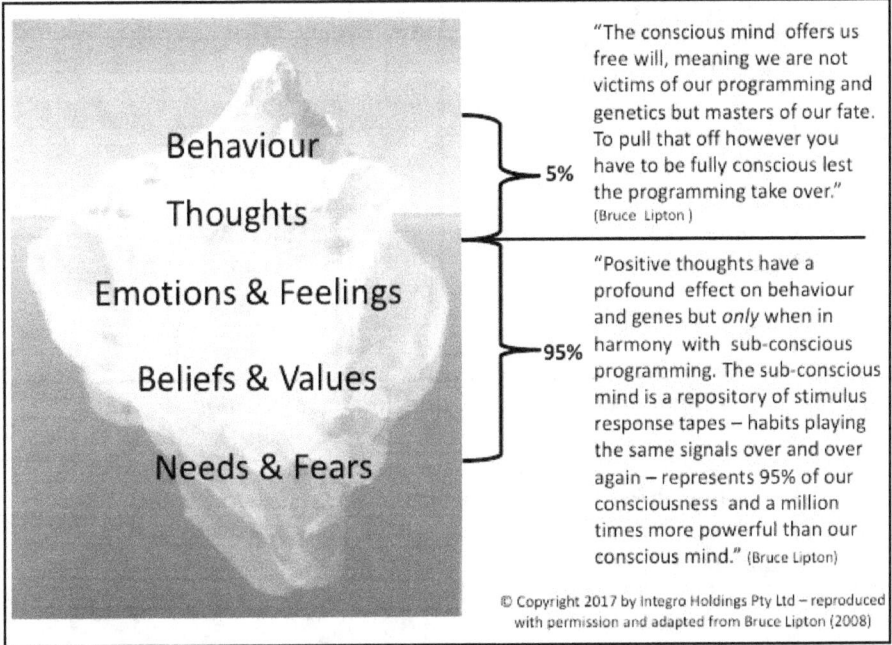

- Consider the following life scripts you may have in Chapter 2. These are a starting point for any limiting beliefs you may be holding on to. Even a positive life script can be limiting e.g. "being positive" if overdone idealises the world and can have us deny difficulties and challenges that are presented in our lives.

Figure A.3: LIFE SCRIPTS & THEMES (from Chapter 2)

• Be strong	• Driving people crazy
• Losing my mind	• Committing suicide
• Being the best	• Carrying my cross
• Saving sinners	• Building empires
• Being helpful	• Being miserable
• Having a ball	• Walking on eggshells
• Trying hard	• Missing the boat
• Bossing others	• Sorry for being alive
• Do it my way	• Getting stepped on
• Stumbling but recovering	• Looking for a pot of gold
• Succeeding then failing	• I have to be perfect
• Never getting anywhere	• It has to be perfect
• Saving for a rainy day	• Be perfect
• I have to get it right	• Give it to me
• I can't be wrong	• Being responsible
• I've got it wrong	• Pleasing others
• It's not enough	• I need to win
• I'm not enough	• I can't lose
• Being positive	• Do the right thing
• Poor me	• I'll do it my way
• Follow the rules	• It's hard to trust

Adapted and expanded from James and Jongeward – Born to Win (1971)

- Decide which buckets these life scripts belong to. See Chapter 2 to refresh how these are core drivers e.g. if you chose "pleasing others" as a life script, if you don't do that, which bucket is emptied; likely it will be the "love bucket"

Figure A.4: Core Drivers – The Six Buckets

| LONGEVITY | POWER | KNOWLEDGE |
| FREEDOM | PLEASURE | LOVE |

- How disturbing is it for you to have it emptied? It's as disturbing for as long as it lingers and/or is carried from situation to situation
- Consider how much the limiting belief or life script you have chosen mirrors either the "Perfection" or "Discovery" approaches outlined below

Figure A.5: Perfection & Discovery Approaches

When how we perceive ourselves and others....

....is judged against	....is open to
PERFECTION	**DISCOVERY**
we are driven by:	we are motivated by:
• Right/wrong	• Enquiry/creativity
• Judgements	• Acceptance
• Failures	• Learning
• Unwillingness to risk	• Willingness to risk
• Anxiety	• Excitement
• FRUSTRATION	• FASCINATION

Does a discovery approach close off the search for excellence? Not at all! We start by acknowledging how we feel about a situation and then look at what we can learn, for better ways of doing things, for new doors that are opening in the future. Being willing to risk is more likely to achieve excellence than a model of perfection which is limited by definition of what's right and how people ought to be.

Adapted by the Conflict Resolution Network from Thomas Crum – "The Magic of Conflict" (1998)

- Begin to reframe the limiting belief using the processes. The positive intention of a limiting belief is often the most difficult component to detect. It is though critical to uncover to move past the limitation you have been living with. Remember, every limiting behaviour, thought, feeling and belief, be it negative of positive has a positive intention. The following examples may assist

Table A.1: Reframing Beliefs (from Chapter 6)

Beliefs	Examples
Limiting Belief	1. I'm not powerful enough 2. I'm not good enough 3. I'm not important
Positive Intention (AKA Payoff)	1. I keep safe 2. Keeps me from falling 3. I get to stay comfortable
Expanding Belief	1. I am empowered and wise 2. I stand for what I believe 3. I am strong and flexible

- You can now take this a step further and review the seven-step process below to further develop your Authentic Self. This next step tracks the source of the limiting often unconscious pattern you have been living.

Figure A.6: SEVEN STEPS TO LIVING AUTHENTICALLY

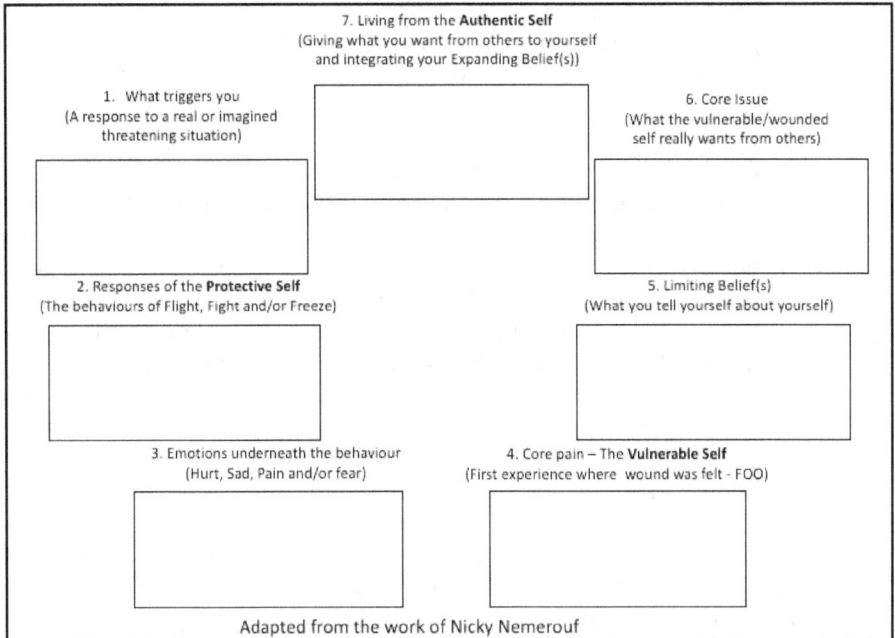

Adapted from the work of Nicky Nemerouf

- Once you have decided an expanding belief in Step 7, set yourself the task of saying it to yourself ten times a day for 33 days in a row (33 X 10). If you miss a day, start again and keep going until you complete 33 sequential days. Notice your process, especially any resistance you have to completing it and how that may reveal yet another unconscious pattern in your life. Journal and track positive changes as you go. At the beginning an expanding belief it may feel like a lie. Well, fake it until you make it then faith it until you make it.

Exercise 5: Early Steps to Developing an Authentic Self

- Take a piece of paper or in your notebook and write down 50 positive qualities about yourself. Yes, that's right 50, no less. Don't ask anyone what they think they might be. You might imagine what they would say though
    - Most people can get to between 20 and 30 and then struggle to reach 50
    - The qualities you have are not just the ones that are easy to access
    - There may be some you have acted on intermittently or some time ago but haven't taken forward at a conscious level or perhaps even judged yourself for not continuing to be that way. It doesn't mean you don't have the quality. There simply may be something else that has overshadowed it. It's these ones we want to re-access and are

usually found in the last 25 or so qualities. For example, as a child, you might have been very sensitive, but things may have happened that have hardened you in some way and today you see yourself as strong and sensitivity is now seen as a weakness. Sensitivity is still a quality you possess and therefore should be listed if you want to re-access it
- Another way to build the list of qualities is to imagine what you admire in others, either people close or have been close to you or public figures. We cannot see in others what is not true for ourselves. If you see this quality in another you possess it at some level. If you want to build that quality into your future, list it, even if you have acted in opposition to that quality. For example, you might admire confidence in someone and feel you lack confidence. If you can identify confidence in someone else at some level you have experienced confidence at some time in your life on something you have done. Even if it is fleeting, you have access to it
- You might find that some of the more elusive qualities are challenging for you to claim. They may even feel like a lie for now
- Your next step is to persevere with the qualities you want more of. If you are "yes butting" yourself you are tapping into your limitations. Go back to Exercise 3 and start the process of unpacking any limiting beliefs you are hanging on to. When you get to developing an expanding belief (Living from the Authentic Self) it can be built around the quality you want to anchor and have more of. Do the 33 X 10 exercise to strengthen what you are seeking
- Once you have 50 qualities group then into themes. You are likely to end up with 4 to 7 or so themes. These themes form the foundation of the essence of who you are. They are the building blocks of your Authentic Self
- As you complete a 33 X 10 process start to notice how your responses to life are changing and how the results you are experiencing are more or less of what you truly want

Chapter 3: Taking Charge of the Past

Exercise 6: Reviewing Your Early Story

- The intention of this exercise is to better understand how our early years influence our adult life. As early as the first few minutes of our life the image we have of our parents is unconsciously imprinted upon us in some way. The image is built and reinforced by the way our caretakers treat us and how they and we interact with society
- Our primary caregivers are our first experience of life so both their positive and negative personality traits are key reference points in our development
- Harvell Hendrix and Helen Hunt (2003) in their book *"Getting the Love You Want"* have developed exercises for couples to assist them to map and improve their adult relationships. They call their process *"Imago Therapy"*. One such exercise is about deepening our understanding about our parents and how they impact our adult lives. It is adapted here.

Step 1

- Take a piece of A4 paper and turn it on its side i.e. landscape, and divide it into four equal columns
- Place a heading in each column as follows:
  - Column 1: Positive parental traits
  - Column 2: Negative parental traits
  - Column 3: Unfulfilled desires
  - Column 4: Positive feelings
- In Column 1 list all the positive traits of your mother or other first primary caregiver
  - List them as you recall them in your earlier years not as you experience her now
  - Use simple adjectives or short phrases
- In Column 2 list all your first primary caregiver's negative traits in the same way as the above step
- In Column 3 write in what you most wanted from your primary caregiver but never received
- In Column 4 write down what you most liked and enjoyed about being with your primary caregiver

Step 2

- On the same piece of paper list all the positive traits of your father or a second primary caregiver underneath your mother's or first primary caregiver
    - Again, as you recall him when you were young
    - Use the same steps as in Step 1
- Then in Column 2 list your father's or a second primary caregiver's negative traits underneath your mother's or first primary caregiver
- In Column 3 write in what you most wanted from your father or second primary caregiver but never received
- In Column 4 write down what you most liked and enjoyed about being with your father or second primary caregiver

Step 3

- Consider other people in your life who have had a substantial influence on you in your early years e.g. siblings, grandparents, uncles, aunts, early school teachers
- Add them one by one to the list and go through Steps 1 and 2 as you did with your primary caregivers
- If you haven't already run out of paper take another A4 sheet and place it landscape under the one you already have; extend the columns and continue until you feel complete

Step 4

- Look back on all you have written down and select the top three positive and negative traits across the entire list that have had the greatest impact on you
- Circle the corresponding unfulfilled desires and what you enjoyed in Columns 3 and 4 respectively
- Combine the unfulfilled desires into a single sentence beginning with: "What I wanted most but did not get was..."
- Do the same for what you liked and enjoyed most: "What I liked and enjoyed the most was..."

Step 5

- Select a new page and develop what we might call a life script. Harvell Hendrix and Helen Hunt refer to this as your "childhood agenda"
- Fill in the blanks to the following:
    - "I am trying to get a person who is _____ _____ (fill in the three negative traits from Column 2) to become _____

(fill in the three positive traits from Column 1) _____ so I can get _____ *(fill in my unfulfilled desires from Column 3)* and feel _____ *(fill in positive childhood feelings from Column 4)*

Step 6

- From the previous steps, reflect on any images that may still be present for you today, especially with your partner or past partners if single
- Notice how you energetically respond to each of the words in the sentence. Record your feelings.
- How might the ideas you have uncovered push or have you drift into Persecutor, Rescuer and/or Victim?
- What Protective Selves and Vulnerabilities may have developed from this history?

Harvell Hendrix and Helen Hunt suggest: "We are products of our past, no matter how free we think we are. When we begin to see the connections between what happened to us as children and what is happening in our relationships, we see that there are no coincidences. The conflicts in our relationship are no accident; it is no quirk of fate that our partner is 'just like' our mother or father, or some other significant person in our childhood. We are reliving our childhood in the hope of getting it right this time.

This happens because our unconscious mind seems to have no sense of linear time. Our adult... partner literally is, in our timeless unconscious, our early caretakers. In unconsciously choosing a partner who has the same wounding behaviours that our caretakers had we are unconsciously trying to correct that early experience and get them to meet the needs we did not get met in childhood. But we can only do this if we understand what's going on. In becoming aware... you take the first step in learning what needs to be healed."

- What does this all mean for you and your relationship(s) now?

Move on to Exercise 7 to experience how transactions between yourself and a significant other map today.

Exercise 7: Mapping Current Transactions in Your Relationship(s)

- Take a recent exchange between you and someone close to you that was less than ideal and created some disturbance for you and/or the other person
    - Map the exchange by drawing arrows between the two of you, including any undertone that may have been present
    - Use full arrows for what was obvious in the transaction and broken

    lines if you perceived any hidden agendas from either party
    - See example diagrams earlier in Chapter 3
    - Be real with yourself about what may surface either in how you might be judging or defending yourself or how you might be projecting your judgements onto the other
- You may find the exchange began a certain way but shifted as the conversation continued
    - If there are clearly points at which the conversation changed perhaps you might redraw the diagram below on a piece of paper and draw the exchanges for each section of the conversation
    - You'll know to do this if the lines you are drawing get too cluttered

Figure A.7: MAPPING TRANSACTIONS

PERSON 1	PERSON 2
Parent	Parent
Adult	Adult
Child	Child

- Once you have identified the complete transaction exchange begin to examine the judgements you were holding onto; what beliefs and values were being challenged?
- Ask yourself when you first experienced these judgements, values and beliefs in your life
- What was your first memory of any similar exchanges which may have involved you directly or you witnessed between people you cared about?

- Perhaps it was mum and dad fighting or a parent disciplining a sibling and your reaction to it

- Link any patterns you identify to the current situation and bring awareness to how much of what you were feeling in the present situation reflects what you felt in the past
- To access your reptilian and mammalian brains ask yourself where you have felt the disturbance in your body. Make a note
  - What was that experience – in your stomach, shoulders, head for example?
  - Getting to know your somatic responses is central to detecting transference
- You can refer to other chapters in this book to develop techniques to reframe future responses to similar situations that may arise
- Link the above exchange to Exercise 1 in this chapter
  - What patterns do you see that are still present today that you might let go of?
  - What judgements of yourself and others might you be holding onto?
  - What forgiveness might be required to assist that?
  - Are you resisting forgiveness?
  - What prices do you pay for that?
  - What is the payoff for holding onto any limitations you identify?
  - What is a next step for you?

Chapter 4: Loving Ambiguity and the Unknown

Exercise 8: Assess Your Focus on Order and Chaos

- Assess how much you love the unknown and ambiguous situations
- Review Figure A.9 and assess where you tend to focus by placing an "X" across the line for each item (print a couple of copies off)

Figure A.8: NEED FOR CONTROL AND TOLERANCE FOR CHAOS

- Join the X's to form a histogram. See the following examples
  - Example 1: A strong focus on order and control

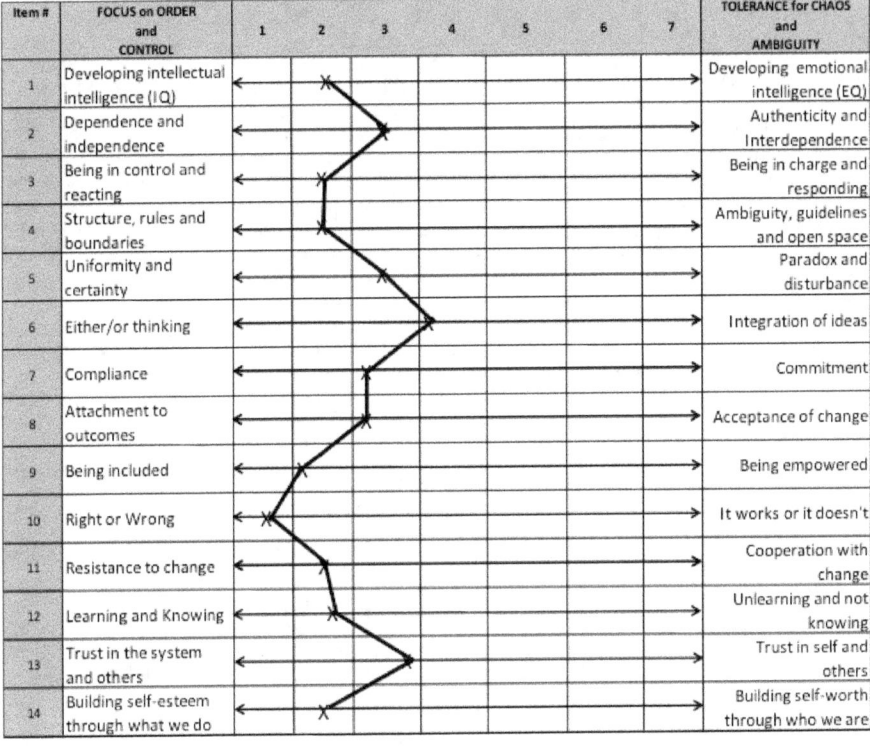

- Example 2: A high tolerance for chaos and ambiguity

Item #	FOCUS on ORDER and CONTROL	1	2	3	4	5	6	7	TOLERANCE for CHAOS and AMBIGUITY
1	Developing intellectual intelligence (IQ)						X		Developing emotional intelligence (EQ)
2	Dependence and independence						X		Authenticity and Interdependence
3	Being in control and reacting				X				Being in charge and responding
4	Structure, rules and boundaries					X			Ambiguity, guidelines and open space
5	Uniformity and certainty						X		Paradox and disturbance
6	Either/or thinking					X			Integration of ideas
7	Compliance						X		Commitment
8	Attachment to outcomes						X		Acceptance of change
9	Being included					X			Being empowered
10	Right or Wrong			X					It works or it doesn't
11	Resistance to change					X			Cooperation with change
12	Learning and Knowing					X			Unlearning and not knowing
13	Trust in the system and others						X		Trust in self and others
14	Building self-esteem through what we do				X				Building self-worth through who we are

- Enter the scores from your histogram in the first figure in this exercise next to the "X" and total them as in the examples below
  - Example 1: A strong focus on order and control

Item #	FOCUS on ORDER and CONTROL	1	2	3	4	5	6	7	TOLERANCE for CHAOS and AMBIGUITY
1	Developing intellectual intelligence (IQ)		2.6						Developing emotional intelligence (EQ)
2	Dependence and independence			3.5					Authenticity and Interdependence
3	Being in control and reacting		2.5						Being in charge and responding
4	Structure, rules and boundaries		2.4						Ambiguity, guidelines and open space
5	Uniformity and certainty			3.5					Paradox and disturbance
6	Either/or thinking				4.2				Integration of ideas
7	Compliance			3.2					Commitment
8	Attachment to outcomes			3.2					Acceptance of change
9	Being included		2.1						Being empowered
10	Right or Wrong	1.6							It works or it doesn't
11	Resistance to change		2.5						Cooperation with change
12	Learning and Knowing		2.7						Unlearning and not knowing
13	Trust in the system and others			3.9					Trust in self and others
14	Building self-esteem through what we do		2.5						Building self-worth through who we are
	TOTALS	1.6	17.3	17.3	4.2	0.0	0.0	0.0	40.4 *
	Example 1	High need for order and control			Mid Range	High tolerance for ambiguity and the unknown			Place the total score * on the above line appropriately along the 'My score' line below
	Score Range	14		35		56	77	98	
	My score *				40.4				
	Implications	This score indicates you are likely to have a high to moderate need for control and order				This score indicates you are likely to have a moderate to high tolerance for ambiguity and the unknown			

- Example 2: A high tolerance for chaos and ambiguity

Item #	FOCUS on ORDER and CONTROL	1	2	3	4	5	6	7	TOLERANCE for CHAOS and AMBIGUITY
1	Developing intellectual intelligence (IQ)						6.1		Developing emotional intelligence (EQ)
2	Dependence and independence						6.8		Authenticity and Interdependence
3	Being in control and reacting					5.2			Being in charge and responding
4	Structure, rules and boundaries					5.8			Ambiguity, guidelines and open space
5	Uniformity and certainty						6.7		Paradox and disturbance
6	Either/or thinking						6.3		Integration of ideas
7	Compliance						6.4		Commitment
8	Attachment to outcomes						6.4		Acceptance of change
9	Being included					5.4			Being empowered
10	Right or Wrong				5.6				It works or it doesn't
11	Resistance to change					5.6			Cooperation with change
12	Learning and Knowing					5.6			Unlearning and not knowing
13	Trust in the system and others						6.7		Trust in self and others
14	Building self-esteem through what we do					5.4			Building self-worth through who we are
	TOTALS	0.0	0.0	0.0	5.6	33.0	45.4	0.0	84 *
	Example 1	High need for order and control			Mid Range	High tolerance for ambiguity and the unknown			Place the total score * on the above line appropriately along the 'My score' line below
	Score Range	14		35	56	77		98	
	My score *						84		
	Implications	This score indicates you are likely to have a high to moderate need for control and order				This score indicates you are likely to have a moderate to high tolerance for ambiguity and the unknown			

- How do you think your responses mirror how you approach life?
  - If your score was relatively low: "I agree I don't like change and resist it preferring to feel in control as I react to arising situations"
  - If you score was relatively high: "I am relatively comfortable with change and feel in charge of myself as I respond to emerging situations"
- What results do you get from your approach?
  - Physically, e.g. stress levels and health
- Emotionally, e.g. frustration, calmness
- Mentally, e.g. resistant thoughts, acceptance and cooperation
- Spiritually, e.g. meaning making of change affects on one's life
- How would you prefer to be in light of your responses?
  - Consider mapping your preferred or ideal scores and examine the gap between the current state and what you want
- What specifically would you like to change in your response to ambiguous and unknown circumstances?
  - Review Chapters 2, 4 and 6, *Living Freely*, *Embracing Vulnerability and Authenticity* and *Intentionality* to assist your response to this question

Chapter 5: Unconditional Relating

Exercise 9: Knowing Your Primary/Disowned Selves

- Take a piece of A4 paper and divide it into four parts as follows
- Only read the rest of the exercise when you have completed it. It's like someone telling you the end of a movie before you have seen it

Figure A.9: ASSESSING PRIMARY/DISOWNED SELVES

Step 3 List the opposite characteristics to the ones you dislike and judge about others	**Step 1** List the characteristics you dislike and judge about others
Step 4 List the opposite characteristics to the ones you like and admire about others	**Step 2** List all the characteristics you like and admire about others

- Follow the above steps in each of the four sectors
- Cluster like ideas
- Those qualities you listed in Step 1 characterise your Disowned Selves that are likely to play out in your Negative Bonding Patterns with others

- The opposites in Step 3 are those qualities that form your Primary Selves – the parts of you that you think are important to your survival, well-being and success
- Those qualities in Step 2 characterise your Disowned Selves that are likely to play in your Positive Bonding Patterns with others
- The opposites in Step 4 are those qualities that also form part of your Primary selves – those parts you perhaps want to deny and try to hide but know they exist
- What do the above lists reveal about your relationships with others, especially your primary relationship or those with your children and other close family members?
- Where and how do they play out?
- Where do you estimate your relationship dynamics place you in the Building Relationships framework? *"Disconnected"*, *"Unbalanced"*, *"Conditional"*, *"Committed"*? Perhaps you have elements of more than one. Relationships are not binary. They are multidimensional and dynamic. The frameworks are represented here for convenience.

Figure A.10: DISCONNECTED RELATIONSHIP (from Chapter 5)

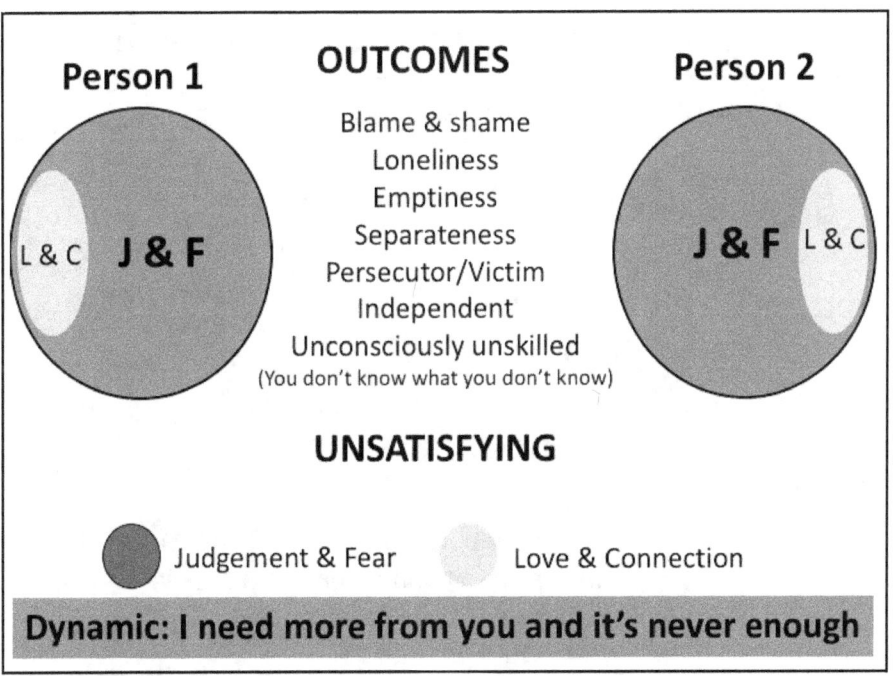

Figure A.11: UNBALANCED RELATIONSHIP (from Chapter 5)

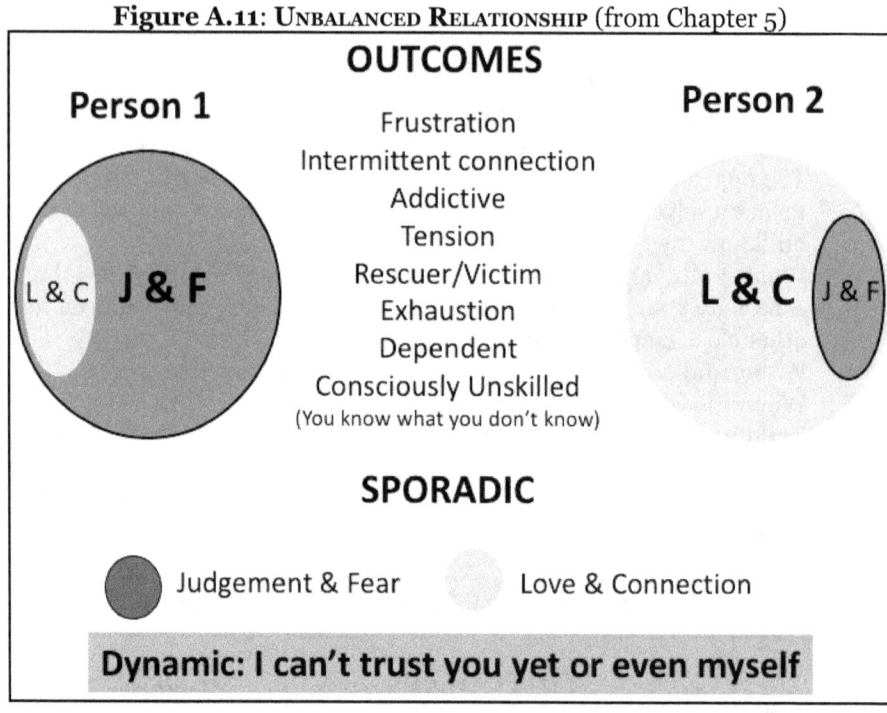

Figure A.12: CONDITIONAL RELATIONSHIP (from Chapter 5)

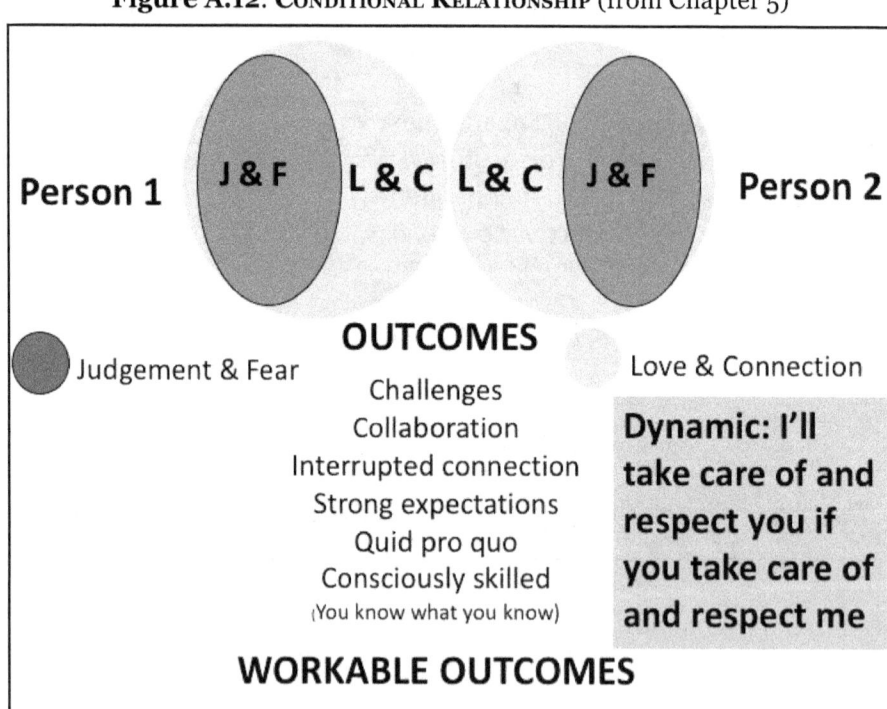

Figure A.13: COMMITTED RELATIONSHIP (from Chapter 5)

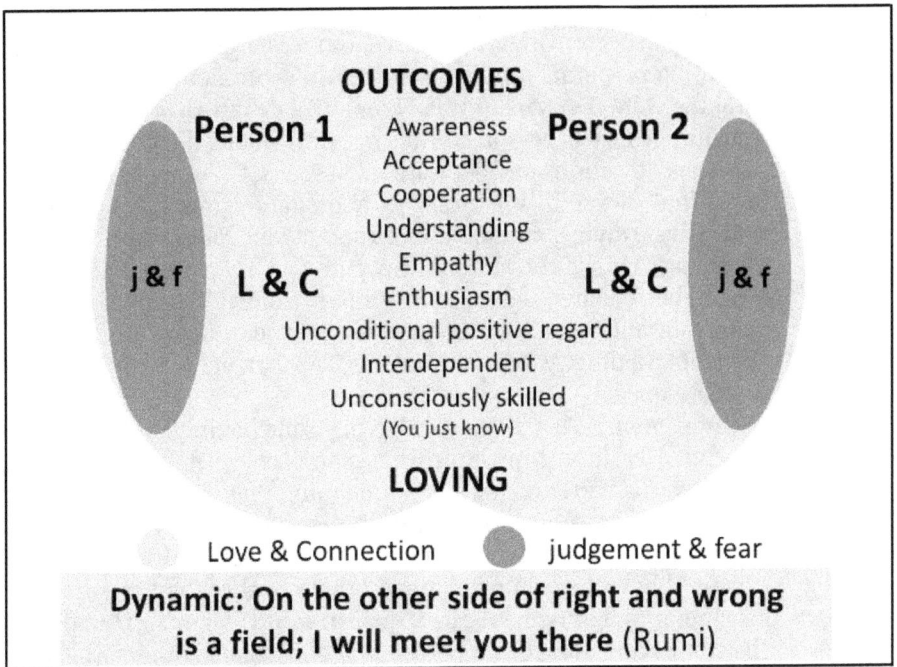

- What next steps would you like to take to improve your relationships with others?

Exercise 10: Relationship Assessment

- Drs John and Julie Gottman's theories are highly compatible with a committed relationship as described above. They propose:
  - Building Love Maps: How well do you know your partner's inner psychological world, his or her history, worries, stresses, joys, and hopes?
  - Sharing Fondness and Admiration: The antidote for contempt, this level focuses on the amount of affection and respect within a relationship. (To strengthen fondness and admiration, express appreciation and respect.)
  - Turning Towards Each Other: State your needs, be aware of bids for connection and respond to (turn towards) them. The small moments of everyday life are actually the building blocks of relationship
  - The Positive Perspective: The presence of a positive approach to problem-solving and the success of repair attempts

- Managing Conflict: We say "manage" conflict rather than "resolve" conflict, because relationship conflict is natural and has functional, positive aspects. Understand that there is a critical difference in handling perpetual problems and solvable problems
- Making Life Dreams Come True: Create an atmosphere that encourages each person to talk honestly about his or her hopes, values, convictions and aspirations
- Creating Shared Meaning: Understand important visions, narratives, myths, and metaphors about your relationship
- Trusting: This is the state that occurs when a person knows that his or her partner acts and thinks to maximise that person's best interests and benefits, not just the partner's own interests and benefits. In other words, this means, "my partner has my back and is there for me."
- Commitment: This means believing (and acting on the belief) that your relationship with this person is completely your lifelong journey, for better or for worse (meaning that if it gets worse you will both work to improve it). It implies cherishing your partner's positive qualities and nurturing gratitude by comparing the partner favourably with real or imagined others, rather than trashing the partner by magnifying negative qualities, and nurturing resentment by comparing unfavourably with real or imagined others. (https://www.gottman.com)

- Examine Gottman's views above and give yourself a score out of 10 for each of the nine points (maximum = 90)
    - Ask your partner to do the same
    - Go a step further and assess what you think your partner would say
    - Also ask them to assess what you say
    - Compare your answers
    - Notice the gaps
    - Affirm the correlations and celebrate
    - Talk about the gaps
    - How the conversation goes will mirror one of the four types of relationships in Chapter 5, "*Unconditional Relating*". How did you go?
- Another way of viewing relationships that reinforces the notion of a committed relationship is Robert Sternberg's (1997) "*Triangular Theory of Love*". He suggested three pillars of love, "*commitment*", "*passion*" and "*intimacy*" and the different relationships that occur when one of the pillars is lacking
- The following diagrams summarise his theories and more can found about them at: https://en.wikipedia.org/wiki/Triangular_theory_of_love (Figures A.13, A.14 and A.15)

Figure A.14: RELATIONSHIP PILLARS – CONSUMATE RELATIONSHIP

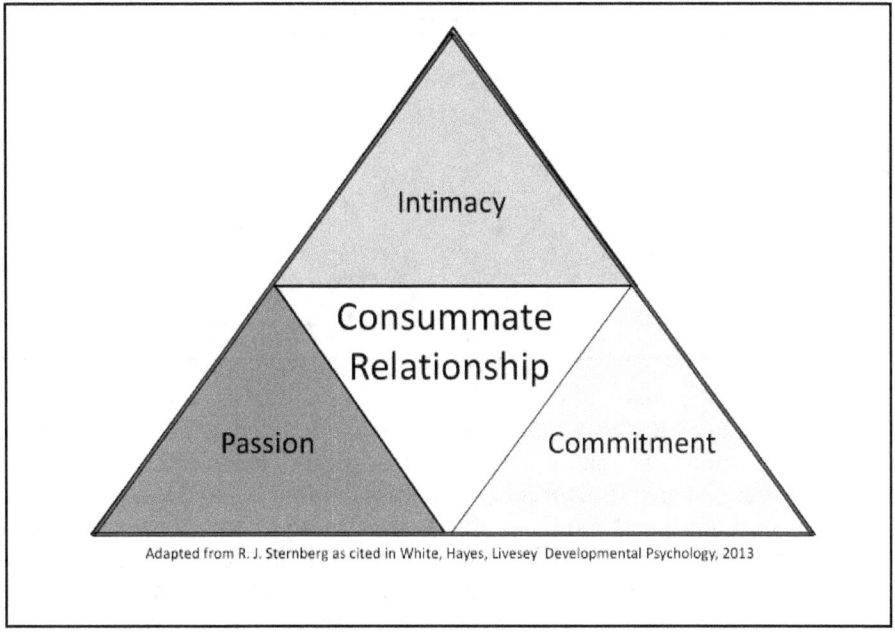

Figure A.15: RELATIONSHIP PILLARS - INFATUATED & ROMANTIC RELATIONSHIPS

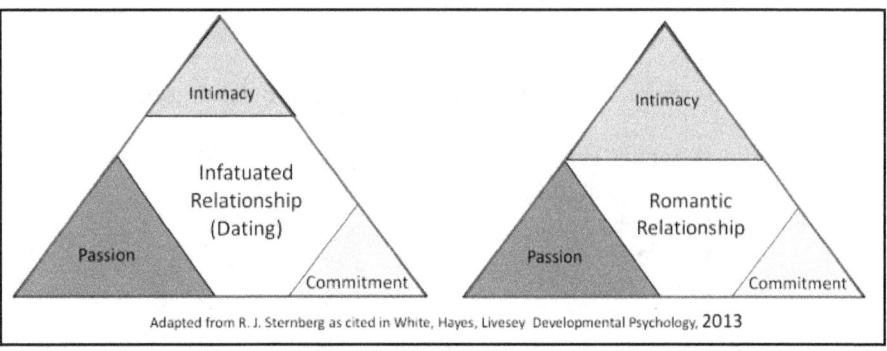

Figure A.16: Relationship Pillars - Friendship & Empty Relationships

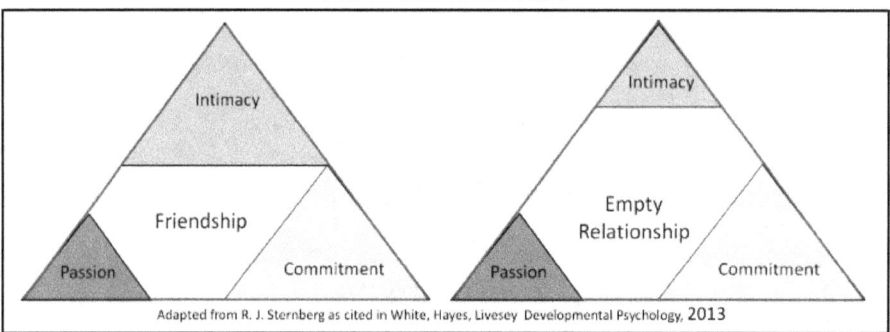

Adapted from R. J. Sternberg as cited in White, Hayes, Livesey Developmental Psychology, 2013

- Robert Sternberg (as cited in White, Hayes and Livesey, 1968) describes intimacy as "feelings that create closeness, bondedness and connection in relationship"; passion as "the expression of desires and needs such as self-esteem, nurturance, affiliation, dominance, submission and sexual fulfilment"; and commitment as "both a short-term decision to love someone and a long-term decision to maintain that love."
- Assess where you broadly land in Robert Sternberg's frameworks.
- What do the responses to the last two exercises mean to you?
- Go on to the next exercise to begin a process of better understanding what you might do to improve your relationship

Exercise 11: Your Relationship Current State

- What are you regretful or remorseful about?
- What do wish the other was regretful or remorseful about in relation to you?
- Who or what are you judging (including in yourself)?
- What is the biggest judgement you have?
  - On the other?
  - On yourself?
- What can you forgive?
  - In the other?
  - In yourself?
- Which one is harder if either?
- Why do you think that is?
- What can't you forgive now or is the most difficult to forgive?
  - About the other?
  - About yourself?
- How significant do you feel?
  - To the other?
  - To yourself?

- How much love do you feel?
  - Towards the other?
  - Towards yourself?
  - From the other?
- How much love do you act upon? E.g. how often do you do things you don't really want to do for your partner but do it simply because you love them and you know they will enjoy it and your action is without hooks or agendas?
  - Towards the other?
  - Towards yourself?
- Given any or all the above, what is a next step for you?
  - Consider what you want to change in yourself
  - Consider what you would like from the other

Exercise 12: Relationship Sharing Exercise

- Share the following with your partner (Figure A.16)

Figure A.17: RELATIONSHIP SHARING

- The limiting judgements I hold on you are....

- What I value about you is....

- What I have been unwilling to share with you up until now is....

- What I would like to see you do more of is....

- What I would like to see you do less of is....

- What I am willing to do to support you more is....

- What I would request of you to support me more is....

- What I will do to support myself from here on in is....

- Go through the whole series of statements whilst your partner listens in silence
- Stay with the statements, i.e. be careful not to wander off into general conversation or explain why you feel as you do
- The listener's responses are confined simply to *"thank you"* at the end, i.e. no interruptions
- Before beginning go through the Appendix, *"Listening for Potential"* in Chapter 3, *"Taking Charge of the Past"*
- As you are listening to your partner notice any inner defensive patterns (Chapter 1, *"Living Freely"* – Figure 1.1, *"The Power/Control Triangle"*) and/or the neutrality of your *"Authentic Self"* in Chapter 2, *"Embracing Vulnerability and Authenticity"*
- How challenging or otherwise might this be?
  - If you are anxious about this exercise consider seeking some professional assistance to facilitate the discussion
- When the process is complete discuss your experiences with each other
  - Notice where this discussion lands you in the *"Relationship Pathway"* and *"Building Relationships"* models in Chapter 5, *"Unconditional Relating"*
- What is a next step for you?

Chapter 6: Intentionality

Exercise 13: Setting Personal Intentions and Goals

- Do you set personal goals?
  - Name a few key ones
- Does the process of setting goals work for you or not?
  - Consider the extent to which you complete what you start in the time you decide
- What goals have you avoided setting?
- What outcomes and results are you getting?
  - (*Intentions are the results you get not the goals you set*)
- Do the outcomes and results match your goals?
- Are you satisfied with your outcomes and results in life?
- Do you want more?
- If not what uncertainties, fears or concerns might be lurking underneath?
- What do these uncertainties, fears or concerns want for you – what are their true intentions?
- What underlying intentions are presented to you now?
- How are they trumping your stated goals?
- What might you be pretending not to notice?
  - These are usually issues and challenges you somewhat know are there but ignore, bypass or dance around
- What realignment can you apply to your goals and intentions?
  - Adjust your intentions and goals and/or move into greater acceptance of what you are in
- How clear are you now?
- If not 100% clear go back and review what might be blocking a Level 7 (Senge) commitment

Exercise 14: Aligning your personal intentions with those around you

- Think of a time when you have really wanted something and it hasn't happened
  - What was the outer goal?
- When you look back, what might have been your inner intention? E.g. Not risk failure or rejection
  - Consider if a limiting or disenfranchising belief was present or a fear/need took hold
- What goals have you set yourself recently?

- What are others' stated goals and how ambitious are they in your mind?
  - Think of your partner if you have one, family, friends, club if you belong to one, your business if you own one, your organisation if you work for someone else and any other significant groups to you
- As you answer this consider your beliefs, hopes and fears about their achievability
  - This may provide insight into whether your inner intentions align with a desired result
- What inner intention do you have for yourself in relation to others' goals? E.g.
  - Head down and keep out of trouble
  - Take risks to challenge the status quo
  - To be a powerful influencer
  - To do just enough/more than enough to support the organisation/club/partner to move forward
- Notice if your body feels expanded and balanced or disquieted and out of balance, even disturbed when you answer these questions
  - What does that tell you about your intention/goal alignment?
- What challenges and opportunities present themselves with your current level of inner and outer alignment?
- What will it take for you to bring your inner intentions into alignment with yours and others' stated goals?
- How resolved are you to do that? (What is your inner intention?)
- Having answered this last question what is your intention now?
- Continue this cycle of questions until you feel fully aligned or decide not to align them. Be authentic with yourself
- How are you feeling now?

COMPANION EXERCISES TO SUPPORT YOUR UNDERSTANDING AND GROWTH

Chapter 7: Sacred Living

Exercise 15: Exploring Your Sacred Living Journey

- Review Figures 2 and 5 to 12 from Chapter 7
  - They are repeated here for convenience

Figure A.18: ASKING QUESTIONS

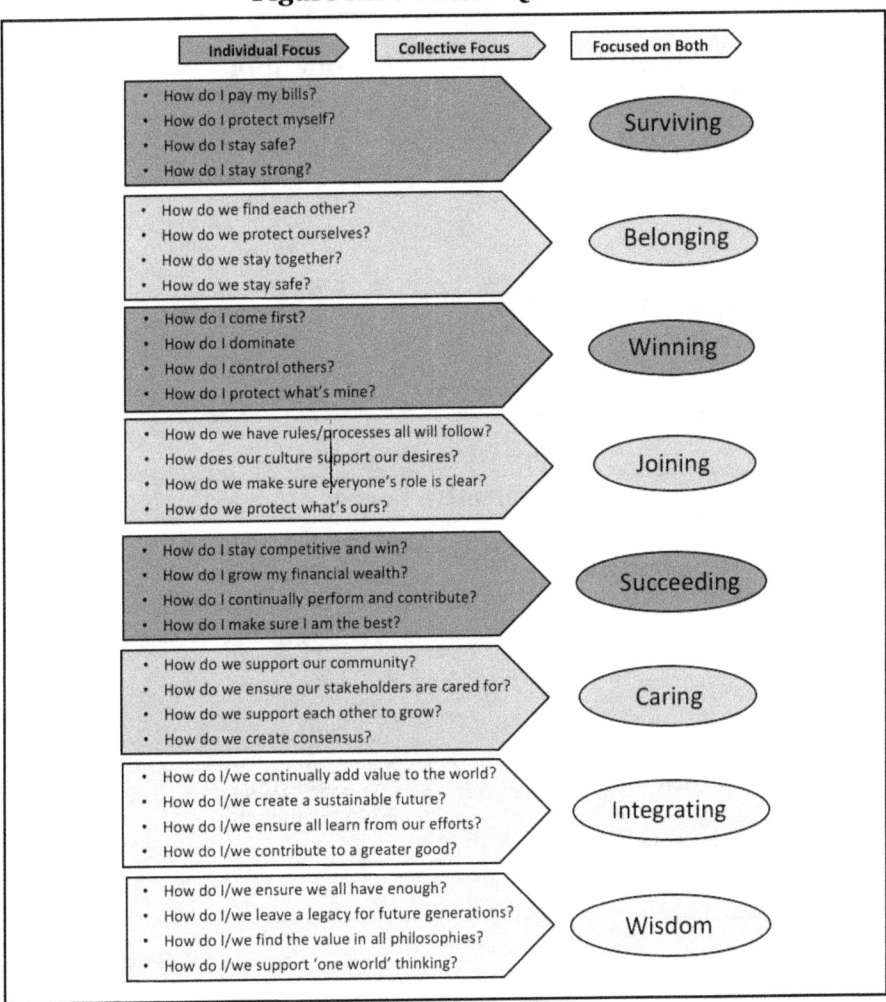

Adapted from the work of Clare Graves, edited by Cowan and Todorovic - Never Ending Quest (2005); Beck & Cowan – Spiral Dynamics (1996)

Figure A.19: SURVIVING

Individual Focus	

• **Limiting beliefs**
  - I must stand alone
  - I must be wary
  - I must move
	• **Intentions**
	  - To pay my bills
	  - To protect myself
	  - To stay safe
	  - To stay strong

• **Expanding beliefs**
  - I can take care of myself
  - I am strong
  - I am vigilant
	• **Essence**
	  - Independence

Figure A.20: BELONGING

Collective Focus	

• **Limiting beliefs**
  - I must belong
  - I must obey
  - I must submit
	• **Intentions**
	  - To be included
	  - To protect the group
	  - To stay together
	  - To ensure the group is safe

• **Expanding beliefs**
  - I am connected
  - I am accepted
  - I am safe
	• **Essence**
	  - Ritualistic

Figure A.21: WINNING

Individual Focus	
• **Limiting beliefs** - I will be overpowered - I must win - I must dominate	• **Intentions** - To be first - To dominate - To control others - To protect what's mine
• **Expanding beliefs** - I am powerful - I can win - I am in control	• **Essence** - Exploitative

Figure A.22: JOINING

Collective Focus	
• **Limiting beliefs** - I must conform or comply - I must follow the rules - If you are not with me you are against me	• **Intentions** - To have rules and processes all will follow - To have a culture that supports our desires - To make sure everyone's role is clear - To protect what's ours
• **Expanding beliefs** - I am supported - I know what is important to me - I am of value	• **Essence** - Conforming

Figure A.23: SUCCEEDING

Individual Focus	

• **Limiting beliefs**
  - I must have more
    than enough
  - I must be competitive
  - I must be seen
    to be successful
	• **Intentions**
	  - To stay competitive and win
	  - To grow my
	    financial wealth
	  - To perform
	  - To be the best

• **Expanding beliefs**
  - I am skilled, confident
    and successful
  - I have the resources
    to be successful
  - I know how to thrive
	• **Essence**
	  - Material gain

Figure A.24: CARING

Collective Focus	

• **Limiting beliefs**
  - I must take care of
    everyone
  - If I don't show care
    I will be rejected
  - I can never do
    enough for others
	• **Intentions**
	  - To support our community
	    and the earth
	  - To ensure all stakeholders
	    are cared for
	  - To support each other to
	    grow
	  - To create consensus

• **Expanding beliefs**
  - I am a loving, caring
    human being
  - I support my community
  - I know how to value people
	• **Essence**
	  - Humanitarian

Figure A.25: INTEGRATING
Focused on the Individual and the Collective

- **Limiting beliefs**
  - I can't hold to my integrity in all situations
  - It's too hard for me to always be ahead of the game
  - I am not big enough alone to do this

- **Intentions**
  - To continually add value to the world
  - To create a sustainable future
  - To ensure we all learn from our efforts
  - To contribute to a greater good

- **Expanding beliefs**
  - I am strategic
  - I add value
  - I believe in myself

- **Essence**
  - Systemic flex flow

Figure A.26: WISDOM
Focused on the Individual and the Collective

- **Limiting beliefs**
  - What I have to sacrifice is too great
  - I can't change the world
  - It's too hard for me to stay loving

- **Intentions**
  - To leave a legacy for future generations
  - To ensure we all have enough
  - To find the value in all philosophies
  - To support 'one world' higher thinking

- **Expanding beliefs**
  - I am whole
  - My loving lifts others
  - I am intuitive and wise

- **Essence**
  - Sacred living

- Take note of the questions, limiting and expanding beliefs, and intentions put forward for each of the figures that predominantly apply to you and make a note of them below
    - The beliefs that strike the strongest chord with me are:

<u>Questions</u>   **<u>Level</u>**

<u>Limiting Beliefs</u>   **<u>Level</u>**

Expanding Beliefs   _Level_

Intentions   _Level_

- Where (what level) does the above review predominantly land you?
- Where do you feel your second and third levels are located in this framework?
    - Often these levels are adjacent to your predominant choice
- What does this mean for you?
    - Change or no change?
- If you wish to initiate change in your life what are your next steps to improve your satisfaction, contentment, joy and loving in life?
    - Self: e.g. Take a Yoga class once a week
    - Family and friends: e.g. Have dinner with the whole family and/or selected friends once a week
    - Work and career: e.g. Define my next job/career intentions for the next year within the next week
    - Social/group and/or personal activities: e.g. Play golf once a week; join a walking club by the end of the month; buy a subscription to the Opera House
    - Financial needs: e.g. Review or create a budget over the next two weeks; set financial goals for the next year
    - Community contribution: e.g. Decide any/which charities to contribute to for the next 12 months; participate in a fund raiser within the next 3 months
- Priorities: e.g. Examine blockages to the above activities and develop approaches to overcome them; decide the life balance I want across the contexts of personal time, relationship/family focus, work/career, social time and community contribution dimensions
- Future generations: e.g. Select a group or cause you would like to make a contribution to; make enquiries within a month
- Notice if you found one area easier to respond to than others
    - Consider those areas you found more challenging or were resistant to respond to
    - Review the beliefs you have identified both limiting and expanding
    - Identify how they link to how you have answered the above questions
    - What do you now want to change if anything?
    - How does your final set of responses correlate with you creating more contentment, joy, peace and love in your life?
    - Continue this cycle until you feel satisfied with your responses and clear you will act on them

Exercise 16: Your Quest(s)

Embracing fears is essential to lifting consciousness and tapping into our potential greater good outcomes. Fears can be couched in the six core drivers outlined in Chapter 2, *"Embracing Vulnerability and Authenticity"*: Longevity – how do I stay healthy and survive; Power – how do I control or not be controlled; Knowledge – How do I build capability and apply it; Freedom – how am I free to choose; Pleasure – how do I get to enjoy life; Love – how am I recognised, respected, acknowledged, liked and loved. When we look at these core drivers and link them to the questions outlined above we can see where our current sacred focus might reside.

Figure A.27: INTEGRATING CONSCIOUSNESS & CORE DRIVERS

Consciousness	Core Drivers					
	Longevity	Power	Knowledge	Freedom	Pleasure	Love
Wisdom	How do we find meaning in life?	How do we focus on continuous expansion?	How do we find what we can't yet know, feel or see?	How do we support a better world to be?	How do we fulfill all our dreams?	How do we sustain loving it all?
Integrating	How do I make the best of all that is available?	How do I inspire others and support integration efforts?	How do I share and spread the knowledge of all?	How do I continually create breakthroughs for the greater good?	How do I celebrate humanity?	How do I love it all?
Caring	How do we look after others and the environment?	How do we make a difference in the world?	How do we keep learning about our ecological needs?	How do we support others to be free?	How do we feel good about the differences we are making?	How do we show others the way of the greater good?
Drive	How do I sustain material success?	How do I realise more of what I want?	How do I keep up with the latest developments?	How do I create my own boundaries?	How do I live the way I want?	How do I promote recognition from others?
Joining	How do we ensure we comply with our rules?	How do we secure positonal places of control and influence?	How do we keep abreast of the 'system'?	How do we hold purposeful discipline that permits us choice?	How do we enjoy what the 'system' permits?	How are we admired for our integrity?
Winning	How do I demonstrate leadership?	How do I take control and lead and not be lead?	What and who do I know that can help me lead and dominate?	Who has authority over me and who do I have authority over?	What indulgences does my leadership and dominance enable me to have?	How do I ensure that others want to follow me?
Belonging	How do we make sure we know our place and fit in?	What is my position in the group?	Who can I ask for advice?	What rituals can I take part in?	How do we mix and enjoy with each other?	How do we ensure the group stays together and individuals feel they belong?
Survival	How do I survive?	How do I dominate my environment?	What do I need to know about my environment?	What boundaries are safe or unsafe for me?	How do I enjoy where I am?	How do I identify and connect with my environment?

The intersecting point between core drivers and consciousness levels provides a quest(s) that may guide your actions. Consider your most prominent core drivers and how you focused on the questions asked earlier to determine your current quest(s).

- What quest(s) have you chosen as a centrepiece of your life from the above matrix?
- Do you have an aspirational quest(s) that might appeal to you but feel you are not quite ready for?
- What do you notice shows up for you about any gap between your current and aspirational focus?

- Consider thoughts, feelings, beliefs (limiting and/or expanding), needs and fears
• What are your next steps to build a sacred life?
• What will challenge you to take them?
• What will support you to take them?
• How are you feeling moving forward now?
  - Continue revisiting this process until a sense of well-being and enthusiasm emerges as you answer this question
• What is your next step?

References, Recommended Readings and Movies

An eclectic selection of readings that have influenced this work

(Authors in alphabetical order within alphabetical categories)

Biographies

Do, A. (2010) *The Happiest Refugee*. Sydney: Allen & Unwin
Greig, G. (1999) *The King Maker – The Man Who Saved George VI*. London: Hodder & Stoughton
Kirby, M. (2011) *A Private Life*: Sydney: Allen & Unwin
Mandela, N. (1994) *Long Walk to Freedom*. Great Britain: Abacus Books
Mandela, N. (2010) *Conversations with Myself*. London: MacMillan Publishers
Obama, B. (2004) *Barack Obama – Dreams from My Father*. New York: Random House
Pausch, R. (2008) *The Last Lecture*. Sydney: Hachette Livre Australia
Suzuki, D. (2003) *A David Suzuki Collection – A Lifetime of Ideas*. Vancouver: Greystone Books
Vujicic, N. (2012) *Life Without Limits – How to live a ridiculously good life*. Sydney: Allen & Unwin
White, R. C. (2009) *A. Lincoln*. New York: Random House

Business, Organisation and Societal Focus

Adizes, I. ((1988) *Corporate Life Cycles – How and Why Corporations Grow and Die and What to do About It.* New Jersey, USA: Prentice Hall
Allen, D. (2003). *Ready for Anything.* New York: Penguin Group
Beck, S. E., Cowan, C. C. (1996) *Spiral Dynamics.* Malden MA: Blackwell Publishing Limited
Bolman, L. G., Deal, T. E. (1995) *Leading with Soul – An Uncommon Journey of Spirit.* San Francisco; Jossey - Bass
Branson, R. (2011) *Screw Business as Usual.* UK: Random House
Deming, E. (1986) *Out of the Crisis.* Cambridge, Mass. USA: Massachusetts Institute of Technology
Diamond, J. (2005) *Collapse – How Societies Choose to fail or Survive.* London: Penguin Books
Dunphy, D. (1981) *Organisational Change by Choice.* Australia: McGraw Hill
Fisher, R., Ury, W. (1986) *Getting to Yes.* London: Century Hutchison Limited
Gordon, T. (1977) *Leader Effectiveness Training.* Toronto: Bantum Books
Graves, C. W. (2005) *The Never Ending Quest.* Santa Barbara, CA: ECLET Publishing
Handy, C. (1989) *The Age of Unreason.* London: Arrow Books
Hodge, B., Dimitrov, V. (2003) *Language and Theory of Everything: Linguistics at the Edge of Chaos.* Sydney NSW: University of Western Sydney
Kohn, A. (1999) Punished by Reward. New York: Houghton Mifflin Company
Kotter, J. P., Heskett, J. L. (1992) *Corporate Culture and Performance.* New York: The Free press
Kouzas, J. M., Posner, B. Z. (2002) *The Leadership Challenge.* San Francisco: Jossey-Bass
Macoby, M. (2004) *Why People Follow the Leader: the power of transference.* Boston: Harvard Business Review, Vol.82 (9)
Obolensky, N. (1994) *Practical Business Re-engineering.* London: Kogan Page Limited
O'Brien, J.K. (2009) *Opportunities Beyond Carbon – Looking Forward to a Sustainable World.* Melbourne: Melbourne University Press
O'Brien, J. K. (2015) *Visions 2100 – Stories from Your Future.* Fremantle W.A.: Vivid Publishing
Quinn, R. E. (1996) *Deep Change – Discovering the Leader Within.* San Francisco: Jossey-Bass
Rock, D. (2006) *Quiet Leadership.* New York: Harper Collins Publishers
Rosenhead, J. (1998) *Complexity Theory and Management Practice.* http://www.human-nature.com/science-as-culture/rosenhead.html
Schein, E. (2003) *DEC is Dead, Long Live DEC.* San Francisco: Berrett-Koehler Publishers, Inc

Senge, P. M. (2006) *The Fifth Discipline: the art and practice of the learning organisation*. London: Random House

Wilber, K. (2001) *A Brief History of Everything*, 2nd edition. USA: Shambhala

Personal Growth

Adams, D. (1979) *The Hitchhiker's Guide to the Galaxy*. New York: Pocket Books

Berne, E. (1967) *Games People Play – The Psychology of Human Relationships*. Harmondsmith: Penguin

Bradshaw, J. (1990) *Home Coming – Reclaiming and Championing Your Inner Child*. New York: Bantum Books

Cameron, J. (1993) *The Artist's Way*. London: Pan Books

Demartini, J. F. (2010) *Inspired Destiny – Living a Fulfilling and Purposeful Life*. USA: Hay House

Dyer, W. (1976) *Your Erroneous Zones*. New York: Avon Books

Dyer, W. (2004) *You'll See It When You Believe It*. USA: Hay House

Fulghum, R. (1990) *All I Really Need to Know I Learned in Kindergarten: The Essay that Became a Classic*. New York: Villard Books

Harris, T. A., (1973) *I'm OK – You're OK*. New York: Avon

James, M., Jongeward, D (1971) *Born to Win*. MA, USA: Addison-Wesley Publishing Company Inc.

Jeffers, S. (1987) *Feel the Fear and Do It Anyway*. London: Century

Kiley, D. (1983) *The Peter Pan Syndrome – Men who never grow up*. London: Corgi Books

King, P. (2004) *Your Life Matters – The Power of Living Now*. Sydney: Random House

McKissock, M., McKissock, D. (2012) *Coping with Grief*, 4th edition. Australia: ABC Books, Harper Collins Publishers

McWilliams, P., Roger, J. (1997) *You Can't Afford the Luxury of a Negative Thought*. Los Angeles: Prelude Press, Inc

Peck, S. M. (1985) *The Road Less Travelled: a new psychology of love, traditional values and spiritual growth*. London; Sydney: Rider

Peck, S. M. (1990) *The Different Drum: community-making and peace*. London: Arrow

Peck, S. M. (1993) *Further Along the Road Less Travelled*. New York: Touchstone

Roger, J., McWilliams, P. (1991) *Do It! Let's get Off Our Buts*. Los Angeles: Prelude Press, Inc

Rowland, M. (1993) *Absolute Happiness – The Way to a life of Complete Fulfilment*. Sydney: Self Communications Pty Ltd

Sheehy, G. (1976) *Passages – Predictable Crises in Adult Life*. London: Bantum Books

Stengel, R. (2010) *Mandela's Way – Lessons on Life*. London: Virgin Books
Stone, H., Stone, S. (1993) *Embracing the Inner Critic*. New York: Harper Collins Publishers
Stone, H., Winkelman, S. (1989) *Embracing Our Selves: The Voice Dialogue Manual*. Mill Valley, California: Nataraj Publishing
Walsch, N.D. (1996) *Conversations with God, Book 1: An Uncommon Dialogue*. Rydalmere, N.S.W: Hodder & Stoughton
Zander, R. S., Zander, B. (2000) *The Art of Possibility*. London: Penguin Books

Psychology

Cozolino, L. (2014) *The Neuroscience of Human Relationships – Attachment and the Developing Social Brain, 2nd edition*. New York U.S.A: W. W. Norton & Company Inc
Daloz, L (1999) Mentor: *Guiding the Journey of Adult Learners*. San Francisco, CA: Jossey-Bass
Eysenck, M. W., Keane, M. T. (2015) *Cognitive Psychology*. East Sussex, UK: Psychology Press
Goldberg, I., Goldberg, H. (1996) *Family Therapy*. Pacific Grove, CA: Brooks/Cole Publishing Company
Herman, J. L. (1992) *Trauma and Recovery*. London: Harper Collins
Hoff, L. A. (1995) *People in Crisis*. San Francisco: Jossey-Bass
Jung, C. G. (1975) *The Practice of Psychotherapy: essays on the psychology of the transference and other subjects, 2nd edition*. Princeton, N.J: Princeton University Press
Lipton, B. H. (2008) *The Biology of Belief: Unleashing the Power of Consciousness*, Matter & Miracles.Carlsbad, California: Hay House
Vaughan, G. M., Hogg, M. A. (2011) *Social Psychology*. Frenchs Forrest, NSW: Pearson Australia
White, F., Hayes, B., Livesey, D. (1968) *Developmental Psychology – From Infancy to Adulthood, 3rd Edition*. Frenchs Forest, NSW: Pearson Australia
Wilson, H., Kneisel, C. (1996) *Psychiatric Nursing, 5th edition*. Menlo Park, CA: Addison-Wesley Nursing

Relationships and Family Dynamics

Alexander, S., Taylor, C. (2014) *Dating & Mating*. Sydney: Grownups Guide Publishing
Biddulph, S. (2010) *The new manhood: the handbook for a new kind of man*. Warriewood, NSW: Finch Publishing

Biddulph, S. (2013) *Raising Boys: why boys are different – and how to help them to become and well-balanced men, 4th edition*. Warriewood, NSW: Finch Publishing

Cornelius, H., Faire, S. (2006) *Everyone Can Win: Responding to Conflict Constructively, 2nd edition*. Pymble, N.S.W: Simon & Schuster

Crum, T. (1998) *The Magic of Conflict: turning a life of work into a work of art, 2nd edition*. USA: Simon and Schuster, Inc., Touchstone Books

Dickson, A. (2006) *Difficult Conversations*. London: Piatkus Books limited

Fisher, R., Ury, W., with Patton, B. editor (2012) *Getting to Yes: negotiating an agreement without giving in, 3rd edition*. London: Random House Business Books

Gordon, T. (1975) P.E.T. – *Parent Effectiveness Training: the tested new way to raise responsible children*. New York: New American Library 1975

Gottman, J. (2015) *The Seven Principles for Making Marriages Work*. USA: Harmony Books

Green, C. (1984) *Toddler Taming - A parent's guide to (surviving)the first four years*. Sydney: Doubleday Australia

Hendrix, H., Hunt, H. L (2003) *Getting the Love You Want: A Guide for Couples*

James, M., Jongeward, D. (1978) *Born to Win: Transactional Analysis with Gestalt Experiments*. New York: New American Library

Jansen, D., Newman, M., with Carmichael, C. (1998) *Really Relating: how to build an enduring relationship*. Milsons Point, NSW: Random House

Stone, H., Stone, S. (1989) *Embracing Each Other*. Novato, CA: Nataraj Publishing

Stone, H., Stone, S. (2000) *Partnering – A New kind of Relationship*. Novato, CA: Nataraj Publishing

Spirituality

Chopra, D. (1996) *The Seven Spiritual Laws of Success*. London: Transworld Publishers

Dimitrov, V. (2003) *Spirituality as Experience at the Edge of Chaos*. Sydney: University of Western Sydney (UWS)

Dyer, W. (1997) *Manifest Your Destiny – The Nine Spiritual Principles for getting everything you want*. USA: Harper Collins Publishers

Millman, D. (1984) *The Way of the Peaceful Warrior*. Tiburon, CA: H. J. Kramer, Inc

Oriah. (1999) *The Invitation*. New York: Harper Collins Publishers

Roger, J. (2009) *Spiritual Warrior: The Art of Spiritual Living*. Los Angeles: Mandeville Press

Roger, J., Kaye, P. (2009) *Serving & Giving, Gateways to Higher Consciousness*. Los Angeles: Mandeville Press

Roger, J., Kaye, P. (2010) *Living the Spiritual Principles of Health and Well-Being*. Los Angeles: Mandeville Press

Tolle, E. (2005) *A New Earth – Awakening to Your Life's Purpose*. New York: Penguin Books

Zukov, G. (1990) *The Seat of the Soul – An Inspiring Vision of Humanity's Spiritual Destiny*. London: Random House

Recommended Movies (In alphabetic order)

- A FEW GOOD MEN
  - A journey through hidden agendas to find the truth
- ALEXANDER
  - A blockbuster movie about power, passion, winning, loss and death
- AMAZING GRACE
  - A biography about championing a seemingly unwinnable cause
- ANTOINE FISHER
  - A biography about finding who you are notwithstanding your history
- AS GOOD AS IT GETS
  - A story that moves beyond judgement and prejudice to friendship, support, romance and acceptance
- AS IT IS IN HEAVEN
  - A musical trip about finding and owning your unique voice and blending it with others
- AVATAR
  - A sojourn of finding the higher ground no matter what you are faced with and living your ultimate authentic truth
- BEACHES
  - A story about deep friendship, it's trials and intimacies, and ultimately loss, grief and moving forward
- BILLY ELLIOTT
  - A film about transcending social scripts
- BLACK OR WHITE
  - A story of conflict and prejudice that leads to understanding and forgiveness
- BRIDEGROOM
  - A documentary about acceptance, loss, grief and possibility
- CASABLANCA
  - A classic story about love, friendship, jealousy and hatred amongst unlikely players
- CASTAWAY
  - A story of how to cope with isolation and loneliness in extreme conditions
- COLLATERAL BEAUTY
  - A movie about loss, grief, withdrawal, letting go, recovery and deep connection and enduring love

- **Dances with Wolves**
  - A journey into isolation, self-discovery and connection
- **Dead Poets Society**
  - A film about aloneness, reconnection, personal growth and empowerment
- **Death at a Funeral**
  - A comedy drama about family secrecy, separation and reconnection
- **Devil's Advocate**
  - A dissension from the ideals of law into the trappings of power and lust
- **Elizabeth**
  - A period study of politics, power and longevity against incredible odds
- **Enigma**
  - A story of self-belief the reward and price paid in the face of incredible opposition at a personal, community and world level
- **Erin Brockovich**
  - A biography about integrity, putting things right, notwithstanding personal circumstances
- **Field of Dreams**
  - A film about having faith in possibility
- **First Wives Club**
  - A fun movie about dysfunctional relationship revenge
- **Ghandi**
  - The story of freedom from oppression and spirited independence on personal and world levels
- **Good Will Hunting**
  - A film about rising above one's circumstances from resistance to cooperation
- **Hidden Figures**
  - A true story of steadfastness, upliftment and inspiration in the face of repression, prejudice and isolation
- **Hotel Rwanda**
  - A movie about how altruism can exist amongst even the extreme cruelties of genocide
- **Interstellar**
  - A futuristic view of survival, loneliness, aloneness, sacrifice, ingenuity, hope, connection, humanity, love and possibility
- **Invictus**
  - The story of Nelson Mandela and his engagement with the Rugby World Cup to help unite South Africa
- **Inside Out**
  - An animated movie about the many voices in our heads; how they fight and how they can unite

- **Lion**
  - A true story of losing your way, finding an unexpected life, returning home and finding our routes to know our sense of place
- **Love Actually**
  - A romantic comedy about the many and varied forms of love
- **Mamma Mia**
  - An adaptation of seemingly unrelated ideas from popular songs into a romantic musical narrative that explores unconventional family and social structures
- **Mandela: Long Walk to Freedom**
  - A biography about perhaps the most amazing man of the 20th century and perhaps for many centuries; an epic about personal empowerment, steadfast resolve, understanding and reconciliation notwithstanding what is presented
- **Milk**
  - A biography about the first gay man elected to public office in America
- **Ordinary People**
  - A film about family dynamics, conflict and power, determination and finding a way
- **Other People**
  - A snapshot of diversity, family dynamics, loss and grief
- **Pay It Forward**
  - A journey of loss grief, hope, recovery and inspiration
- **Schindler's List**
  - A statement about what it takes to remain courageous and genuinely caring for mankind in a cruel and evil world
- **Slum Dog Millionaire**
  - A film about resolve, hope and rising up from impoverished circumstances
- **Steel Magnolias**
  - An insight into the power of women to bond, connect, love and lift through it all
- **Stepmom**
  - A movie about separations, transitions, loss, rejoining and finding higher ground
- **Sully**
  - A flight into integrity, courage and personal resolve to paradoxically take the higher ground
- **The Bucket List**
  - A film about ageing, dying and loving it all
- **The Colour Purple**
  - A journey into societal bigotry and reactions to it

- **THE FAMILY STONE**
  - A reflection of family dynamics, diversity, acceptance and unconditional loving
- **THE FIRM**
  - A look into corporate power, manipulations, deceit and finding yourself beyond it
- **THE HELP**
  - A movie about prejudice, servitude and dignity amongst bigotry
- **THE KING'S SPEECH**
  - A biography about self-trust and expression
- **THE LEGEND OF BAGGER VANCE**
  - A movie about the inner game of Golf or any sport for that matter
- **THE LION KING**
  - Animated movie about values, family and group dynamics
- **THE PEACEFUL WARRIOR**
  - A biography about American Olympic athlete Dan Milman
- **THE STORY OF US**
  - A film about the juxtaposition of dysfunctional family dynamics and deep commitment
- **THE THEORY OF EVERYTHING**
  - A story of mastering impossible odds and contributing to the world
- **TOOTSIE**
  - More than a comedic look into sexism in the late 20th century
- **VICEROY'S HOUSE**
  - A historical story about finding unity in the face of enormous separation at individual, community, national and international levels
- **WAR AND PEACE**
  - A journey through life at the individual and world levels
- **WHEN HARRY MET SALLY**
  - A film that shows how long and short term relationships can change and evolve

Author's Biography

Warmth, compassion, wisdom and insight: these are just a few of the words that John's clients have used to describe his unique counselling and coaching style. He combines deep know-how in both the business world and psychotherapy. With more than 40 years of experience improving people's lives at individual, group, organisation and community levels.

John's talent is releasing his clients' understanding of who they are so they can transform not only themselves and their organisations but their communities as well, even at the global level. John's mission is to help his clients for the greater good of all. The best way to understand John's success is to read **what others say about him** at the end of this biography.

Psychotherapy and Counselling Background

Some 15 years ago, having witnessed such a wide range of challenges and issues in the business world, John began to transition to the more personal focuses of individual growth, relationships and family dynamics. He began this transition initially by adding to his business qualifications gaining credentials in counselling, psychotherapy and social ecology (a field focused on the deeper values of collective systems). Today he supports individuals, couples, families and community groups (including his own professional association and peers) challenged with and who want to grow through:

- Stress related anxiety, depression, anger, dependencies, enduring worry and overwhelm
- Loss resulting from:
    - Divorce, relationship breakup, family crisis, parental separation from children
    - Job loss, retrenchment, financial loss and business failure
    - Death and grieving

- Transitions requiring new approaches to life:
  - Partnerships, marriage, new relationships, new born arrivals, blending families
  - Relocation between countries
  - Career changes and direction
  - Retirement adjustment
- General life pressures
  - Work-life balance
  - Family conflict
  - Financial strains
  - Long term unemployment

John assists his clients to build tools that sustain more understanding, joy, spontaneity, enthusiasm, loving and inner peace; a supportive pathway to better life choices. In his work with clients he found that many coming to see him floundered between sessions. The chapters in this book began with him writing articles for them with companion exercises to work with if they chose to. He found their learning, resolve and desired outcomes became more meaningful to them and sustainable change better manifested in their life.

Business, Facilitation and Coaching Background

In the business world John's consulting focus has been on long-term business strategy, leadership, restructure and transformation outcomes. His international clients have included Fortune 500 corporations such as IBM, JPMorgan, Zurich Insurance and Financial Services, BOC Gases, Digital Equipment Corporation (DEC – now Hewlett Packard), MCI WorldCom (now Verizon). Australian engagements have included iconic organisations such as Qantas, Telstra, Optus, Origin Energy and Goodman Fielder. Australian government bodies have also been an area of success for John covering local councils, state and federal departments and instrumentalities. Among his many accomplishments, he has worked with the Australian Sports Commission to successfully develop strategies for the 2000 Sydney Olympic Games and for the Australian Olympic Diving Team where unprecedented results were achieved. His overall experience ranges from local start-ups to world leaders.

John has had his work published in national and international journals and books on business transformation. Details are built into the chapters of this book where appropriate. As far back as 1984, he had several articles published in an Australian national leading business journal of the time Rydges Business Journal. This was an extensive research study of the top 1000 Australian companies sponsored by Deloitte's and IBIS Consulting on the effectiveness of pay for performance schemes and their impact on organisation success. Attesting the study's success was the decision by Delloite's to have 4,000 booklets separately printed for distribution to their clients.

John's Credentials

Academic Qualifications

- Masters of Applied Science (Social Ecology) – University of Western Sydney (UWS)
- Graduate Diploma in Psychology – Charles Sturt University (CSU)
- Graduate Diploma in Counselling – Australian College of Applied Psychology (ACAP)
- Bachelor of Business – Charles Sturt University (CSU)

Vocational Qualifications

- Lectured at:
  - University of Technology Sydney (UTS) MBA program – Leadership
  - Australian College of Applied Psychology – Leadership, Counselling and Group Dynamics
- Doctorate in Spiritual Science – Peace Theological Seminary (Treatise Pending)
- Masters in Spiritual Science – Peace Theological Seminary
- Voice Dialogue Practitioner - Australian Institute of Relational Training
- NET (Neuro Emotive Technique) Practitioner – NET Australia
- NLP (Neuro Linguistic Programming) Practitioner – Inform Training and Research
- Conflict Resolution Skills Program Facilitator – Conflict Resolution Network
- Advanced facilitation training programs in the USA - Insight Seminars.
- Advanced Human Resource Management Program – Babson College MA, USA

Accreditations

- Leadership & Cultural Inventories - The Leadership Circle (TLC),
- Lifestyle and Cultural inventories (LSI/OCI, GSI) - Human Synergistics
- CPP – Cognitive Process Profile - Cognadev
- Spiral Dynamics Values Profile (VOP) – Cognadev
- Motivational Profile (MP) - Cognadev
- Values Assessment - RBA Corptools
- Team Management Profile – Team Management Systems TMS
- DISC - Integro Learning Systems
- Published in Rydges Business Journal (1984)
  - Deloitte Australia & IBIS Research Project – 1000 organisations: Seven Articles published:
    - Systems: Handling the Sweaty Dynamite of Pay Systems

- Economy: Understand the Economy to Put Packages in Perspective
- Performance: Stimulate Productivity, Stem Mediocrity, Reward Performance
- Capacity: How to Earn the Capacity to Pay People Properly
- Communication: The Golden Rule to Get Value for What You Pay
- Personnel (HR): Personnel Departments – Pull Up Your Performance Socks
- Cut Anomalies to Cut Costs, Turnover and Staff Dissatisfaction
- Sited in three publications (see recommended readings)
  - Business Processing Engineering (UK) – Facilitating major transformation project
  - Vision 2100 – Stories from Your Future: Raising Consciousness
  - Opportunities Beyond Carbon – Looking Forward to a Sustainable World: Acknowledgement by the author

Memberships

- Clinical Member Psychotherapy and Counselling Federation of Australia (PACFA # 24853)
- Member Australian Counselling Association (MACA # 4725)
- Member of the College of Clinical Counsellors
- Member of the College of Clinical Supervisors
- Registered with the Australian Registry of Counsellors and Psychotherapists
- Member, Australia Counselling
- Member, Voice Dialogue Australia
- Minister, Ministry of Spiritual Inner Awareness (MSIA)
- Fellow of the Australian Institute of Executive Coaches (#F250105)

What others say about John's work

This Book

"It is **an awesome compilation** of a great deal of work, research, thought, synthesizing of a whole lot of material. The number of theories, approaches, systems, thoughts, etc. you have studied and used both in your life and in the book is **nothing short of amazing**. The presentation with the graphs and graphics adds to clarity. **The story is compelling**.

"I think you have written **a wonderful book** and shared an amazing amount of information and presented a lot of material for people to work with.

"Be very proud of yourself for the huge accomplishment that your book is !! And maybe even more so, the huge accomplishment that your own personal happiness and spiritual growth is. What do you Aussies say... 'good on ya'... did I get that right?"

(Faculty Member MSIA Peace Theological Seminary (PTS) Doctorate in Spiritual Science)

Psychotherapy and Counselling

"John Harradine is a kind, **insightful**, intelligent man who **knows how to get to the core of an issue straight away**... I would highly recommend John to anyone; male/female, young/old. **He knows how to relate to anyone in any circumstance**... If you need some direction or you are at a crossroads, **you can be assured he will guide you up the right path**. If you feel like you are falling into a pit, John will be there, not to rescue but to guide you to where you become so clear it seems like he has known you all his life... **With all the professionals I have come across in my line of work and the field of psychotherapy, John is No. 1**." (Health worker)

"Thank you for your support this year and **indeed I could not be here without you** and really appreciate everything you have done. You're like a superhero, just without the cape." (Lawyer)

"John's **insights and techniques are spot on**, and we have seen ourselves **grow, as individuals, and as partners**, under his mentorship. We can't recommend him highly enough, and would never go to anyone else for our relationship or mental health needs." (Private couple)

"John didn't take sides or told us things we wanted to hear; in fact, he genuinely **brought unforeseen matters to the surface** and worked with us toward

a tangible and lasting solution. His approach is very welcoming and easy to absorb, and his tips and examples are extremely helpful." (Private couple)

One of John's clients published her experience of counselling with him after a year working with her partner on their relationship. Here are some highlights reprinted with permission. For the whole article, see Google Elephant Journal: Emotional Health is the New Sexy (http://www.elephantjournal.com/2014/11/emotional-health-is-the-new-sexy) – 59037 views as at 19th September 2016.

"I'm seeing a counsellor."

My face burns and I look down at the floor. I don't want to see the pity reflecting in your eyes – I know what you think. At least, I tell myself a story about what you think... I want to set the record straight once and for all, so gather round my friends and hear my truth: **therapy is brave**. Therapy is **empowering**. And therapy is **sexy**. I'll tell you why.

Therapy is brave.

Every bone in my weary body screamed at me to run away – to stay safely wrapped in the warm cosy blanket of ignorance, to bury the feelings deeper where they couldn't hurt me. I stayed in that chair. And I returned to it every week for a year... It takes a certain kind of brave to sit with the agonising pain of grief as it crushes your chest – to acknowledge guilt, to accept loneliness, with tears streaming down your face. **There is a warrior in all of us waiting for that opportunity.**

We all need a witness in this life. I believe it's one of the reasons we connect with others so deeply – to know that someone cares enough about us to see us, to really see us for who we are as we move through life's journey.

He questions me in ways that make me **think beyond my comfort levels**, to see **an alternate perspective**. My current ways of thinking have not always served me well and he is not afraid to push me hard beyond them, even if it makes me cry. ... Exhausting? Yes. **Valuable? Beyond measure**. I am **more myself than I have ever been**, which is the **best gift I could have given myself** in this thirtieth year of my life.

Therapy is empowering.

It gives me the **ability to recognise negative patterns and behaviours**, and the **tools and awareness to deal with them** without melting down. It lets me get **comfortable with ambiguity** and **to sit with my sadness without dissolving into it** to a point where I can't cope or recover from it.

I can apply these **lessons across the board**: at home, at work, walking down the street. I can understand the motivations and fears that drive people and myself, which is **powerful beyond words**. ...I finally understand that no one in this world has the power to *make* me feel anything. ...I create, promote and allow the feelings and behaviours that I want in my life and I give to myself the things that I want to experience.

Therapy is sexy.

There is nothing more attractive than a person prepared to own his or her shit. We are all messed up in some way or another; it's just a matter of how, and to what degree. To accept that fact is to **be a real adult in this world – to take responsibility for our own happiness and to stop blaming others** when life is hard, or when they don't meet our expectations.

If a man is willing to face his issues, my god is he a man in my eyes. If he is able to work on himself with the intention of **becoming the best version of himself** that he can be, **for himself**, and subsequently for **his relationships, that is a serious turn-on**. I know that **he is going to show up for me, for his family, and he is going to address the issues that he doesn't want to pass onto his kids.**

The fact that you care about your mental health is as significant to me as you taking care of yourself physically. **Mental grooming is way more important than working on your washboard abs** (though I won't deny, I like those too).

We don't have to be perfect; heaven knows that I'm not. **We just have to be willing to participate in our own growth, and that will speak to my mind, my soul and to my body in ways you could never imagine.**

Business, Coaching and Facilitation

Computer Services Sector

"The success of the workshop was largely **due to the process you designed**... and the **skilful way** you navigated the team through to an **entirely satisfactory outcome**... The workshop was **well paced** and your **ability to read the mood of the group was extremely perceptive.**" Senior executive, international computer services provider

"We could **not have gotten to the point** where we are **without your help**. ...you did a **better job** of facilitating that session **than any he (worldwide VP Operations) had ever seen**... your **dedication** to the outcome was **an inspiration to our team.**" Senior executive, international computer services provider

Consumer Services Sector

"John is an **incredibly insightful and powerful coach**. He can get 'right to the core' of an issue and has an **exceptional ability** to understand both situations and real motives. These combine to make him **truly able to change lives.**" CEO, international consumer goods provider

"I have been involved in many restructures and this was the **fastest, smoothest, biggest and best yet**, owing very largely to John's process and facilitation skills. ...**he is the good oil for the smooth running of your business**, at the most important level – human interaction." Chief Operating Officer (COO), ASX listed national consumer goods provider

Financial Services Sector

"The Strategy work has been **stunningly successful** – but, without the prior groundwork, simply would not have occurred... John has been able to measure, explain and coach improved inter-and intra-team performance... Teamwork is improving, interaction is easier and this shows in the results. ...now there is **an agreed roadmap and aligned path**. ....John Harradine can take a great deal of credit for that." Chief Information Officer (CIO), international financial services sector

"It is really **an amazing job** that you've done. The exercise has proved to be **extremely useful** even though the core team has been working together for months. It brought them **from an unconscious state to working together to consciously care and value each other's ideas** and it also helped the team from getting stuck." Senior executive, Asian financial services provider

Government and Not For Profit (NFP) Sector

"It's **very difficult to put into words** what I felt and am still feeling. It will **be one of the most rewarding achievements for me in this position**... On top of that, the group who went to the course begrudgingly on the Tuesday came **away a very united team, more understanding and trusting of each other** three days later." Executive Director, Peak Australian Olympic sports organisation

"John's skill is evident. ...Another **outstanding skill** is in **facilitation** and **assisting people to step up to the challenge in front of them**." Senior Strategy Executive, state health care provider

"Your **professionalism, tenacity** and **dedication** have been **extremely positive**... you **promised a lot** and you **gave more than you promised**. Your process is **indeed different, challenging** and **for the most part a lot of fun**. As the workshop progressed my respect for your professionalism grew as **you clearly know your 'stuff'**." Director of operations, Australian government peak general sports body

"Your **keen observation of process**, together with your **use of 'gut feel'** meant that the **outcomes** we achieved were **far beyond our expectations**. ...to build the **commitment to relationships** within the team, and the **degree of trust that was achieved, is truly memorable**." Deputy Director General, state government training and industrial relations department

"The process and the people were **outstanding**! The success of the process was largely due to their expertise. Words which spring to mind include – **enthusiastic, dedicated, professional, sincere, highly skilled** and also **empathetic**. They were **a real credit** to your company. Please pass on my personal thanks for their great efforts." Chief Information Officer, state health department

Resources and Engineering Sector

"Whilst personnel achieved new heights in group dynamics, the synergy and dynamism displayed by your team was at **another level again**. The **skilful blend of pleasure and pain** utilised to **engender peak performance** was a **delight to enjoy and observe**. Employees who were previously filled with doom and gloom, and long treasured negativity, are now leading the way by constantly **espousing the virtues of 'such a powerful experience'**." Senior executive, international engineering provider

"I have worked with John on a personal level and in a business capacity since 2006 (to 2013). Through this time, I have benefitted from John's **wisdom, insightfulness, warmth** and **caring** to undertake some **truly amazing personal growth** and **transformation**. From the insights and awareness I have gained **I have no doubt I am a more conscious person** which has made me more at ease with what is and **has positively impacted my life** at and away from work and **generated improved business outcomes. What sets John apart** is his **willingness to work with me** to understand myself as well as my business opportunities and challenges and **then propose an integrated program** of work focused on **strategic outcomes** for the business **that are sustainable** and, because of the greater awareness of who and how I am and how this impacts the decisions I make, are **also transferable from one business to another**. John is not wedded to any particular paradigm and I have personally experienced his **ability to design fit for purpose programmes** and refine and redesign in the moment to **deliver outstanding results**." Senior executive, Top 50 ASX listed resources organisation

"Over the past seven years... I have always found John's professionalism, insight and ability to constructively challenge to be central to the value he has provided to me and my teams... John does not shy away from challenging the mentee, however always approaches his work in a manner that is respectful, and targets a positive outcome. In particular, I note John's **underpinning recognition that only through reflection upon a leader's own motivations and personal belief structures can that leader fully grow to be their best in both their professional role, and their personal endeavours** – not a trivial challenge in this era of quick fixes! With a strong desire to push the mentee in a supportive yet challenging manner, John has shown the unique knack of obtaining the **optimum benefit** from his engagement, conscious that there is a personal and/or business outcome that is the destination around which the mentoring and coaching work is aimed. John **strategically plans and guides, always flexible and willing to evolve and adjust the work plan based on emergent requirements**." CEO, joint venture, international resources sector

"None of these people (past consultants) come close to be able to impart the skill and provide the awareness of developing a strategy and creating a complementary culture with **such professionalism, compassion and sincerity. The value of getting through difficult situations with a win/win outcome is immeasurable**." CEO, national engineering company

"Working with John over several years and in two very different roles has enabled me to grow from a frustrated and grumpy company executive into someone who **is in control of my own destiny** and am utilising my skills more effectively. John's skill in **helping me to see how I was holding myself back** has enabled me to **make a step change for myself, my family and, in time, for the entire industry in which I work**." CEO, national clean energy association

Telecommunications Sector

"I have found his work efforts in the area of human resources/human development, to be **one of the finest to have ever been associated with**." Operations Director, international telecommunications company

"The success and quality output of the sessions run... has been recognised not just in the product development area but in the XX Marketing division as a whole... we feel they **add considerable value to our business**." Senior executive, Top 50 ASX listed Telecommunications provider

What John says about his own work

An Interview with Australia Counselling

In 2013 John was **interviewed** on **Australia Counselling** and featured on their website www.australiacounselling.com.au. Excerpts reprinted here for convenience.

- **How did you become interested in counselling and working as a therapist?**
  - From the time I was 15 I knew I would end up in this field. Family disruption was the trigger and I knew there had to be a better way.
  - I ultimately gained a master's degree in applied science (social ecology) which composites psychology, sociology, quantum thinking and complexity and chaos theory to better understand the deeper value systems (ecology) that drive human behaviour and outcomes.

- **How do you believe people change and what supports long-lasting change?**
  - People change when they are ready and they choose to. Often the paradigms they operate off keep them stuck in habits and beliefs that are no longer effective.
  - Unpacking and understanding belief systems, particularly the unconscious out of sight ones, is central to my work with clients.
  - Whilst the approach is initially cognitive, sustainable change occurs when new expanding belief systems are fully embraced and integrated by the client at a heartfelt and physiological level. The client has new choices to hold for in challenging circumstances rather that retreat to old ways.
  - We don't go up alone so having a tour guide on life's journey who can help point out the scenery that the traveller doesn't notice facilitates better life choices.

- **Tell us about your approach and why you believe the way you work is effective in helping people change.**
  - I take a client-centred and -led approach, i.e. the client explores their own challenges and opportunities.
  - My role is to bring awareness to the experience they are having as they dialogue about presenting issues and possibilities. I aim to assist them see for themselves what is working and what is not working for them.

- A secondary role is to add some educative perspectives and frameworks on ways in which they might think about what they are presenting.
- A third step is to deepen and anchor new awarenesses and strategies they wish to adopt. It is important to work holistically, i.e. on a physical, emotional, mental and for those who are open to it spiritual (not necessarily religious) levels.
- Developing a trusting and supportive therapeutic relationship with the client is central to assisting desired change they are seeking.

- **Tell us what a client can expect to experience in an initial counselling session with you.**
    - At the beginning of any session, I aim to clarify what has brought them here and what they would like out of the session and our work together. I ask about what they might expect. I share some ground rules around confidentiality and ask if they have experienced counselling, coaching or therapy before. Then I ask what has worked or not worked for them before in their previous experience (if they have had that). The underlying intention is to establish rapport and a safe environment for them to explore their needs and desires.
    - The next part of the session is to have them talk about their situation and simply listen, making mental notes of things that might be sitting underneath their story with a view to pursuing some questions with them.
    - When they appear to have finished speaking, I'll typically ask them how it has been right now to talk about this and bring any awarenesses forward they are noticing about their feelings, and what that means to them.
    - We then might work with an approach to move forward and check I with the client's experience for the first session.
    - This sequence varies depending on how the client is responding. It's an in-the-moment emerging process.

- **On a personal note, tell us something that you're passionate about or love to do in your spare time.**
    - I own a boat and have an incredible sense of peace when on the water. I am also a keen competition tennis player, a movie buff, the theatre and eating out are great pastimes.
    - I am passionate about making a difference where I can, especially to family life and relationships.

- I am passionate about my primary relationship, my children and living with joy spontaneity and enthusiasm. That means I am passionate about releasing anything that holds me back from that. To do that I hold to loving it all, the issues, the challenges, the opportunities and possibilities and most of all the present.
- What is that poem again? "The past is history, the future is a mystery; now is the present, which is why they call it a gift."

John can be contacted as follows:

Cremorne Consulting Suites
4/350 Military Rd, Cremorne, 2090
Sydney, Australia

M: +(61) 0 419 953 389
W: +(61) 02 99087911
jeharrad@bigpond.net.au
www.johnharradine.com
http://www.linkedin.com/profile/preview?locale=en_US&trk=prof-0-sb-preview-primary-button

Epilogue

A personal reflection on writing this book

Writing this book has been a challenging, arduous, sometimes draining but also integrating, creative and ultimately satisfying even joyful task. My hat is off to anyone who tries this and especially those who do it more than once and for a living.

It has brought together every aspect of my life over my now 69 years. It has engaged me with trusted friends knowing they have supported me no matter what. Of course, that doesn't mean they like everything I do, but that's also the gift in my learning. To all who are in and have been in my life: I am so grateful for the lifelong learning they have provided whether it be in the form of acknowledgement and love, or criticism and upset I have been gifted by it. That is one big thank you from me to you if you happen to be reading this.

The book began with a series of articles, some of which I had written originally to focus businesses on their desired success. The articles emerged from time spent over many years in that field and witnessing so much dysfunction but also material success. When I decided to move out of that area into full-time psychotherapy, I found some of the articles could be adapted to counselling and began to hand them to my clients. They seemed to find them useful and many found them life-altering, so I set about improving them.

I recalled as I began to write that I was told once I had a book in me. As I write this epilogue it is my eldest son Mark's 41st birthday, so happy birthday Mark (21st September, International day of Peace 2016 – aha!). Mark and Christopher are my two biggest gifts in life and inspire me every day to do better. My relationships with them and Maxx are the most sacred thing on this planet for me.

The style and formatting of the book were at least if not more challenging than the writing of the content. I've always used pictures and frameworks to figure things out. I write as I think and I think in emergent circular ideas, so constructing language linearly is not my bench strength. Although I have gotten better at it over the years, thanks to the likes of Terri, without whom it would have taken a lot longer. Just take a look at the beginning of Chapter 6 – "Intentionality" and the underlying limitations I set up for myself about writing a book. They speak volumes about the limiting patterns I've broken though.

In the end, I broke my own pattern about how a book "should" be written and did it my way. Those who know me well would say the "Harradine Way" and, in the end, that turned out to be an integrative process in itself.

What started to emerge as a set of individual articles began to form into a cohesive methodology:

Chapter 1, *Living Freely* begins the process by examining limiting control roles we play in life (*Persecutor, Victim, Rescuer*) and maps a journey toward the higher ground of possibility and more expanding roles (*Creator, Allower, Promoter*).

Once we understand where we are heading, Chapter 2, *Embracing Vulnerability and Authenticity* takes a dive into exploring how we protect our vulnerability, how we can let go of these protective mechanisms and feel safe, strong and courageous to live more authentically.

As we come to understand our patterns, Chapter 3, *Taking Charge of the Past* creates a window through which we can see where and when our patterns began and how these patterns either contract or expand us today.

Today's world is characterised by an ever-increasing pace of change. As soon as we think something is settled, something else comes along to disturb our status quo. Building capability to adapt to and function well with never-ending changes is essential; else we retreat into old limiting patterns. They may have worked previously but may not be the right strategy for the next change we face. Chapter 4, *Loving Ambiguity and the Unknown* assists us to navigate an unpredictable world with less trepidation and greater confidence and openness to personal growth.

Having looked deeply at who we are and how we function we now turn to the challenging territory of relationships. Our primary relationship in particular challenges how we think we should and should not behave with others. Chapter 5, *Unconditional Relating* leads us through the maze of how relationships work.

If we are equipped to manage our life authentically, deal with the unexpected changes and our relationships are intact, we are much better placed to look to the future, assess what we want and go for it. Chapter 6, *Intentionality* helps to address our real intentions and goals and overcome blockers to our success.

Finally, in Chapter 7, *Sacred Living* aims to lift our consciousness and fully integrate our past, present and future, providing life purpose and direction.

Whilst this may seem like a linear process or journey from A to B, it most assuredly is not. It is iterative, continually revisiting various stopping off points along the way and reconnoitring – more like a maze, eventually finding our way through it. The companion exercises for each of the chapters bring to life how this maze applies to your personal story.

When I integrated my personal story, that's when either the rubber hit the road or the stuff hit the fan. The intention for me in including my story has been transparency, authenticity and wholeness and to demonstrate examples of how the principles in this book can apply in life.

My intention for you is to support you to find the same thing for yourself in your own story. If you respond to the sentiments in the poem below, your own story may unfold for you. I have added point number 11.

Rules for Being Human

1. *You will receive a body.* You may like it or hate, but it will yours for the entire period this time round
2. *You will learn lessons.* You are enrolled in a fulltime school called "life". Each day in this school you will have the opportunity to learn lessons. You may like the lessons or call them irrelevant or stupid.
3. *There are no mistakes, only lessons.* Growth is a process of trial and error, and experimentation. The "failed" experiments are as much a part of the process as the experiment that ultimately works.
4. *A lesson is repeated until learned.* A lesson is repeated to you in various forms until you have learned it. When you have learned it, you can then go onto the next lesson.
5. *Learning lessons does not end.* There is no part of life that does not contain its lessons. If you are alive there are lessons to be learned.
6. *"There" is no better than "here".* When your "there" has become a "here" you will simply obtain another "there" that will, again, look better than "here".
7. *Others are merely mirrors of you.* You cannot love or hate something about another person unless it reflects to you something you love or hate in yourself.
8. *What you make of your life is up to you.* You have all the tools and resources you need. What you do with them is up to you. The choice is yours.
9. *Your answers lie inside you.* The answers to life's questions lie inside you. All you need to do is look listen and trust.
10. *You will forget this.* (Source unknown)
11. *Unless, of course, you don't!*

What to put in your story and what to leave out? What's the balance?

This book encourages you to state who you are and make that carry more weight than what you do. The balance then? To be or to do? I like Frank Sinatra's words: "Do, Be, Do, Be Do!" So, I did and I was, when I wrote both my personal story and the biography from that place. Anything less would diminish transparency and authenticity and therefore the intentions I started with. I invite you to inventory your life and see what shows up.

To close, life is a "coming out" process for all of us in one way or another, and if we break open the eggshell when we are ready, not when others or even ourselves think we "should", we are able to get up and walk away from the eggshells so many of us walk on in our lives, knowing the eggshell has served its purpose to birth us into new awareness. New awareness comes most easily when we move into what I call the four pillars of healing: *acceptance, detachment, forgiveness* and *neutrality* – all concepts explored in this book. They better enable us to break patterns and develop new ones, which in turn can be broken when they no longer serve us.

I hope you have gained something from reading this hand book and doing the exercises and hopefully dance through life with grace, ease, peace and joy. I'm dedicating this work to my Mum (see *"The Story of Us"*) who taught me to get up one more time than I fall no matter the setbacks and even tragedies; to laugh about and with myself, but not at myself. It heals. God bless you Mum! Thank you for taking the time to look in.

My very very best to you all.

John

THE STORY OF US

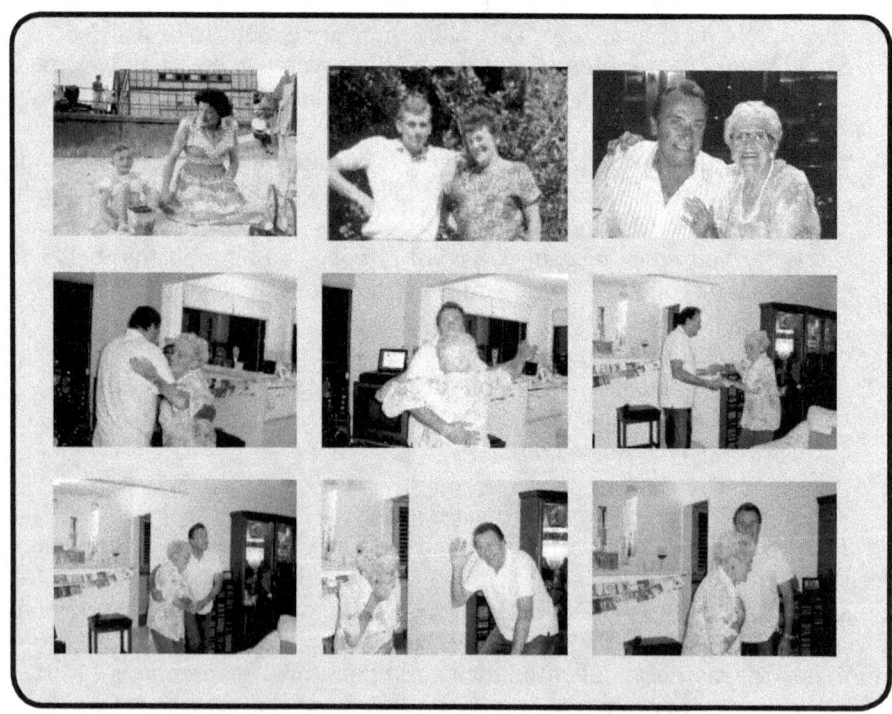

I hope you dance your way through life!

www.ingramcontent.com/pod-product-compliance
Lightning Source LLC
Chambersburg PA
CBHW071909290426
44110CB00013B/1336